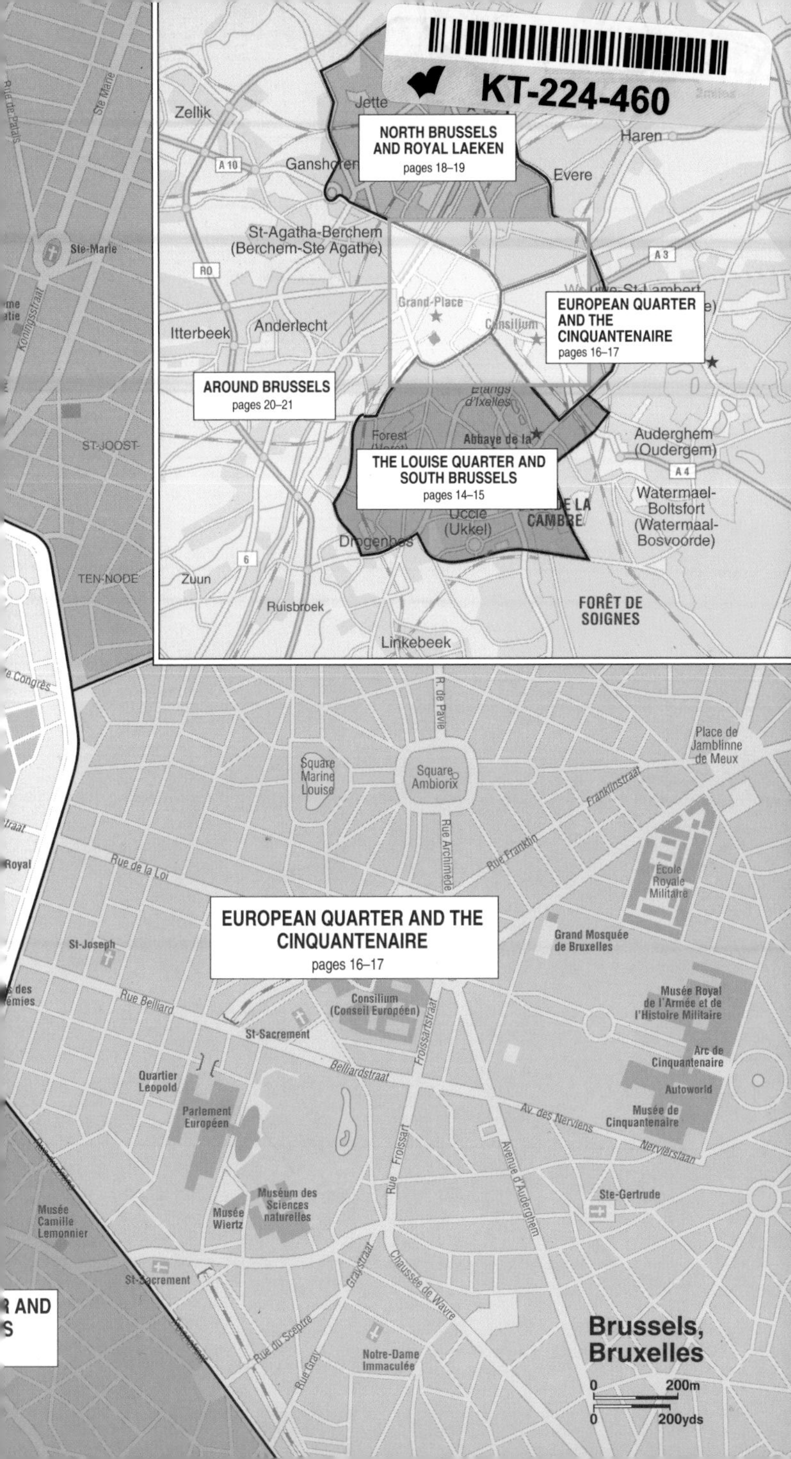
KT-224-460
Zellik
Jette
NORTH BRUSSELS AND ROYAL LAEKEN
pages 18–19
Haren
Ganshoren
Evere
A 10
St-Agatha-Berchem
(Berchem-Ste Agathe)
A 3
R0
Grand-Place
Consilium
EUROPEAN QUARTER AND THE CINQUANTENAIRE
pages 16–17
Itterbeek
Anderlecht
AROUND BRUSSELS
pages 20–21
Etangs d'Ixelles
Forest
Abbaye de la
Auderghem
(Oudergem)
A 4
THE LOUISE QUARTER AND SOUTH BRUSSELS
pages 14–15
Watermael-Boltsfort
(Watermaal-Bosvoorde)
Uccle
(Ukkel)
CAMBRE
Drogenbos
6
Zuun
Ruisbroek
FORÊT DE SOIGNES
Linkebeek
Rue de Palais
Ste Marie
Ste-Marie
Koningsstraat
ST-JOOST-
TEN-NODE
Congrès
Royal
R. de Pavie
Place de Jamblinne de Meux
Square Marie Louise
Square Ambiorix
Franklinstraat
Rue Archimède
Rue Franklin
Rue de la Loi
École Royale Militaire
EUROPEAN QUARTER AND THE CINQUANTENAIRE
pages 16–17
St-Joseph
Grand Mosquée de Bruxelles
Musée Royal de l'Armée et de l'Histoire Militaire
Consilium
(Conseil Européen)
Rue Belliard
St-Sacrement
Froissartstraat
Arc de Cinquantenaire
Belliardstraat
Quartier Leopold
Autoworld
Parlement Européen
Av. des Nerviens
Musée de Cinquantenaire
Nerviërslaan
Rue Froissart
Avenue d'Auderghem
Musée Camille Lemonnier
Musée Wiertz
Muséum des Sciences naturelles
Ste-Gertrude
St-Sacrement
Graystraat
Chaussée de Wavre
Rue du Sceptre
Rue Gray
Notre-Dame Immaculée
Brussels,
Bruxelles
0
200m
0
200yds

INSIGHT GUIDES

BRUSSELS
smart guide

Discovery CHANNEL

Contents

Areas

Below: angel statue on Place des Martyrs.

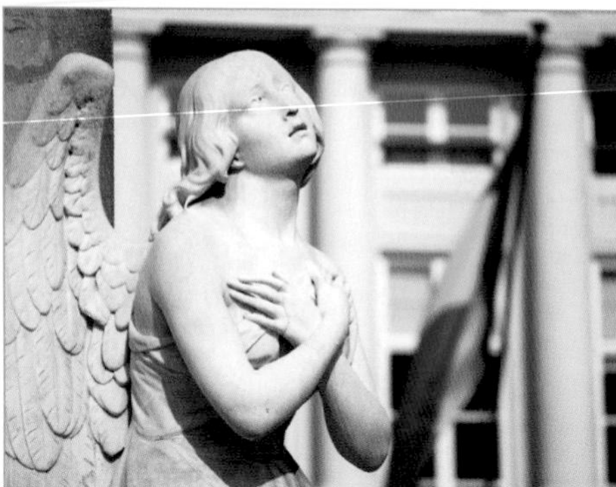

A–Z

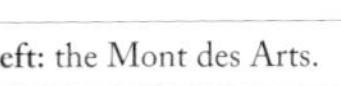

Left: the Mont des Arts.

Below: seafood restaurants on the Quai aux Briques.

Atlas

Brussels

Brussels, capital of Belgium, headquarters of the European Union and Nato, and butt of jokes about boredom and bureaucracy. Those who know the city call it the best kept secret in Europe, for its superb restaurants, cafés, parks, museums, Art Nouveau architecture and transport links, coupled with a loveable refusal to take itself too seriously.

Brussels Facts and Figures

Population: **1 million (Brussels Capital Region)**
Languages spoken: **French (85 percent) and Dutch (15 percent)**
No. of foreign residents: **over 29 percent**
Area: **162 sq km (62 sq miles)**
No. of museums: **100**
No. of World Heritage Sites: **2 (Grand'Place and the major houses of architect Victor Horta)**
International organisations based in Brussels: **European Union (EU) and North Atlantic Treaty Organisation (Nato)**

Location

Brussels is a bilingual French-Dutch region in central Belgium, 80km (50 miles) from the North Sea and surrounded by Dutch-speaking municipalities within the province of Flemish Brabant. Around 10km (6 miles) to the south of the city is the linguistic border between Flanders and Wallonia, the French-speaking southern half of Belgium. The 19 communes (municipal districts) of Brussels Capital Region include Bruxelles-Ville (the City of Brussels), which is the legal capital of Belgium.

Seat of both Nato and the main institutions of the European Union, the city is home to over 50 intergovernmental agencies and has more diplomats and journalists than Washington D.C., plus hordes of lawyers, lobbyists and politicians.

Character

Business and tourism chiefs trumpet their city as the 'capital of Europe', but the typical *Brusseleir* is more modest, bemused as to why anyone would ever want to identify 10 famous Belgians. *Bons vivants* who uphold the tradition of Burgundian feasting and Brueghelian merriment, they have a quirky, Surrealist edge and are proud of their mongrel heritage, of the anarchic underbelly of their city and of the fertile arts scene that results from being at a crossroads of Latin and Germanic cultures.

Although one of few countries where the vote is compulsory, Belgians have little faith in official bodies, which are widely seen as corrupt, despite recent reforms of the police and judiciary, and the political class is considered self-serving and incompetent. This view was compounded in 2007 when the ruling coalition failed to form a government for nine months due to political stalemate over the Flemish demand for more devolution to the regions.

Population

For decades, wealthier families decamped out of the city to greener suburbs rather than challenge crass town-planning decisions to raze beautiful neighbourhoods and erect urban motorways and dreary offices. But as the city has grown more cosmopoli-

Below: La Chaloupe d'Or on the Grand' Place.

tan it has undergone a renaissance, with renewed efforts to preserve what remains of its heritage. Brussels may not have the immediate appeal of Paris, Rome or Amsterdam, but each quarter has a distinct charm, from the fashionable Dansaert, chic Sablon and sharp-suited EU quarter to down-to-earth Marolles, arty Ixelles and bohemian Saint-Gilles.

The population is equally diverse, with nearly one in three residents holding foreign nationality. In addition to large communities of Moroccans, Turks and Congolese, who are over-represented in menial jobs and unemployment rates – which hover around 20 percent – there are thousands of immigrants from other EU countries, the US and elsewhere, working in international institutions and business. English is increasingly used as a lingua franca, and wealthier foreign residents enjoy an excellent quality of life: an EU civil servant earns three times as much as their Belgian equivalent.

Between the two, the native Belgian population has started to feel priced out of their city, neglected by decision-makers using Brussels as a pawn in disputes between Flanders and Wallonia. As the linguistic communities grow further apart, many believe the break-up of Belgium is inevitable. Deciding the fate of Brussels may present the biggest test the country has ever had to face.

Highlights

▲ **Grand'Place** The heart of old Brussels and a 360° panorama of Gothic and Baroque beauty.

▶ **Musée Horta** A time-capsule of Art Nouveau survives in the former home and studio of architect Victor Horta.

▲ **Vieux Marché** The daily flea market provides a colourful snapshot of the city's cosmopolitan cha acter – and some rare bargains.

▶ ***Moules-frites*** A steaming pot of mussels with fries and mayonnaise is the national dish, in season from mid-July to February.

▲ **Forêt de Soignes** A cathedral-effect beech forest which extends for 44 sq km (17 sq miles).

▶ **Atomium** This gigantic model of an iron molecule epitomises the city's sense of Surrealism.

Grand'Place

Every visit to Brussels should begin on the Grand'Place, a cobbled square at the heart of the city which offers a stunning panorama of Gothic-meets-Baroque architecture. But the medieval town hall and former guildhouses are not just a museum piece: they form the core of the living town, both as a backdrop for pageants, festivals and markets, and as the seat of local government. Radiating from here into the narrow streets nearby is a no-nonsense warmth typical of the Belgian people: an appreciation of tradition and ceremony as long as it is followed by a hearty dinner and a chilled glass of beer.

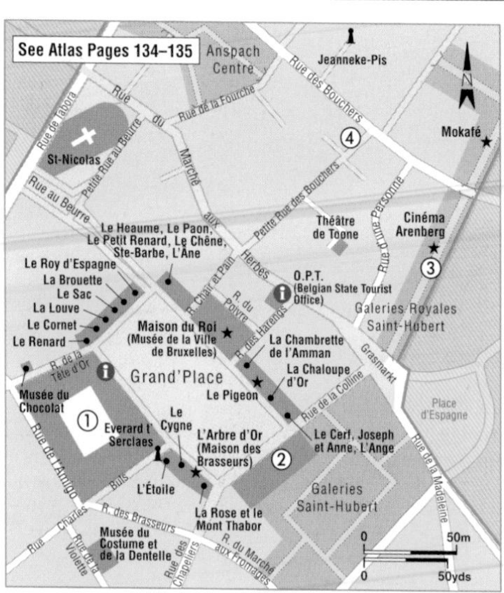

Grand'Place

The former market square became the centre of civic life in the Middle Ages when wealthy crafts guilds competed to build the most ornate premises. The **Hôtel de Ville** ① (town hall) is a pinnacled Gothic delight completed in 1444. By a stroke of fortune, the building survived a 1695 bombardment by French troops that destroyed most of the square and some 4,000 other buildings. United in indignation, the city guilds determined to rebuild the square in even finer form.

Each house has a distinctive identity and decoration: no. 1, **Le Roy d'Espagne** (King of Spain, now a café with a superlative view) was the bakers' house, while **Le Cornet** (the Horn, no. 6) was the boatmen's house, with anchors, rigging and other nautical elements adorning the facade. **L'Arbre d'Or** (the Golden Tree) at no. 10 was the brewers' guild (the **Maison des Brasseurs**), and is now a brewery museum; **Le Pigeon**, at no. 26, was the guild of painters, and occupied by Victor Hugo during his exile in Brussels; **Le Cygne** (the Swan) was the butchers' guild, and, later, a tavern where Karl Marx and Friedrich Engels worked on their *Communist Manifesto*. Today it is a gastronomic restaurant. Just around the corner, the recumbent statue beneath the arcade on Rue Charles Buls is folk hero **Everard 't Serclaes**, who in 1356 freed the city from the tyrannical Counts of Flanders. Five times alderman of the city, he was brought to this house on his deathbed in

Below: L'Arbre d'Or.

Left: the Grand'Place.

1388. The 19th-century bas-relief is said to bring luck to those who touch it.

Facing the Hôtel de Ville is the **Maison du Roi**, an 1873 reconstruction of an earlier building and now a museum of city history, the **Musée de la Ville de Bruxelles**.

The southeastern flank of the square has a uniform facade: **La Maison des Ducs de Brabant** ② (House of the Dukes of Brabant) is actually six houses, one of which is the Hotel Saint-Michel. No duke ever lived here: the name comes from the busts carved on the facade.

SEE ALSO ARCHITECTURE, P.24; HOTELS, P.61; MUSEUMS AND GALLERIES, P.76; RESTAURANTS, P.100

Galeries Royales Saint-Hubert ③

This glass-roofed shopping arcade was the largest of its kind in Europe when built in 1846–7, dedicated to the royals of newly created Belgium. Sheltered from the elements, it is ideal for wandering and window-shopping, with old-fashioned stores and upscale boutiques. Brussels' reputation as chocolate mecca was born here in 1912, when the grandson of Swiss chocolatier **Neuhaus** devised a bite-sized filled chocolate: the praline. The two-screen **Cinéma Arenberg** is the best art-house cinema in town, while café **Mokafé** is good for hot chocolate, cake and people-watching.

SEE ALSO BARS AND CAFÉS, P.28; FILM, P.51

Below: Galeries Royales Saint-Hubert.

Ilôt Sacré ④

The quarter between Rue du Marché aux Herbes and Rue de l'Ecuyer is known as the 'Sacred Isle', after a campaign to preserve it from bulldozers in the 1950s. Best-known for its tourist-trap restaurants on the patio-heated Rue des Bouchers and Petite Rue des Bouchers, it is a crush of restaurants with striking shell-fish displays and pushy waiters eager to attract passing trade. Notable exceptions to the rip-off rule are **Aux Armes de Bruxelles**, which has no tables outside, and Chez Léon, a no-nonsense mussels joint. A modern, female version of the Manneken-Pis, **Jeanneke-Pis**, squats contentedly on Impasse de la Fidélité off Rue des Bouchers. Towards the Bourse, the **Eglise Saint-Nicolas** contains an unexpected memento of the 1695 bombardment: a cannonball lodged 3m (10ft) up a stone pillar in the nave.

SEE ALSO CHURCHES, P.37; RESTAURANTS, P.100

The Grand'Place plays host to a variety of festivities during the year, including the Ommegang, a medieval pageant in early July. In summertime, a kitsch *son et lumière* show animates the space at dusk, and there are frequent free classical and rock concerts, as well as the Jazz Festival and the Summer Festival. In December, a large Christmas tree and full-size Nativity scene with live animals take up residence. *See also Festivals, p.48.*

The Lower City

Brussels grew up around the River Senne in this area until it was covered in the 19th century. Now the only flowing liquid is in the bars around Saint-Géry and the Rue du Marché au Charbon, where hip young Belgians sport Flemish designer chic from the boutiques on Rue Dansaert. This is the heart of Brussels cool: after years of neglect, when the middle classes left the city centre for greener suburbs, artists and young families have repopulated the area, renovating historic properties in minimalist style. As a result, the area has all the buzz of the city centre, but with a lived-in feel that you might never want to leave.

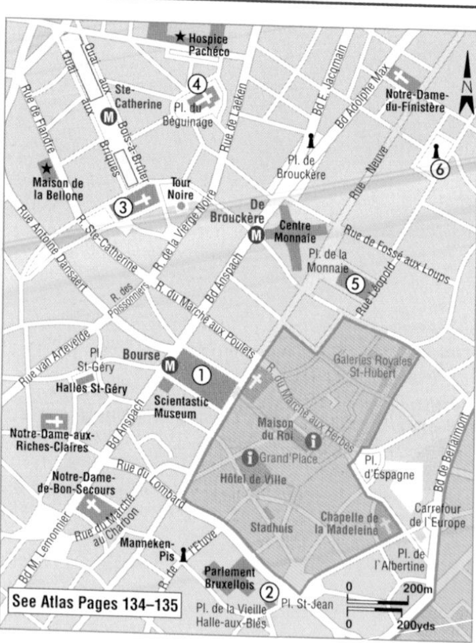

Above: the Manneken-Pis.

Bourse

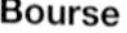

Built in the form of a Classical temple but with lashings of ornamentation, the broad steps of the **Bourse** ① (stock exchange) are a popular meeting point. **Boulevard Anspach** is a Hausmann-style thoroughfare that cuts through the centre, the north–south trams running below ground. To the east of the street is the quaint **Quartier Saint-Jacques**, a bohemian and gay quarter centred around **Rue du Marché au Charbon**.

Tourists file from the Grand'Place down Rue de l'Etuve to snap the **Manneken-Pis**, the bronze urinating boy statue that is the enduring symbol of Brussels. He is as likely to be dressed as undressed: costumes created for his diminutive form to mark feast days or charitable causes are displayed in the Maison du Roi on the Grand' Place. Up the hill, on **Place de la Vieille Halle-aux-Blés** with its relaxed pavement cafés, the **Fondation Jacques Brel** ② keeps alive the memory of Belgium's most famous troubadour (1929–78), still loved by old and young.

SEE ALSO GAY AND LESBIAN, P.56–7; MUSIC, P.86

Quartier Dansaert

On the opposite side of Boulevard Anspach is the Dansaert district. **Place Saint-Géry**, with its covered market building and hip cafés, is named after a bishop regarded as the founder of Brussels (c.AD600). This historic neighbourhood was in a state of neglect until 10 years ago,

Left: stock exchange facade.

In 977, Charles, Duke of Lower Lorraine, built a fortress on Saint-Géry island in the River Senne. But the river which gave birth to the city is sadly no longer visible. Grown filthy after centuries of use as the common sewer, it was built over in the 1870s, and the historic quarters on its banks were flattened to build the boulevards Midi, Lemonnier and Anspach. *See also Environment, p.40.*

when Flemish creative types moved into the upcoming fashion district around **Rue Dansaert**. A spirit of craftsmanship prevails in many boutiques, where you can meet designers and pick up unique items of clothing, jewellery and accessories. The area around the canal is alive with loft developments, galleries and bars, although deprivation is still palpable around this western district.
SEE ALSO FASHION, P.44–7

Place Sainte-Catherine

The Baroque tower of **Sainte-Catherine** ③ is all that remains of the 17th-century church; the rest was rebuilt in the 19th century by Joseph Poelaert (of Palais de Justice fame). Alongside the church, fish and seafood restaurants line the former quaysides. Although increasingly trendy, **Rue de Flandre** retains a few old-fashioned shops, and several restaurants recall the offal-eating habits of the modest population who once inhabited these streets. The **Maison de la Bellone** at no. 46 is a centre for performing arts in a sumptuous Baroque house.

A surprising tranquility pervades the streets around the **Eglise Saint-Jean-Baptiste au Béguinage** ④, a 17th-century Rococo church built for a community of lay nuns *(béguines)*, once 1,200 strong but dissolved in the 19th century.
SEE ALSO CHURCHES, P.37

Symbolic Squares

An audience uprising at the **Théâtre Royal de la Monnaie** ⑤ opera house on **Place de la Monnaie** lit the touchpaper for the Belgian Revolution in August 1830. A performance of Auber's opera *Masaniello*, about the Neapolitan rebellion of 1647, whipped opera-goers into a frenzy, prompting them to rush out and join a workers' demonstration, moving on to storm the Palais de Justice in protest at Dutch rule.

The neo-Classical **Place des Martyrs** ⑥, to the east of the Rue Neuve pedestrianised shopping street, commemorates 450 'martyrs' who died fighting for independence from the Netherlands.
SEE ALSO ARCHITECTURE, P.24

Right: Place Sainte-Catherine.

The Marolles

The wedge of ancient Brussels between Notre-Dame de la Chapelle and Saint-Pierre hospital is named after the convent of the Apostolines of Mariann Colentes ('Maricolles'), who cared for lepers exiled here in the Middle Ages. It is a close-knit working-class quarter with a reputation for standing up to the ruling elite. Creeping gentrification in the past 25 years has brought antiques dealers and higher rents, but has done little for the elderly poor and a large immigrant population. The colourful flea market on Place du Jeu de Balle is a fantastic sight, surrounding by cafés serving soup and *stoemp* to a backing of Brussels dialect and live accordion.

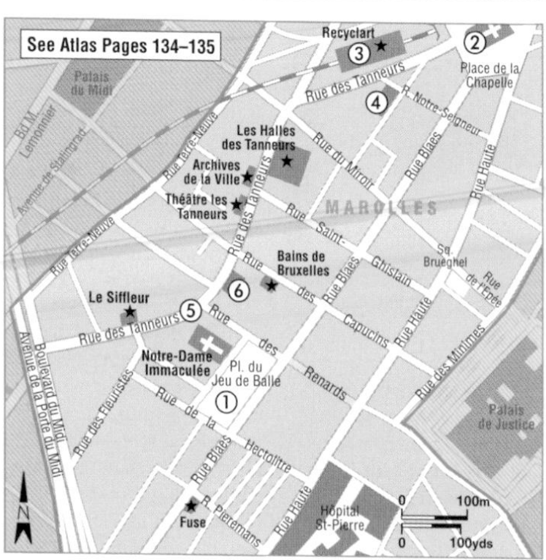

Vieux Marché

The **Vieux Marché** ① flea market on **Place du Jeu de Balle** is one of Brussels' best-loved attractions. Every day, a cornucopia of items old and new, from antiques to rusty nails, is laid out on the cobbles of the sloping square. If many sellers have a speciality – period furniture, chandelier parts, old books, antique linen, 1960s lamps – as many others will lay on their tarpaulin anything from broken dolls to battered saucepans. Traders can smell a tourist at 50 paces and ask ridiculous prices for junk (especially at weekends), so haggling is essential. When the market packs up towards 2pm, crowds pick over the detritus left behind before the rubbish trucks move in. Around the square are a variety of cafés aimed at the eclectic market clientele. The **Bains de Bruxelles** (public baths) in the northwest corner of the square comprise an Art Deco pool on the third floor, and hot baths on the ground floor for the many local residents whose lodgings lack a private bathroom.

SEE ALSO MARKETS, P.75

Place de la Chapelle

The square at the Sablon end of the district is home to the **Eglise Notre-Dame de la Chapelle** ② where artist Pieter Brueghel the Elder married Mayken Coeke in 1563, and where he is buried. Further down the hill, the **Gare de la Chapelle** ③ is a small station that is a destination for more than the commuters who alight each day. Decorated in and out with graffiti, it houses artistic lab and social project **Recyclart**. In a transformation begun in the 1990s, the station ticket

Left: the Recyclart project.

Left: Vieux Marché flea market.

offices and waiting rooms were transformed into workshops, exhibition spaces and a café-restaurant in the former station buffet, complete with priceless retro detailing. The non-profit organisation lays on studio space, courses for jobseekers, club nights and mini festivals in the square outside.

The skinny 16th-century **Eglise des Brigittines** ④ was formerly the church of a Brigittines convent. Long deconsecrated, in recent years it has been transformed into a performance venue for theatre and contemporary dance. A modern seven-storey extension in steel and glass provides space for dressing rooms, rehearsal studios and a café.
SEE ALSO CHURCHES, P.38; NIGHTLIFE, P.90

Rue Haute and Rue Blaes

The area's two parallel main streets are known for their antique and interiors stores and restaurants, with the more upmarket at the Sablon end. On Rue Haute, there is a lovely Art Nouveau facade on the leather goods store at no. 158. The Espace Jacqmotte at no. 139 is a former coffee-roasting factory converted into business units and upscale apartments. In an area where cafés used to close early in the evening and allow the homeless to sleep slumped over their tables, there is a growing buzz at night, thanks in part to the lift from the upper city that has brought an influx of life. Square Pieter Brueghel and **Rue de l'Epée** have several cafés, as does Rue des Capucins, and coachloads of techno fans make a regular pilgrimage to **Fuse**, at the southern end of Rue Blaes.

On the cobbled Rue des Renards are several small galleries and restaurants.
SEE ALSO NIGHTLIFE, P.88

> The Marolles district is often dubbed the Brueghel quarter, after its most famous former resident, 16th-century painter Pieter Brueghel the Elder, who trained in Antwerp and Italy before settling in Brussels. Famous for his 'genre paintings', depicting scenes of everyday life, he was known locally as 'Peasant Brueghel' for his habit of dressing in peasants' clothing and mingling with guests at weddings and other celebrations to draw inspiration for his paintings.

Rue des Tanneurs ⑤

Across from the **Archives de la Ville** (city archives) in a former fabric store at no. 65, is an Art Nouveau former wine warehouse, Le Palais du Vin (no. 60), which has undergone a stunning transformation into **Les Halles des Tanneurs**, a lofty space that combines the best of old and new. The cleaned-up facade shows off the ornamentation and sgraffito medallions identifying principal wine-growing regions. Inside, there's a café on the ground floor, and a bookshop and gourmet restaurant on the mezzanine.

At no. 75, the **Théâtre les Tanneurs** presents cutting-edge French-language theatre and dance, and involves the local community by offering cut-price tickets to those who live nearby. Brussels homeowners in search of a suitable brass door handle or letter box cover for their Art Nouveau house head to **Le Siffleur**, an Aladdin's cave at no. 141, stuffed with period and reproduction glass lampshades, chandelier parts and brass fittings, and many more to order.
SEE ALSO THEATRE AND DANCE, P.121

The Upper City

This eastern half of central Brussels is the seat of royalty, the law and government. It ascends the Coudenberg hill, once the site of a great medieval palace, still partly visible as subterranean ruins. The area was remodelled under Austrian rule and again by King Leopold II. A royal avenue cuts through the district, starting at the Palais de Justice, passing the exclusive Sablon quarter to the grandiose Palais Royal and Parc de Bruxelles before heading out to the royal family's primary residence in Laeken. A clutch of cultural venues perches on the hill, below which the cathedral stands in Gothic majesty.

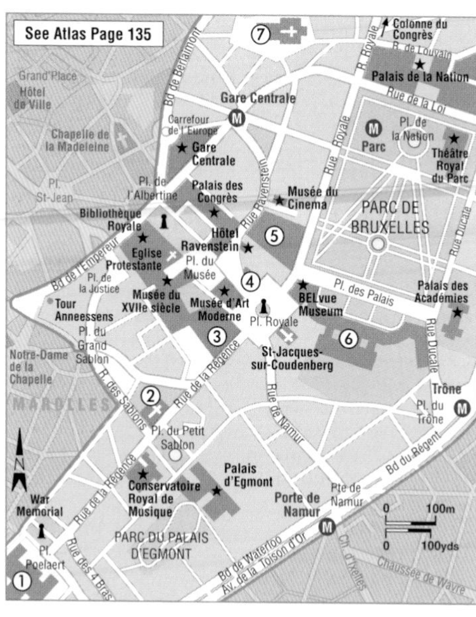

Above: Sablon is home to some of Brussels' finest chocolatiers.

Palais de Justice ①

Leopold II's mammoth courthouse was designed to inspire fear and respect among the lower orders, many of whom lost their homes to make space for the building. The parapet offers a superb view of the Basilica and Atomium.

SEE ALSO ARCHITECTURE, P.24

Sablon

Situated just outside the route of the 14th-century city wall, the **Place du Grand Sablon** derives its name from the sand that was quarried here to build the fortification. In 1568, 19 noblemen were beheaded on the square for signing an appeal to the Spanish rulers calling for an end to the persecution of Protestants. Today it is a rarefied quarter of art and antiques dealers and top-notch chocolate stores and eateries. Well-turned-out Belgians strut their stuff at weekends, when even the stalls of the antiques market are dressed to impress, with dapper red and green awnings.

Beyond the 15th-century **Eglise Notre-Dame du Sablon** ② is the **Petit Sablon**, a pretty garden on the site of the former city burial ground, encircled by 48 bronze statues depicting the trades guilds of yore. At the top of the square is the 16th-century **Palais d'Egmont**, which now houses the Belgian foreign ministry. Tucked behind is the **Parc du Palais d'Egmont**.

SEE ALSO CHURCHES, P.38; FOOD AND DRINK, P.55; MARKETS, P.75; PARKS AND GARDENS, P.97

Place Royale

The elegantly proportioned square was built under the rule of Charles of Lorraine, the

Left: the Musée des Instruments de Musique.

18th-century governor of the Austrian Low Countries. His apartments, in the pretty **Place du Musée** to the west of the square, are now a museum of 18th-century life, the **Musée du XVIIIe siècle**. Opposite, the 15th-century **Hôtel Ravenstein**, a nobleman's house, is a rare survivor from the Burgundian period.

The collections of the **Musées Royaux des Beaux-Arts** ③ bear witness to the illustrious record of painting in the Low Countries, with works by Van Eyck, Brueghel, Bosch, Rubens, Ensor and Magritte.
SEE ALSO MUSEUMS AND GALLERIES, P.80

Mont des Arts

The cultural mecca between Place Royale and the Gare Centrale includes the wrought-iron splendour of the **Musée des Instruments de Musiques** ④, designed in 1899 by Art Nouveau architect Paul Saintenoy for the Old England department store, and reopened a century later to display a world-class collection of instruments. Victor Horta's Art Deco **Palais des Beaux-Arts – Bozar** ⑤ is a maze on seven levels, with a fabulous concert hall, exhibition halls and theatres. Nestled in its side is the **Musée du Cinéma**, which shows classic and art-house films, including silent movies with live piano accompaniment.
SEE ALSO FILM, P.51; MUSEUMS AND GALLERIES, P.80

Parc de Bruxelles

The largest park in the city centre gained its geometric layout, inspired by Masonic symbols, in the late 18th century. On its south side stands the **Palais Royal** ⑥, official residence of the Belgian monarch but used for state occasions only and open to the public in summer. On the northern edge of the park is the **Théâtre Royal du Parc**, facing the **Palais de la Nation**, seat of the Belgian Parliament and Senate.

Further along Rue Royale towards the Botanique, the **Colonne du Congrès** commemorates the founding of Belgium in 1830. A statue of Leopold I, first 'King of the Belgians', stands atop the column; the four female figures at its base symbolise the fundamental rights granted to citizens of the new state: freedom of education and religion, freedom of the press and freedom of assembly.
SEE ALSO PARKS AND GARDENS, P.96; THEATRE AND DANCE, P.121

Cathédrale Saints-Michel-et-Gudule ⑦

Brussels' 13th-century cathedral only gained the rank of cathedral in 1962, when Brussels merged with the diocese of Mechelen (seat of the primate of Belgium). The twin-towered Gothic beauty stands amid dismal office blocks on a thoroughfare created when the north–south rail link was cut through the city in the 1950s.
SEE ALSO CHURCHES, P.38

Beneath the cobbles of Place Royale, the footings of the original Palace of Brussels can be viewed in the **Coudenburg** archeological site. Built from the 12th century for the dukes of Brabant, it was later occupied by Charles V, Holy Roman Emperor, and the Archdukes Albert and Isabella. Famed for its beauty and grandeur, the palace was destroyed by a monumental fire in the winter of 1731 – it is said that the locals attempted to extinguish the flames with beer as the water supply was frozen. *See also Museums and Galleries, p.79.*

The Louise Quarter and South Brussels

Visitors who venture outside central Brussels to bohemian Saint-Gilles, stylish Châtelain, arty Flagey or the African-tinged Matongé are rewarded in spades. The urban southern districts are among the city's most attractive, with excellent shopping on Avenue Louise and Place Brugmann. The birthplace of Art Nouveau, many buildings here boast ornate detail in iron, wood and stained glass. This is also the gateway to the green spaces outside Brussels: the Bois de la Cambre and the Forêt de Soignes.

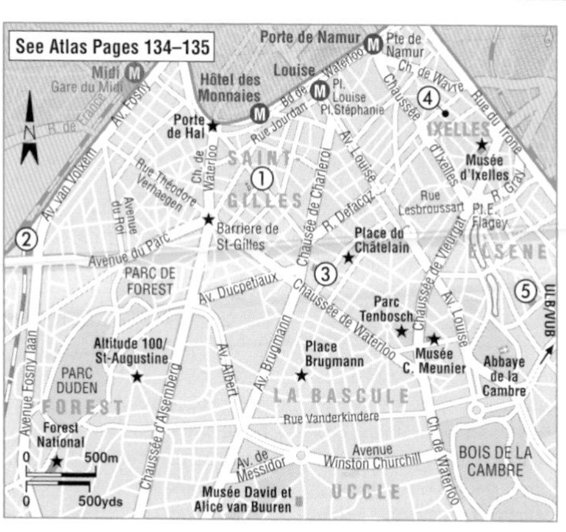

Saint-Gilles and Forest

The commune of Saint-Gilles ①, which rises up the hill to the southeast of the Gare du Midi, gets better the higher you climb. Artists and immigrants inhabit the lower quarters around the **Parvis Saint-Gilles** and its *bobo* cafés and street market.

Things get smarter beyond the **Barrière de Saint-Gilles**, a former tollgate for roads into Brussels, and today a cobbled roundabout well suited to a study of the chaotic priority-to-the-right rule that applies on Belgian roads.

The more suburban **Forest** commune is quieter and greener, but faces similar regeneration challenges. Contemporary art museum **Wiels** ②, in the former Wielemans brewery, has brought a dash of style to the lower part of the commune, otherwise best-known for its Audi car factory and the **Abbey de Forest** on Place Saint Denis. Dating from the 12th century, but extensively rebuilt following a fire in the 18th century, the latter is now a brasserie and reception venue. Superb views can be enjoyed at the from **Altitude 100**, the highest point of Brussels and site of the imposing Art Deco St Augustine's Church, while midway up the hill are two lovely parks and concert

Above: the Ixelles ponds.

arena **Forest National**.
SEE ALSO MUSEUMS AND GALLERIES, P.82; MUSIC, P.87

Châtelain

The heights of Saint-Gilles around the Chaussée de Charleroi include the **Musée Horta** ③, studio and home of the pioneering architect, thanks to whom Brussels can claim to be the world capital of Art Nouveau. This is at the boundary with Ixelles commune, whose **Châtelain** neighbourhood has a villagey atmosphere favoured by young professionals. Chic restaurants, cafés and boutiques, and pretty local **Parc Tenbosch**, make this one of the most desirable spots in town. **Place Brugmann**, to the southwest, is a little more straight-laced but has irresistible boutiques. It sits on

Left: Rue l'Abbaye.

Belgium's historic ties with the Congo are much in evidence in the streets between the Chaussée d'Ixelles and Chaussée de Wavre. Known as the **Matongé**, after a district in Kinshasa, its African hair salons and fashion stores inject a joyful vitality to the area. Rue Saint-Boniface draws on this local colour with its hip bars and restaurants. A mixed local and Euro crowd, and the proximity of several cinemas, keep it lively late into the night.

the border of Uccle, a suburban commune with immense detached properties and a haughty air.
SEE ALSO ART NOUVEAU, P.26; MUSEUMS AND GALLERIES, P.81; PARKS AND GARDENS, P.98

Avenue Louise

This prestigious (if characterless) thoroughfare extends from **Place Louise** to the **Bois de la Cambre**, a landscaped park and woodland. The chestnut-lined avenue was commissioned in 1847 to honour King Leopold II's eldest daughter, Princess Louise-Marie (her younger sister Stéphanie got a nod part-way up, at Place Stéphanie). A well-heeled francophone clientele – often with accompanying miniature doggie – frequents the upscale shops and malls at the city end of the avenue, beneath whose length passes a dual-carriageway to shuttle commuters out of the city. Shopaholics' heaven continues from Place Louise along the inner ring road towards Porte de Namur. The exclusive **Boulevard de Waterloo** – Gucci, Chanel, Hermès and the like – is on the city side, while **Avenue de la Toison d'Or** (and the shopping arcades behind) on the Ixelles side is more your average high street.
SEE ALSO PARKS AND GARDENS, P.94; SHOPPING, P.116

Flagey

Ixelles was always a haven of progressives and intellectuals, a tradition upheld by the municipal **Musée d'Ixelles** ④, with its fine collection of post-Impressionist and *fin de siècle* paintings. Near the lush Ixelles ponds on **Place Flagey**, the former public radio building is a triumph of Art Deco style. It preserves the memory of its pioneering recording studios in its reincarnation as a successful concert and film venue. Children will love the **Musée des Enfants** ⑤ nearby, where they can explore art, theatre and science in hands-on activities.
SEE ALSO CHILDREN P.34; MUSEUMS AND GALLERIES, P.81; MUSIC, P.86; PARKS AND GARDENS, P.94–5

Right: Flagey's Café Belga.

The European Quarter and the Cinquantenaire

Brussels' international character can best be explored in this district, home to some of the most privileged and deprived residents of the country. Euro-lovelies party on Place du Luxembourg, while down in Saint-Josse, Turkish and African families inhabit a municipality with the lowest average income in Belgium. Decades of regrettable planning decisions have left their mark, but a new architecture project for the EU Quarter aims to integrate the European institutions better into their surroundings.

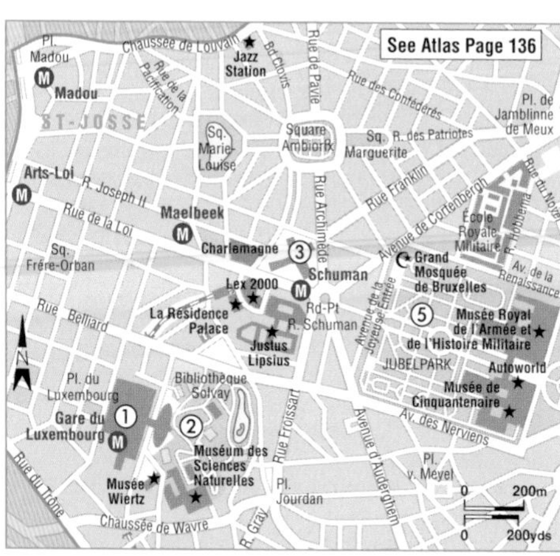

Place du Luxembourg

This neo-Classical square, built around the **Gare du Luxembourg**, is now somewhat dwarfed by the latest extension to the European Parliament. Its cafés are the preferred watering hole for staff and interns of the European Parliament and attendant lobby firms.

SEE ALSO BARS AND CAFÉS, P.33

European Parliament

The glass-and-chrome home of the **European Parliament** ① occupies two buildings joined by a bridge across Rue Wiertz. Inside is a mini town, with a hairdresser's, newsagent, banks, a gym, canteens and coffee bars, as well as committee rooms, offices and a voting chamber. For three weeks each month, meetings are held here; in the fourth, everyone relocates to the principal chamber in the French city of Strasbourg, in a move increasingly criticised as a waste of taxpayers' money.

Parc Leopold ②

A pretty park on a steep escarpment, which cascades down to the former Maelbeek valley (hence the lake). The excellent **Muséum des Sciences Naturelles**, home to a

Below: the imposing arches of the Cinquantenaire, home to two major museums.

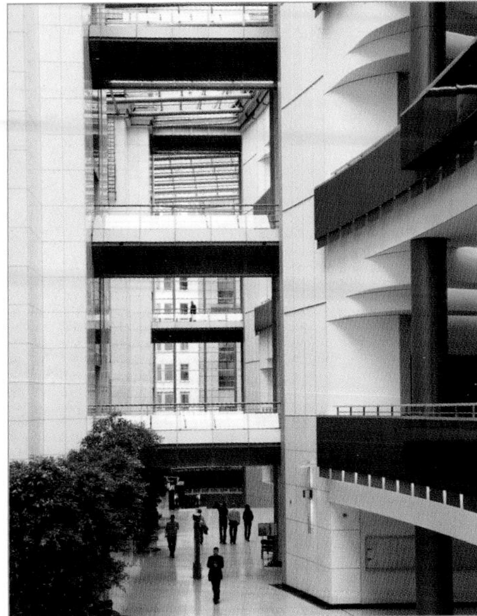

Left: European Parliament.

collection of iguanodon skeletons, is one of several former scientific institutions located within the park.
SEE ALSO MUSEUMS AND GALLERIES, P.83; PARKS AND GARDENS, P.97

Place Jourdan

Much of this area is rather sleepy out of office hours, but Place Jourdan retains a stronger community spirit, with a popular weekend market and arguably the best *frites* stand in the city, **Maison Antoine**. An added bonus: most cafés on the square accept that clients eat fries from the stand in their establishments, in exchange for buying a drink.
SEE ALSO MARKETS, P.75; RESTAURANTS, P.112

Schuman

The hub of this area is Rond-Point Schuman, a congested roundabout and the epicentre of EU decision-making. Facing each other at the top of Rue de la Loi are the principal powerhouses of the European Commission, which occupy the cruciform **Berlaymont** ③ building, and the Council of Ministers, whose seat is the rose-marble and tinted-glass **Justus Lipsius**.

The vast Council of Ministers building has been outgrown by recent EU enlargements. Its extension is the curved-facade glass building a little further down Rue de la Loi, the **Lex 2000**. Between the two and set back from the road is the Art Deco **Résidence Palace**, a former luxury apartment complex that once had banqueting halls, a theatre, rooftop restaurant and a frescoed swimming pool. It is now an office building used by Belgian government officials.

Tranquil Squares

To the north of Schuman and the canyon-like highways of Rue Belliard and Rue de la Loi are the green squares **Marie-Louise** and **Ambiorix**, lined with prestigious properties dating from the Art Nouveau period. The most remarkable is the ornate Maison Saint-Cyr at 11 Square Ambiorix, designed by a pupil of Victor Horta.
SEE ALSO ART NOUVEAU, P.27

Cinquantenaire

The **Parc du Cinquantenaire** ④, created to celebrate Belgium's 50th year of independence in 1880, is a green haven for office workers and local families. Within the park are several major museums – the **Musée du Cinquantenaire**, the **Musée Royal de l'Armée et de l'Histoire Militaire, Autoworld** – and the city's principal mosque. The streets around the park are popular with wealthy Belgian families, senior Eurocrats and diplomats, who shop and dine in the Mérode and Georges Henri neighbourhoods.
SEE ALSO CHILDREN, P.34; MUSEUMS AND GALLERIES, P.82–3; PARKS AND GARDENS, P.97

The 'Berlaymonster'

All EU directives are issued from the 1960s Berlaymont building, which underwent a major refurbishment in the 1990s to remove asbestos. By the time it reopened in 2004, the building had become a byword for Belgian incompetence and bureaucracy: the works had taken 13 years, five years longer than the original construction and at an undisclosed cost. The College of Commissioners now meets in a panoramic 13th-floor chamber (formerly a helipad). Security is tight, and visits possible only on annual open days.

North Brussels and Royal Laeken

This large area follows the extension of Rue Royale out through a regeneration zone around the Brussels–Charleroi canal to the royal park in Laeken, and beyond to the Heysel plateau. Punctuated by strange landmarks such as the Atomium, the immense 20th-century Basilique du Sacré Cœur, and a small house in Jette where Surrealist René Magritte dreamed up his artworks, it reveals parts of Brussels that most visitors never see, including some secluded green spaces.

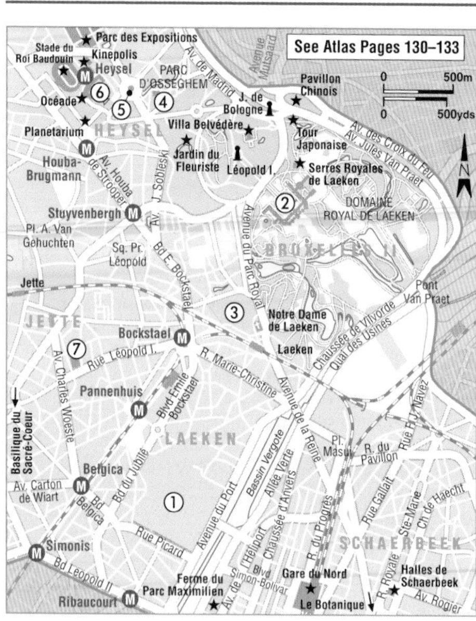

Canal District

One of the most exciting urban developments is taking shape on the west bank of the canal, around **Tour et Taxis** ①, a vast former customs depot. Built 1904–7, the impressive collection of buildings is named after the Von Thurn und Tassis family, an Austrian dynasty who founded the European postal service and who originally owned the site. An exhibition hall and business centre with a top-notch restaurant have been created; housing and community space are in the pipeline.

Across the canal, sandwiched between the Art Deco Citroën garage and some grim tower blocks, the **Ferme du Parc Maximilien** city farm is an unexpected slice of rural life in town, and holds regular activity sessions to teach kids about ecology.
SEE ALSO CHILDREN, P.35

Above: Notre-Dame de Laeken.

Laeken

The Belgian royals live in the **Château Royal** ② in the vast **Domaine Royal de Laeken**. Built under Austrian rule in the late 18th century, it was remodelled by Leopold II, who added the stunning **Serres Royales** (Royal Glasshouses; open to the public for a few weeks each spring) in 1895 to house exotic species brought back from the Congo.

On the fringes of the estate, the ornate **Pavillon Chinois** and **Tour Japonaise** (now museums of oriental art) were both also commissioned by Leopold II, the start of an unfulfilled project to fill his park with exotic architecture.

The **Cimetière de Laeken** ③ is the oldest cemetery in

Left: Cimetière de Laeken.

Brussels (17th century) and surrounds part of a semi-ruined 13th-century church; the current Notre-Dame de Laeken is a neo-Gothic extravaganza. Part of the underground network laid for coffins in the 19th century can be viewed from a flight of steps at the back of the cemetery.

In the lee of the Atomium, the open-air **Théâtre de Verdure** ④ (Theatre of Greenery) is an unjustly overlooked spot within the Parc d'Osseghem, formed for the Universal Exhibition in 1935 and now used for music festivals in summer.
SEE ALSO MUSEUMS AND GALLERIES, P.84; PARKS AND GARDENS, P.94, 98

Heysel

The Heysel plateau was developed to accommodate the pavilions of the World Fairs in 1935 and 1958. Queen among the 1958 structures is the **Atomium** ⑤ a model of an iron molecule magnified 165 billion times. A full renovation to replace the aluminium casing in recent years has restored its shine, and new lights make it twinkle at night. Very odd, but essential viewing, and the inside can be explored too.

King Leopold II (1835–1909) founded the Congo Free State as a private colony in 1885, after hiring explorer Henry Morton Stanley in 1876 to establish him a colony. His rule over the large territory became an international scandal in the early 1900s, following revelations of abuse, enslavement and murder of the native population (estimates of the death toll range from 2 to 15 million). In 1908, the Belgian Parliament forced the king to cede his territory to the state, and crowds booed his funeral cortège. Even so, Leopold II is also remembered as 'the builder king' for the grand construction projects undertaken during his reign.

The rest of the Heysel plateau is devoted largely to leisure pursuits – the **Kinepolis** multiplex, National Planetarium, the **Stade du Roi Baudouin** sports stadium and popular family attractions **Bruparck**'s ⑥ **Mini-Europe** and the **Océade** fun pool.
SEE ALSO ARCHITECTURE, P.25; CHILDREN, P.35; FILM P.51

The Northwest

In the district of Koekelberg, another hill overlooking the city, the fifth-largest church in the world stands in stark majesty – and a mix of Art Deco and neo-Gothic styles. The **Basilique du Sacré Cœur** was built 1905–70 in a vain attempt to give Brussels its own Montmartre.

In the nearby commune of Jette, the **Musée René Magritte** ⑦ celebrates the life of the Belgian Surrealist in the house he occupied for much of his life.
SEE ALSO CHURCHES, P.39; MUSEUMS AND GALLERIES, P.84–5

Schaerbeek

Northeast Brussels has a chequered image, with pockets of deprivation and sleaze around the **Gare du Nord** in Saint-Josse, as well as more affluent suburban areas. Art Nouveau is well represented by the **De Ultieme Hallucinatie**, a quirky bar-brasserie on Rue Royale, and the **Maison Autrique**, now a museum. A beautiful glass-and-steel former covered market on Rue Royale-Sainte-Marie houses French-language cultural centre **Les Halles de Schaerbeek**, while **Le Botanique** puts on concerts and exhibitions in the former botanical garden glasshouses.
SEE ALSO ART NOUVEAU, P.27; BARS AND CAFÉS, P.33; MUSIC P.87

Around Brussels

You don't have to travel far out of Brussels to discover a pastoral idyll of rolling hills, grazing cattle and romantic castles. The southern outskirts of the city are particularly well supplied with dainty châteaux and parkland, and residential property here fetches a high price. The immediate periphery of Brussels is in the Flemish region, and it is here that the nation's linguistic divide is most keenly felt. An earlier conflict – and Napoleon's great defeat – is recalled in Waterloo, one of Belgium's earliest tourist destinations. For less bloody history, the old university town of Leuven is just a short train ride away.

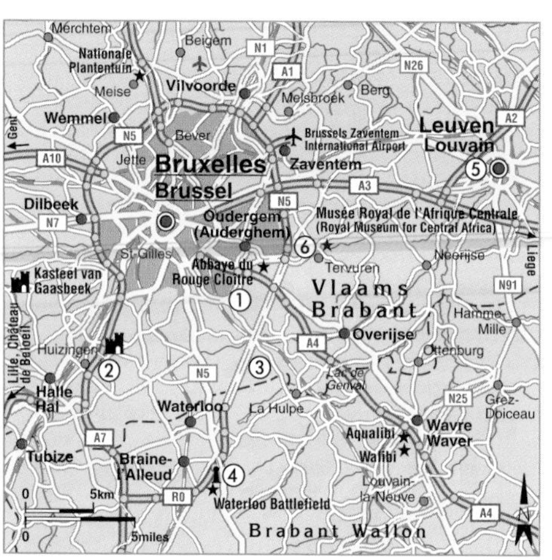

in Meise, north of Heysel, which became the **Nationale Plantentuin** (National Botanical Garden) in 1944, when the collection outgrew its city home. The glasshouses alone are worth the visit.

Southeast of Brussels, the **Lac de Genval** is a good focal point for a civilised stroll, while the nearby **Solvay Park** is home to the **Fondation Folon** ③, dedicated to the work of Brussels-born artist Jean-Michel Folon (1934–2005), known for his illustrations for books such as Aldous Huxley's *Brave New World*.

SEE ALSO MUSEUMS AND GALLERIES, P.85

Forests and Castles

Quick getaways from Brussels to nearby beauty spots are made easy by excellent public transport links and a fast highway network from the city centre. The closest taste of deep green to Brussels is the **Forêt de Soignes**, ① a beautiful, cultivated beech forest in the south of the city, extending to Tervuren. The Abbaye du Rouge Cloître in Oudergerm is a good starting point for walks, and has a pleasant café.

Southwest of Brussels, the **Kasteel van Gaasbeek** is a turreted château surrounded by ponds and parkland. It dates from the 13th century, when it served to protect Brussels from attacks from Hainaut and Flanders. What remains today is the 19th-century rebuild, recently scrubbed clean. The **Kasteel van Beersel** ② is the real thing: a moated medieval stronghold, whose towers and turrets can be explored. The nearby provincial park at **Huizingen** has an outdoor pool, rowing lake, gardens and playgrounds. Another moated castle, 12th-century but much restored, sits amid the spacious country estate

Waterloo

Military history buffs and costumed re-enactors make a beeline for a site south of the small town of Waterloo, the **Butte du Lion** ④ (Lion Mound), which marks the area where an allied army defeated the French Emperor Napoleon Bonaparte in June 1815, leading to his final abdication. The Mound was built in 1825 using soil from the battlefield, at a spot near the centre of the allied armies' position, where the Prince of Orange was wounded. The related museums, a painted panorama and a waxworks, are in need of

Left: Butte de Lion.

Beware confusion when approaching Leuven ('Louvain' in French) by road, bus or rail. Signs for '**Louvain-la-Neuve**' (New Leuven) designate an entirely separate town, 20km (12 miles) to the south. The latter was built in the 1960s when the old university split along linguistic lines, and the French-language institution relocated here. A campus town designed for pedestrians, it is desolate out of term-time. Two of Belgium's largest fun parks are in the vicinity, outside nearby **Wavre**. **Walibi**'s 40 rides include some terrifying experiences; Aqualibi is a sub-tropical water theme park. *See also Children, p.35.*

modernisation, but have a faded charm.

Historic Leuven

The oldest university in the Low Countries was founded in **Leuven** ⑤, a medieval cloth town that reached its zenith in the 12th and 13th centuries, after which Brussels became dominant. Now a lively student town with plentiful cafés and bars, it makes for a pleasant trip away from the capital. Chief among its attractions are the **Grote Markt**, where the 15th-century **Stadhuis** is like a Brabant Gothic wedding cake, with pretty turrets and pointy windows. The **Sint-Pieterskerk**, across the square, is a late-Gothic cruciform basilica containing two paintings by Dirk Bouts, the city painter from 1468 until his death in 1475. About 10 minutes' walk away is the **Groot Begijnhof**, one of Belgium's best preserved *béguinages*, founded around 1230 and once home to 300 lay nuns. Its cobbled streets and tiny brick dwellings are peacefully atmospheric.

Tervuren ⑥

Once the location of a grand park and 17th-century royal palace occupied by Albert and Isabella, the small town of Tervuren regained favour in the 19th century, when King Leopold II built a grand boulevard linking it to Brussels, and constructed the **Musée Royal de l'Afrique Centrale** to display his Congo collection, mementoes brought back by Henry Morton Stanley and other explorers. Nearly 50 years after the Congo gained independence in 1960, the museum's curating team is still trying to shake off the stain of being associated with a brutal colonial regime, which seems somewhat unjust. After all, most of Brussels was built on the plunder of the resource-rich African country.
SEE ALSO MUSEUMS AND GALLERIES, P.85

Below: the Musée Royal de l'Afrique Centrale, in Tervuren.

A–Z

In the following section the city's attractions and services are organised by theme, under alphabetical headings. Items that link to another theme are cross-referenced. All sights that are plotted on the atlas section at the end of the book are given a page number and grid reference.

Architecture

In a city whose two most recognisable monuments are a tiny statue of a urinating boy and a gigantic copy of an iron molecule, architects enjoy a dubious reputation. Popular protest greeted the building of the Palais de Justice in the 1870s, while in recent decades the term *bruxellisation* was coined to describe the crass demolition of historic buildings to make way for office blocks and urban motorways. Thankfully, some treasures have survived, due largely to sustained campaigning by heritage groups. This section highlights the best of these; *see also Art Nouveau, p.26–7.*

Pre-16th Century

Hôtel de Ville

Grand'Place; tel: 02 279 43 65; www.brucity.be; Tue–Sun 10am–5pm; guided visits in English: Tue–Wed 3.15pm, Apr–Sept also Sun 10.45am and 12.15pm; admission charge; metro: Gare Centrale or De Brouckère, tram: 3, 4, bus: 48, 95; map p.135 D2

This masterpiece of Flemish Gothic, built 1402–44, is adorned with 297 statues and a 96m (316ft) openwork spire. The south wing and Baroque courtyard were added in the 18th century. The municipal wedding chamber is where leaders of the nine corporations formed in 1421 met to decide on local affairs: the guilds' coats of arms still adorn the walls. Visitors can climb the spire, within which nestles a statue of St Michael, patron saint of Brussels, crushing the devil (a copy replaces the bronze original).

Below: the Hôtel de Ville.

La Porte de Hal

Boulevard du Midi; tel: 02 534 15 18; www.mrah.be; Tue–Fri 9.30am–5pm, Sat–Sun and public holidays 10am–5pm; admission charge; metro: Porte de Hal, tram: 3, 4, bus: 27, 48; map p.135 C4

The sole survivor of the seven city gates from the outer medieval wall, built in the 15th century but much restored, is a formidable fortified tower. It served as a prison from the 16th–18th century, but is less fearsome since it was reopened as a museum of Brussels history.

MUSEUMS AND GALLERIES, P.78

16th–18th Centuries

Place des Martyrs

Place des Martyrs; tel: 0477 21 07 33 (crypt visits only); metro: De Brouckère, tram: 3, 4, bus: 38, 66, 71; map p.135 D1

A neo-Classical square built in 1775 by architect Claude Fisco and restored in the past 10 years in an example of 'facadism': the facades were supported while the buildings behind were entirely reconstructed. A monument and crypt were added to the square after 1830, to honour the 450 'martyrs' who died fighting the Dutch for Belgian independence. Group visits of the crypt can be arranged.

19th Century

Palais de Justice

Place Poelaert; tel: 02 508 64 10; Mon–Fri 8am–5pm, closed public holidays and July; free, guided tours on written request; metro: Louise, tram: 92, 94; map p.135 D4

The monolith Brussels lawcourts were designed to intimidate the lower orders and inspire awe of the judicial system. Joseph Poelaert designed it in 1862, and it was

Left: the Atomium.

20th Century

Atomium

Square de l'Atomium; tel: 02 475 47 75; www.atomium.be; daily 10am–7pm, Thur until 10pm; admission charge; metro: Heysel, tram: 23, 51; map p.130 C2

Possibly the strangest monument imaginable, a 102m (335ft) tall copy of an iron crystalline molecule designed by engineer André Waterkeyn for the 1958 World Fair. The nine aluminium spheres are linked by tubes containing escalators and staircases. Never intended to survive, it proved so popular that funding was found for a full renovation. Five spheres are open to the public today, including the top one – a café and restaurant.

SEE ALSO RESTAURANTS, P.112

Flagey

Place Sainte-Croix; tel: 02 641 10 20; www.flagey.be; free; guided tours on written request; tram: 81; bus: 38, 60, 71

Once home to the former National Institute for Radio Broadcasting (NIR), this Art Deco building was designed to resemble a passenger liner. It gained world renown for the acoustic excellence of its recording studios and concert halls. It is now a cinema and music venue.

SEE ALSO BARS AND CAFÉS, P.32; MUSIC, P.86

The Architecture Foundation (55 Rue de l'Hermitage; tel: 02 642 24 50; www.civa.be; Tue–Sun 10.30am–6pm; admission charge; tram: 81, 94, bus: 54, 71) is located within a large complex (CIVA) devoted to architecture and comprising a library, archives and bookshop. Opposite lies **La Loge Museum of Architecture** (86 Rue de l'Hermitage; tel: 02 649 86 65; www.aam.be; open for exhibitions only, Tue–Sun noon–6pm, Wed until 9pm; admission charge).

completed in 1883. Costs spiralled to 12 times the estimate, equal to the country's entire public works budget for one year; 3,000 homes in the Marolles were razed, and Poelaert became a figure of hate, inspiring the Brussels dialect insult *schieven architek* (twisted architect), which continued to be used long after he had gone mad seeing his project come to fruition.

Palais Royal

Place des Palais; tel: 02 551 20 20; www.monarchie.be; late July–early Sept Tue–Sun 10.30am–4.30pm; free; metro: Trône, tram: 92, 94, bus: 27, 38, 71; map p.135 E3

The royal family live in the Château de Laeken and use this official residence purely for business and state occasions, opening its doors to the public for six weeks in summer. Begun in 1820 under the reign of King William (and remodelled by Leopold II in 1904), it occupies the site of the former Palace of the Dukes of Brabant (whose remains lie in the Coudenberg archeological site).

SEE ALSO MUSEUMS AND GALLERIES, P.79

Right: the Palais Royal.

Art Nouveau

In 1893, when great tracts of Brussels were being built, two architects, Victor Horta and Paul Hankar, started employing organic forms that broke with tradition. 'Art Nouveau' used the materials of the industrial age to evoke floral, feminine forms in ironwork. The style caught on, and soon hundreds more homes, shops and cafés were built in a similar style. This chapter highlights the best surviving Art Nouveau buildings in Brussels. Besides cafés and shops, only five are permanently open to visitors, but two of these are museums. A walking tour is an ideal way to take in the rest.

For further information on Art Nouveau in Brussels visit www.brusselsartnouveau.be. The tourist office produces a map of four walking itineraries for visitors to discover Art Nouveau properties around the city, as well as a detailed background to the style.

Upper City

Musée des Instruments de Musique (MIM)
Montagne de la Cour 2; tel: 02 545 01 30; www.mim.fgov.be; Tue–Fri 9.30am–5pm, Sat–Sun 10am–5pm; admission charge; tram: 92, 94, bus: 27, 38, 71; map p.135 D3
The ironwork-and-glass facade of this former department store, designed in 1904 by Paul Saintenoy, stops passers-by in their tracks and now houses a museum.
SEE ALSO MUSEUMS AND GALLERIES, P.80

Louise Quarter and South Brussels

Hôtel Ciamberlani
Rue Defacqz 48; not open to the public; tram: 92, 94, 97, bus: 54
Architect Paul Hankar's affection for Moorish touches is visible on the facade of this private home (1897) designed for artist Albert Ciamberlani. The first-floor windows illuminate the former artist's studio.

Hôtel Hannon
Avenue de la Jonction 1; tel: 02 538 42 20; www.contretype.org; Wed–Fri 11am–6pm, Sat–Sun 1–6pm; admission charge; tram: 4, 23, 92, bus: 54
Commissioned in 1902 by engineer Edouard Hannon (1853–1931) for his friend, architect Jules Brunfaut (1852–1942), this mansion is a head-turning example of the style. Run by photographic organisation Contretype, it hosts temporary photo exhibitions.

Hôtel Otlet
Rue de Livourne 48; not open to the public; tram: 92, 94, 97
This grand corner house was designed by architect Octave Van Rysselberghe, with an interior by Henri van de Velde, built 1894–8. A more classical style of Art Nouveau, it alludes to the Italian Renaissance.

Hôtel Stoclet
Avenue de Tervuren 281; not open to the public; tram: 39, 44
One of the most striking buildings in Brussels, this mansion was built by Viennese architect Joseph Hoffman in 1905–11 in a style that foretells the shift to Art Deco. No expense was spared for owner Baron Stoclet: the facade is coated in white marble and gilded mouldings, while the interior, including a Gustav Klimt frieze for the dining room, was created by the Wiener Werkstätte (Viennese workshops), which Hoffman founded.

Maison Paul Hankar
Rue Defacqz 71; not open to the public; tram: 92, 94, 97, bus: 54
The home that Paul Hankar had built for himself, in 1893, was his first major work and launched the new style. It has wide bow windows, visible use of ironwork on the facade and sgraffito beneath the cornice.

Musée Horta
Rue Américaine 25; tel: 02 543 04 90; www.hortamuseum.be; Tue–Sun 2–5.30pm, except public holidays; admission charge; tram: 81, 92, 97, bus: 54, 60

Left: the front of the Musée des Instruments de Musique.

Possibly the best example of the style: two houses that Victor Horta designed as his own home and studio (built 1898–1901), which highlight the movement's insistence on the equal artistic merit of decorative and fine arts.
SEE ALSO MUSEUMS AND GALLERIES, P.81

Rue Vanderschrick

Rue Vanderschrick 1–25; not open to the public; tram: 4, 23, 55 (Parvis St-Gilles or Porte de Hal), bus: 48

A terrace of 17 houses built by architect Ernest Blerot: all slightly different but with typical flourishes in the pediments and gables, and ornate wooden bays. At the end of the street, café-restaurant **La Porteuse d'Eau** is a well-executed but soulless replica of the Art Nouveau original.

European Quarter and the Cinquantenaire

Maison Cauchie

Rue des Francs 5; tel: 02 673 15 06; www.cauchie.be; first weekend of each month 10am–1pm and 2–5.30pm or by arrangement; admission charge; metro: Merode, tram: 81, bus: 27, 61, 80

A spectacular facade sets this house apart from its neighbours. Architect Paul Cauchie built it for himself in 1905 and it is remarkable for its sgraffito – a design technique in which a layer of plaster in a contrasting colour is applied wet, and then an outline scratched away to reveal the colour beneath.

Maison Saint-Cyr

Square Ambiorix 11; not open to the public; metro: Schuman, bus: 22, 60, 63; map p.136 B2

A highly ornate house with ironwork balconies on all four floors, built by Horta pupil Gustave Strauven in 1903 as the private residence for painter Georges Léonard de Saint-Cyr. After falling into terrible disrepair as successive owners failed to raise the funds needed to restore the listed building, it is now undergoing renovation.

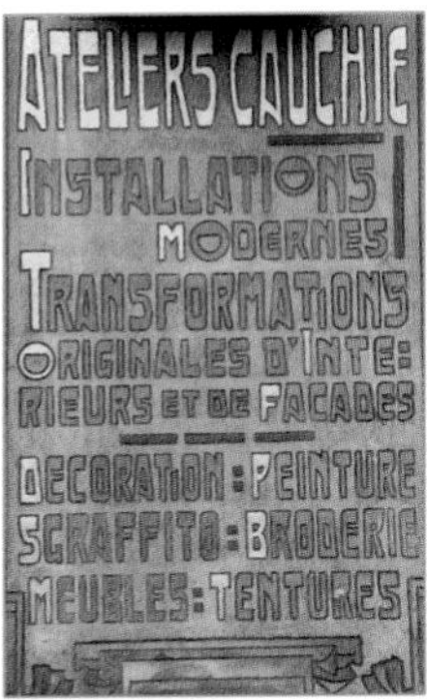

Below: Maison Cauchie.

North Brussels and Royal Laeken

Hôtel Cohn-Donnay (De Ultieme Hallucinatie)

Rue Royale 316; tel: 02 217 06 14; www.ultiemehallucinatie.be; brasserie open Mon–Fri 11am–1am, Sat 5.30pm–1am; free entrance to brasserie; metro: Botanique, tram: 92, 94

Paul Hamesse undertook a renovation of this 1850 house in 1904, adding a frontage to the neo-Classical facade and remodelling the interior, influenced by the Glasgow School (Mackintosh) and the Viennese Succession, with a hint of the nascent Art Deco style.
SEE ALSO BARS AND CAFÉS, P.33

Maison Autrique

Chaussée de Haecht 266; tel: 02 215 66 00; www.autrique.be; Wed–Sun noon–6pm; admission charge; tram: 90, 92, 93; bus: 59, 65, 66

The house which launched Art Nouveau in Brussels: Victor Horta's first private commission, for his friend Eugène Autrique, was built in 1893 using some of the new techniques of the industrial age. A major restoration in the 1990s uncovered original paint layers and room partitions, long since changed. The visit is presented as a journey into the memory of a house through layers of time and space.

Bars and Cafés

No visit to Brussels would be complete without a frequent pit-stop in one of the many excellent cafés and bars, and those who stray off the tourist map will be rewarded by a warm welcome and good-value drinks. The most fashionable spots are around Place Saint-Géry and Rue du Marché au Charbon, with another hub at Place du Luxembourg for a good-looking Euro crowd. This section highlights the best in a city with innumerable options, whether you want an extensive beer list or a cup of coffee. For bars whose prime draw is their dance floor and DJ sessions, *see Nightlife, p.88–91.*

Grand'Place

Floris Bar

Impasse de la Fidélité 12; tel: 02 514 44 34; www.floris-bar.be; daily 8pm–6am; metro: De Brouckère, tram: 3, 4, bus: 63, 66, 71; map p.135 D2

In a tiny cul-de-sac inhabited by Jeanneke-Pis, the Manneken's modern sister, this spirits bar specialises in absinthe, the aniseed-flavoured drink known for driving French poets mad: 300 varieties are available. Lively cellar bar **Delirium Café** opposite is under the same ownership and boasts 2,000 different beers.

Goupil le Fol

Rue de la Violette 22; tel: 02 511 13 96; Sun–Thur 5pm–5am, Fri–Sat 5pm–7am; tram: 3, 4, bus: 48, 95; map p.135 D2

Curious venue with a rather dreamlike quality, which could be attributed to the effects of the house speciality: fruit wine. Located in a former brothel, you can snuggle up with your friends or loved one on an aged, grubby sofa on the upper floors, studying the paintings or old vinyl records that adorn the walls, or stay around the ground-floor bar listening to Jacques Brel and Edith Piaf. Dark, a tad seedy and unforgettable.

Mokafé

Galerie du Roi 9; tel: 02 511 78 70; daily 9am–1am; metro: De Brouckère, tram: 3, 4, bus: 63, 66, 71; map p.135 D2

With a terrace perfect for people-watching in the elegant Galeries Saint-Hubert arcade, this trad café serves good-value meals, cakes and drinks for its prime location, and boasts professional fast service. If not the terrace, the front room overlooking the arcade has more character than the rear, although you'll rarely have the choice. Great hot chocolate.

Lower City

AM Sweet

Rue des Chartreux 4; tel: 02 513 51 31; Tue–Sat 9am–6pm; tram: 3, 4, bus: 46, 58; map p.135 C2

The tea and sweet shop celebrates exquisite flavours, with a tiny tearoom on two creaky floors in an old property. Its long menu features brews from Parisian label Frères Mariage, as well as scrumptious cakes, Parma violets and fine chocolates by Laurent Gerbaud, all of which may also be taken home and consumed with pleasure.

L'Archiduc

Rue Antoine Dansaert 6; tel: 02 512 06 52; www.archiduc.net; daily 4pm–5am; tram: 3, 4, bus: 46, 58; map p.135 C2

A fabulous Art Deco interior modelled on a 1920s liner with club chairs, columns and a grand piano makes for faded grandeur with attitude: service is not fast and the drinks are pricey. If you can take that, it's wonderful for post-shopping drinks (weekend jazz concerts at 5pm) or late into the night. The horseshoe-shaped balcony is good for people-watching through a haze of smoke.

Café Walvis

Rue Antoine Dansaert 209; www.cafewalvis.be; daily 9am–late evening; metro: Comte de Flandre, tram: 51; map p.134 C1

Fashion designers and other

Right: scented tea and handmade sweets at AM Sweet.

Left: beer on tap at L'Archiduc.

There was a time in Brussels when you could take a seat in a café and count on a waiter dropping by to collect your drinks order within minutes. While this is still the norm, recent years have seen the practice ditched in a new generation of establishments, notably those launched by local bar entrepreneur Fred Nicolay – including Café Belga *(see p.32)* and Café Walvis *(see p.28)* – and now getting picked up in newer cafés, such as Maison du Peuple *(see p.32)*.

(mainly Flemish) creatives who work around the affordable end of Rue Dansaert break from work in their respective studios to meet at the 'Whale', facing the canal with a large west-facing terrace. Live concerts twice a month feature edgy local musicians strong on impro jazz.

Le Cercle des Voyageurs
Rue des Grands Carmes 16–18; tel: 02 514 39 49; www.lecercledesvoyageurs.com; Mon, Wed, Thur 11am–11pm, Fri 11am–midnight, Sat noon–midnight, Sun noon–10pm; tram: 3, 4, bus: 48, 95; map p.135 C2
Parlour palms and leather club armchairs give this mansion ground floor the feel of a private club. In fact, it is an unpretentious café-restaurant for anyone who loves to travel, for real or in spirit, and has a reading room of guidebooks and a regular programme of travel-themed films, slideshows and discussion evenings.

Le Cirio
Rue de la Bourse 18–20; tel: 02 512 13 95; daily 10am–1am; tram: 3, 4, bus: 48, 95; map p.135 C2
An original and still one of the best: a *fin de siècle* bar with stripy upholstered banquettes, a gilded ceiling and chandeliers. Regulars include elegant older ladies with small dogs, sipping the house special and Brussels' classic: *half-en-half* (half white wine, half sparkling wine), or businessmen catching up on emails while downing a Duvel.

Au Daringman
Rue de Flandre 27; tel: 02 251 43 23; Tue–Fri from noon, Sat 4pm–late; metro: Sainte-Catherine, bus: 88; map p.134 C1
Tiny bar with working-class roots that's been appropri-

Left: the *fin de siècle* exterior of Le Cirio *(see p.29)*.

like talking to folks at neighbouring tables, who are of all nationalities and income brackets, yet share a love of the city's underbelly.

Monk

Rue Sainte-Catherine 42; tel: 02 503 08 80; www.monk.be; Mon–Thur 11am–2am, Fri–Sat 11am–4am, Sun from 4pm; metro: Sainte-Catherine, tram: 3, 4, bus: 46, 47, 88; map p.134 C2

Like its right-on Flemish clientele, this café has mastered the art of dressing up by dressing down. Modelled on a traditional brown café, with dark-wood furniture, tiled floor and panelled walls, it gets busy late in the evening with tousle-haired night-owls.

A la Mort Subite

Rue Montagne-aux-Herbes Potagères 7; tel: 02 513 13 18; www.alamortsubite.com; daily 10.30am–1am; metro: De Brouckère, tram: 3, 4, bus: 63, 65, 66; map p.135 D2

A beer-lover's haven in beautiful Art Deco surroundings: a long room lined with mirrors and divided by columns. Very touristy, but none the worse for that; it serves its own variety of gueuze, a good selection on draught, and since it also does decent

ated by hip Flemish creatives. Drop in late of an evening and strike up a conversation with trendies and eccentrics young and old. It doesn't try too hard, and therein lies its charm.

Le Fontainas

Rue du Marché au Charbon 91; tel: 02 503 31 12; Mon–Fri 2pm–2am, Sat–Sun 2pm–3am; tram: 3, 4, bus: 48, 95; map p.135 C/D2

Straight bar with a strong gay following that is the centre of the buzz in the Rue du Marché au Charbon. Its 1950s retro look with draping greenery, friendly service and – above all – large terrace on a pedestrianised corner are the secret of its success, as well as the fresh mint tea, good hot chocolate and perky Mojitos. Free Wi-fi too.

Kafka

Rue de la Vierge Noire 6; tel: 02 513 54 89; www.myspace.com/cafekafka; daily 4pm–2am; metro: De Brouckère, tram: 3, 4, bus: 47, 88; map p.135 C2

Nicotine-stained, smoky and packed late at night, the ideal spot for a deep conversation on remaking the global economic system, washed down with a glass of vodka or the local Cantillon beer. Owner Patrice is something of a philosopher, and his clients follow in the same vein; they

Below: Le Cercle des Voyageurs *(see p.29)*.

Many bars and cafés listed in this section also serve good-value meals: spaghetti Bolognese or lasagne are usually the best value, but many menus are a lot more elaborate. Since the smoking ban at the start of 2007, establishments that serve food must be non-smoking, or provide a sectioned-off non-smoking area, although observance of this rule is patchy.

brasserie food, it is all too easy to stay for hours.

Le Pain Quotidien
Rue Antoine Dansaert 16; tel: 02 502 23 61; www.lepainquotidien.be; Sun–Fri 7.30am–5pm, Sat 7.30am–6pm; tram: 3, 4, bus: 46, 58; map p.135 C2
A Belgian chef's quest for the perfect loaf of bread has grown into a successful international chain of café and bakery stores, now in 13 countries. This is the original (and smallest) shop, with the large shared table that is at the heart of the concept. It's perfect for breakfasts, savoury open sandwiches (*tartines*) and to-die-for cakes.

Roskam
Rue de Flandre 9; tel: 02 503 51 54; www.cafe-roskam.be; daily 4pm–5am; metro: Sainte-Catherine, bus: 88; map p.134 C1
Stylish bar that is a perfect antidote to the feeling that you've grown out of Saint-Géry, and a real contender to topple L'Archiduc *(see p.28)* from its increasingly complacent perch. The regular live jazz and world music and reasonably priced cocktails will restore vigour to your stride.

Taverne Greenwich
Rue des Chartreux 7; tel: 02 511 41 67; daily 10.30am–midnight; tram: 3, 4, bus: 46, 58; map p.135 C2
A chess-player's meeting place, untouched by passing trends, the Greenwich is perfect for quiet contemplation over a beer, drinking in a vision of old-school Brussels in a fine period interior. The only sound is the rustle of a newspaper or the slap of a hand coming down on a timer. It also boasts one of the finest toilets in town, in the basement.

Zebra
Place Saint-Géry 35; tel: 02 511 09 01; www.st-gery.be; daily 11am–1am; tram: 3, 4, bus: 46, 58; map p.135 C2
The liveliest square downtown boasts several good cafés, but this is the original and the best, with the sunniest terrace, a small, post-industrial interior, laid-back sounds on the decks and fresh juices, mint tea and hot paninis on the menu. It launched the Saint-Géry revival, and continues to draw artists, students and trend-setters.

> Belgium has long remained impervious to the spread of Starbucks, but that resistance will end in 2009, as the US coffee-to-go chain is set to open its first branch in the country, in Brussels Airport.

Marolles

La Brocante
Rue Blaes 170; tel: 02 512 13 43; Tue–Fri 6am–7pm, Sat–Mon 6am–6pm; bus: 27, 48; map p.135 C4
On a corner of the flea market, this traditional café opens at dawn for market traders – and clubbers exiting nearby techno temple Fuse. An institution of the working-class Marolles, it has live jazz at weekend lunchtimes, cheap local dishes including *stoemp* or 'pressed head' terrine and three dozen small-brewery beers. All of Brussels is here, albeit in bleary-eyed form.

Upper City

Le Bier Circus
Rue de l'Enseignement 57; tel: 02 218 00 34; www.bier-circus.be; Tue–Fri noon–

Below: rue des Chartreux is home to several popular bars, including Taverne Greenwich.

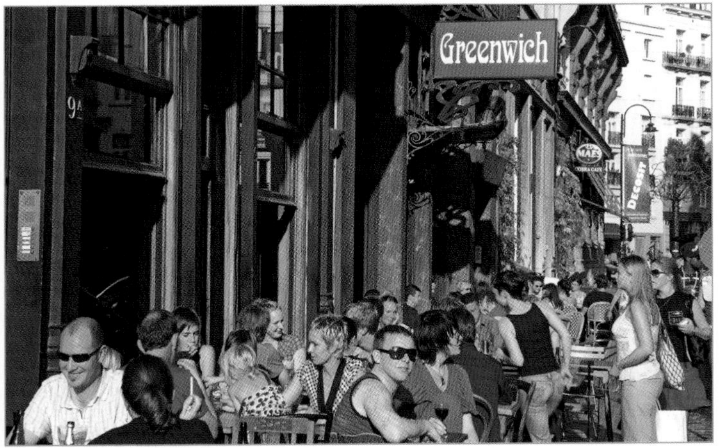

Bar culture in Belgium is convivial, with the emphasis on conversation rather than consumption (note that beers are served in quarter-litre glasses, and only tourists are offered half-litres). Belgians prefer to socialise in small, mixed groups, with the result that large same-sex groups tend to stand out as foreigners on a hen/stag weekend and may not get a warm reception outside Irish bars or tourist spots.

2.30pm, 6–11pm, Sat 6–11pm; metro: Madou, tram: 92, 94, bus: 29, 65, 66; map p.135 E2
A place of pilgrimage for beer fans, with a connoisseur's menu including vintage brews and small brewery produce. White-label Chimay, Chouffe and Bink blonde are on tap, and the last is the closest you'll get to pils in the joint. A recent move to more spacious quarters last year removed some of its rustic charm, and added a restaurant that resembles a works canteen.

Le Flat
Rue de la Reinette 12; tel: 0472 18 98 73; www.theflat.be; Wed–Sat 6pm–2am; metro: Porte de Namur, bus: 54, 71, 80; map p.135 E2
Set out like a stylish apartment, this small lounge bar is perfect for those who like a flutter, as the price of drinks fluctuates in response to demand as if on a stock exchange. Take up a perch in the living room, bathroom or bedroom, and get chatting with your new roommates.

Louise Quarter and South Brussels

Café Belga
Place Flagey 18; tel: 02 640 35 08; www.cafebelga.be; 8am–2am, Sat–Sun until 3am; tram: 81; bus: 38, 59, 60, 71
With an architecture school nearby and many young Eurocrats in the neighbourhood, the café beneath Flagey cultural venue is a runaway success, popular with large groups. It gets rammed on a weekend evening, when you need to battle to reach the bar, but will be rewarded by sight of the gorgeous staff, although they may be too busy posing to serve you. Bar food from 9am–4pm.

Maison du Peuple
Parvis Saint-Gilles 39; www.maison-du-peuple.be; daily 8.30am–midnight, later Sat–Sun; metro: Porte de Hal, tram: 3, 4, 51, bus: 48
The 'house of the people' was built in 1905 as a meeting place for Socialists; Lenin spoke here in 1914. Several changes of function later, in 2008 the ground floor reopened as a bright, hip bar for Saint-Gilles bohemians, with exposed brick walls, a reading corner with armchairs, DJ sets each Fri and Sat from 10pm–2am and twice-monthly live rock gigs. Light snacks and bar meals are served noon–10pm.

L'Ultime Atome
Rue Saint-Boniface 14; tel: 02 511 13 67; www.ultime-atome.com; Mon–Fri 8am–1am, Sat–Sun 10am–1am; metro: Porte de Namur, bus: 54, 71; map p.135 E4
Perenially popular bar-brasserie that is the hub of the Saint-Boniface district, and as good for breakfast à deux as a solo dinner when travelling on business or a late drink with friends after a

Below: former Socialist meeting place, the Maison du Peuple.

Left: many bars offer a wide selection of draught beers.

movie. Competition for a terrace table is fierce on fine days, and the staff are famously cool-mannered. But with the good selection of beers, decent enough food and perpetual buzz, this is one of the best meeting spots in town.

European Quarter and the Cinquantenaire

Fat Boy's Sports Bar and Grill

Place du Luxembourg 5; tel: 02 511 32 66; www.fatboys-be.com; daily 11am–late, 4am Sat–Sun; train: Gare du Luxembourg, bus: 27, 54, 80

Loved and hated in equal measure, the only sports bar in the city worthy of the name has 10 screens and one very large one, and is a melting pot for sports-freaks of all nationalities. The American-style food attracts homesick US citizens and anyone else who fancies a large burger with chilli sauce, and is served lunchtimes and evenings during the week, and non-stop at weekends.

> A standard Belgian coffee is served quite strong in a smallish cup and saucer, with a pot of cream on the side, as well as a sweet biscuit. Alcoholic drinks usually come with a small bowl of peanuts or savoury nibbles. Tea-drinking in cafés is to be avoided unless you are a fan of non-boiling water served with a insipid Lipton tea bag on the side. Even specialist tea shops in Belgium will not serve strong black tea with milk, as, in common with much of Continental Europe, tea-drinking is seen as an upmarket pastime involving mild, scented brews to be sampled like fine wine. On the other hand, herbal teas ('infusions') are widely available, and commonly drunk after dinner by those who don't want coffee.

Piola Libri

Rue Franklin 66–68; tel: 02 736 93 91; www.piolalibri.be; Mon–Fri 11am–8pm (bookshop), noon–3pm (restaurant), 6pm–10pm (wine bar), Sat noon–6pm; metro: Schuman, bus: 21, 79; map p.136 C2

Piola is an old Piedmontese word for 'wine bar', and this place preserves the tradition of the region, serving wines from small vineyards accompanied by complimentary antipasti in warm and convivial surroundings, in this case, an Italian bookshop (the 'libri'). Immensely popular with an Italian-strong EU crowd since it opened in 2007, especially on a Friday for after-work aperitifs, but also for its daily lunch menu and occasional concerts.

Ralph's

Place du Luxembourg 13; tel: 02 230 16 13; www.ralphsbar.be; Mon–Fri 2pm–late; bus: 21, 27, 54

The pulse of 'Plux', so don't expect a seat in the early evening during a European Parliament working week, when the 6–7pm happy hour pulls in a young international crowd, dressed to impress. Tapas and snacks are served in the evening and, as the night wears on, the dancing starts and any language barriers drop clean away.

Tout Bon

Rue du Luxembourg 68; tel: 02 230 42 44; www.toutbon.be; Mon–Fri 8am–7pm, Sat 7am–5pm, Sun 8am–5pm; bus: 21, 27, 54

The breakfast meeting place near the European Parliament, modelled closely on the Pain Quotidien (it used to be a franchise), and good for coffee meetings with tasty pastries, sandwiches and salads from early morning to late afternoon.

North Brussels and Royal Laeken

De Ultieme Hallucinatie

Rue Royale 316; tel: 02 217 06 14; www.ultiemehallucinatie.be; Mon–Fri 11am–1am, Sat 5.30pm–1am; metro: Botanique, tram: 92, 94

Slightly out of the way, but its stunning interior is worth the detour. On the ground floor of a major Art Nouveau establishment, the bar-brasserie is inspired by station architecture, with painted wooden booths, high-backed benches, fans and a metal-and-glass canopy over the bar. The menu is simple and sufficient, with Trappist and other Belgian beers, a wide selection of wines, as well as a broad food menu from snacks and salads to pasta or steak.

SEE ALSO ART NOUVEAU, P.27

Children

Belgians are very family-minded, so those visiting Brussels with children can expect a friendly reception. Restaurants provide high-chairs and child menus and major museums offer child-focused activities. Entry to public swimming pools is cheap, and many parks and gardens have good playgrounds. Taking public transport with small kids is also simple: the metro and buses are pushchair-friendly, and children travel free up to the age of six (locals up to 12 with a transport pass). This chapter provides details of babysitting services plus an overview of attractions likely to appeal to little ones.

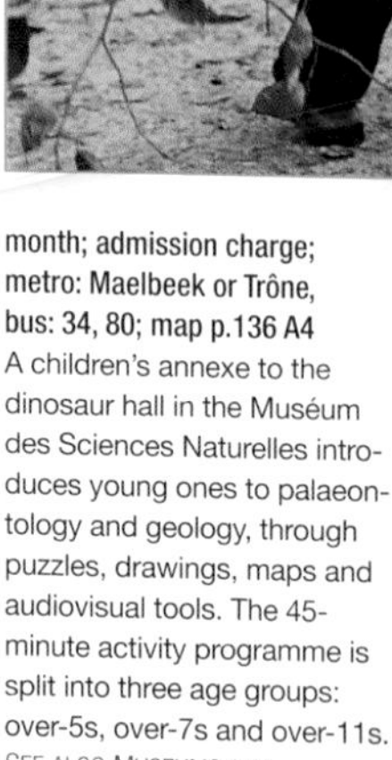

Babysitting Services

The following organisations can help with childcare.

Ligue des Familles
Rue du Trône 127; tel: 02 507 72 11; www.liguedesfamilles.be
Family association which published a newsletter for families and keeps a register of recommended babysitters.

ULB Service Jobs
Avenue Jeanne 44; tel: 02 650 21 71; Mon–Thur 10am–noon, 2–4pm, Fri 10am–noon
The Brussels Free University jobs section can put parents in touch with students who do babysitting work.

Indoor Play Centres

Kid's Factory
Chaussée de Ninove 281; tel: 02 414 11 51; www.kidsfactory.be; Wed–Fri noon–7pm, Sat–Sun and school holidays 10am–7pm; admission charge; metro: Gare de l'Ouest, bus: 20, 85; map p.134 A2
Large indoor play centre with inflatables, mazes and slides, suitable for kids aged 1 to 11, and with free entry for parents and an attractive café. There's another branch in Waterloo, and both are popular for birthday parties.

Best Parks for Children
Parc du Cinquantenaire
Parc Tenbosch
Parc de Bruxelles
Forêt de Soignes/Parc du Rouge Cloître
See also Parks and Gardens, p.94–99.

Museums and Galleries

Musée des Enfants
Rue du Bourgmestre 15; tel: 02 640 01 07; www.museedesenfants.be; Wed, Sat, Sun 2.30–5pm, daily during school holidays; admission charge; tram: 23, 24, 25, bus: 71
Budding scientists, musicians, actors and crafts-people can explore their talent in this much-loved museum in Ixelles. Aimed at kids aged 4–12 years, but younger ones enjoy it too.

Paleo Lab
Rue Vautier 29; tel: 02 627 42 38; www.sciencesnaturelles.be; 45-minute activity programme on Wed 2.30pm, also 3.30pm in summer holiday, Sat–Sun and school holidays 1.30pm, 2.30pm and 3.30pm, closed first Wed of month; admission charge; metro: Maelbeek or Trône, bus: 34, 80; map p.136 A4
A children's annexe to the dinosaur hall in the Muséum des Sciences Naturelles introduces young ones to palaeontology and geology, through puzzles, drawings, maps and audiovisual tools. The 45-minute activity programme is split into three age groups: over-5s, over-7s and over-11s.
SEE ALSO MUSEUMS AND GALLERIES, P.83

Scientastic
Bourse metro station, Boulevard Anspach; tel: 02 732 13 36; www.scientastic.be; Mon, Tue, Thur, Fri 10.30am–5.30pm, Wed, Sat–Sun 2–5.30pm; admission charge; metro: Bourse, tram: 3, 4, bus: 38, 71, 95; map p.135 C2
Despite being located below ground in the rather gloomy Bourse metro station, this hands-on science museum is a favourite with children.
SEE ALSO MUSEUMS AND GALLERIES, P.77

Parks and Gardens

Ferme du Parc Maximilien
Quai du Batelage 21; tel: 02 201 56 09; www.fermeduparc

Left: gathering chestnuts in one of Brussels' many parks.

maximilien.be; winter Tue 1–4.30pm, Wed–Sat 10am–4.30pm, summer Tue 1–6pm, Wed–Sat 10am–6pm; free; metro: Yser, tram: 81, bus: 47, 58, 88; map p.133 D4
A city farm nestled beneath tower blocks where kids can see farm animals at close range and learn the rudiments of ecology and how to protect the environment.

Theme Parks

Mini-Europe

Bruparck, Boulevard du Centenaire 20; tel 02 474 13 13; www.minieurope.eu; admission charge; metro: Heysel, tram: 23, 81, bus: 84, 88; map p.130 B2
A miniature-scale model of Europe's sights – see the gondolas of Venice, Vesuvius erupting, the fall of the Berlin Wall, and a bullfight in Seville – with interactive exhibits.

Océade

Bruparck, Boulevard du Centenaire 20; tel: 02 478 43 20; www.oceade.be; Sat–Sun, school and public holidays 10am–9pm, other times 10am–6pm, closed Mon Sept–June and Tue Sept–Mar; admission charge; metro: Heysel, tram: 23, 81, bus: 84, 88; map p.130 B2
A large water park, with slides, currents and bubbles.

Walibi

Wavre; tel: 010 42 15 00; www.walibi.be; admission charge; opening times vary, so check website; train station Bierges-Walibi is 150m from the park
A family favourite: Belgium's biggest theme park is 20km (12 miles) from Brussels and merits a full-day visit. Large-scale rides and roller coasters, and a tropically heated water park – Aqualibi (separate visit) – with slides, chutes, a white-water route and waterfalls.

Walks and Tours

Comic-Strip Mural Trail

Streets of central Brussels, especially the Lower City; www.brusselsinternational.be
Comic-strip heroes Tintin, Lucky Luke, Asterix and Obelix and others can be seen in larger-than-life form on wall paintings around the city. A walking route that takes in the 34 murals is available from the tourist office.

Right: Mini-Europe.

Churches

Many of Brussels' historic churches bear the scars of the French bombardment of 1695, the Reformation, or of conversion for secular use after the French Revolution. As a result, many display the *zinneke* (mongrel) character that typifies Brussels, combining medieval and Baroque features with modern stained glass or artworks. Visitors will also observe that the religious character of modern Brussels is very mixed. Following the arrival of North African migrants in the mid-1960s, there are now some 80 mosques in the city, many in converted garages and factories, meeting the needs of up to 400,000 Muslims.

Grand'Place

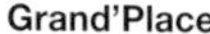

Chapelle de la Madeleine

Rue de la Madeleine 21; tel: 02 502 05 68; Mon–Sat 8am–7.30pm, Sun 7.30–11.30am, 5–8pm; free; metro: Gare Centrale, bus: 29, 38, 66; map p.135 D2

A small oratory in 15th-century Gothic style, the church of Mary Magdalene has had a chequered history. Established in the 13th century, it became a Protestant church from 1579–85, was rebuilt thanks to the generosity of the bakers' guild after the 1695 bombardment, and, following the French Revolution, was converted into a school in 1804, before being returned to the Church in 1840. During mid-20th-century works to bury the north–south rail route beneath the Gare Centrale, all the houses around the church were demolished and it alone

Forty-seven percent of Belgians describe themselves as practising Catholics, and 57 percent as 'belonging to the Catholic Church'. However, an independent study suggests that just 15 percent of the Catholic population regularly attend a religious service. Besides Catholicism, six religions are recognised by the state: Islam, Protestantism, Orthodox, Judaism and Anglicanism. The state education system requires strict neutrality regarding religion on the part of all teachers except teachers of religion. Religious or 'moral' teaching is obligatory; children are instructed in the religion of their choice (any of the six recognised religions) or in non-religious ethics.

Left: Basilique du Sacré Cœur, *(see p.39)*. **Right:** sculpture and stained glass inside the city's cathedral *(see p.38)*.

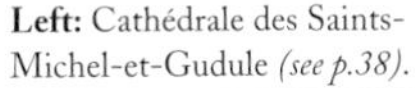

Left: Cathédrale des Saints-Michel-et-Gudule *(see p.38)*.

was spared, although in terrible condition. A major renovation in 1957–8 included the addition of the Chapelle Sainte-Anne on its western flank, complete with an intact 17th-century Baroque facade saved from a nearby chapel.

Eglise Saint-Nicolas
Rue au Beurre 1; tel: 02 513 80 22; Mon–Fri 8am–6.30pm, Sat 9am–6pm, Sun 9am–7.30pm; free; tram: 3, 4, bus: 48, 95; map p.135 D2
Dedicated to the patron saint of shopkeepers and with tiny stores stuck along its flank, Saint-Nicolas is one of the city's earliest churches, dating from 1125 – although considerably remodelled since.

Many Belgian churches contain vast, ornate wooden pulpits dating from the Baroque period and illustrating biblical scenes with life-size figures. Brussels' cathedral contains a fine example, carved in 1699 by Antwerp sculptor Hendrik Verbruggen, and portraying the banishment of Adam and Eve from Paradise. Above them the Virgin Mary, with the Christ Child in her arms, crushes the head of the serpent at her feet.

Romanesque features are visible in the porch, but the oldest surviving section is the choir (1381). The dark interior is decorated with artworks – the *Virgin with Sleeping Child* painting is attributed to a pupil of Rubens, while a copper shrine in front of the pulpit recalls the Martyrs of Gorcum, put to death in Brielle (near Rotterdam) in 1572 after suffering torture at the hands of the Gueux (Protestant Dutch 'Sea Beggars').

Lower City

Eglise Saint-Jean-Baptiste au Béguinage
Place du Béguinage; tel: 02 217 87 42; Mon–Fri 9am–5pm, Sat–Sun 11am–5pm; free; metro: Sainte Catherine, bus: 47, 88; map p.135 D1
At its height, the Brussels *béguinage* was home to 1,200 lay nuns, but was dissolved in the 19th century. The community's church was dedicated to John the Baptist and the Gothic original rebuilt in the 17th century in flamboyant Rococo style, with onion domes, turrets and rich ornamentation. Most recently, it has been painstakingly restored following a fire in 2001.

Above: Eglise Notre-Dame de la Chapelle.

Marolles

Eglise Notre-Dame de la Chapelle

Place de la Chapelle; tel: 02 512 07 37; daily 9am–7pm, winter until 6pm; free; bus: 27, 48; map p.135 D3

This attractive church is a rare blend of Romanesque-Gothic (transept) and pure Gothic (nave). One of the oldest monuments in Brussels, it started as a chapel in 1134, expanding to a full church from 1210 and undergoing repeated repair following a string of fires, sackings and attacks (the incongruous Baroque bell-tower was added after the 1695 bombardment of the city by the French). Artist Pieter Brueghel the Elder and his wife Mayken Coeke, who married here in 1563, are commemorated by a chapel within the church.

Upper City

Cathédrale des Saints-Michel-et-Gudule

Place Sainte-Gudule; tel: 02 217 83 45; www.cathedralestmichel.be; free, admission charge for crypt and treasury; Mon–Fri 7am–7pm, Sat–Sun 8.30am–7pm; free; metro: Gare Centrale, bus: 29, 63, 65; map p135 E2

Brussels' cathedral appears somewhat stranded amid government offices and between the upper and lower town, but it is situated on an ancient crossroads where a place of worship has been recorded since AD 695. The present church was built between 1226 and the early 16th century, using stone quarried 88km (55 miles) east of Brussels. The choir dates from the start of the construction, the Brabant Gothic-style nave and transept from the 14th and 15th centuries, the French Gothic facade and its two 64m (210ft) towers from 1470–85, and the stained-glass windows from the 16th century. During restoration works in the 1990s, a 10th-century Romanesque crypt was discovered. The former collegiate church gained the title of cathedral only in 1962, when it became the seat of the Mechelen-Brussels diocese.

> Catholic Belgium legalised gay marriage in 2003, the second country in the world (after the Netherlands) legally to recognise same-sex marriage. At the time, the Christian Democrats were in opposition and the government was composed of a coalition of Liberals, Socialists and Greens. Initially, foreign nationals could not take advantage of the law unless gay marriage was also allowed in their own country, but this was amended in 2004 to allow non-Belgians to wed if one partner had resided in the country for at least three months. Gay adoption was legalised in 2006.

Eglise Notre-Dame du Sablon

Rue de la Régence; tel: 02 511 57 41; Mon–Fri 10am–6.30pm; free; tram: 92, 94, bus: 27, 95; map p.135 D3

The delicately ornate Sablon parish church was built in 1594 in flamboyant Brabant

Belgium may be a land of religious freedom today, but in the 16th century it witnessed the bloody persecution of Protestants. Two aristocrats, Lamoral, Count of Egmont, and Philip de Montmorency, Count of Hoorn, led the revolt against the Catholic policies of Philip II in the Spanish Netherlands. Egmont pleaded for religious tolerance for Protestants, but remained loyal to the crown, refusing to side with William I of Orange. But in 1567, Philip II sent the Duke of Alva and 10,000 troops to the Low Countries to crush his religious opponents. Backed by the Inquisition, the Duke set up the 'Council of Disorders'. Egmont and Hoorn were charged with high treason and beheaded on the Grand'Place. Around 12,000 of their fellow citizens were also condemned to death. A statue of the two heroes stands in the garden on the Place du Petit Sablon.

Gothic style with five naves to honour the five military guilds of Brussels (an earlier chapel on the site was commissioned by the crossbowmen's guild in 1304). A black marble chapel (1651–76) inside is dedicated to the memory of the von Thurn and Tassis family, creators of the European postal service. It is best viewed after dark, when lights within make its stained-glass windows twinkle like gems.

Eglise Protestante

Chapelle Royale, Place du Musée 2; tel: 02 213 49 40; www.eglise-dumusee.be; 10.30–11.30am during Sun services or by appointment; free; tram: 92, 94, bus: 27, 38, 71; map p.135 D3

A Protestant community had existed unofficially in Belgium since 1525, but only gained legal status and a church in 1804, when it was granted this former royal chapel of Charles of Lorraine, built 1760 and annexed to his palace. With independence in 1830, Belgium gained a king of Protestant faith in Leopold I, its only non-Catholic monarch, who worshipped in the light-flooded neo-Classical chapel. Today it is additionally prized for its acoustics and hosts regular classical concerts.

Eglise Saint-Jacques-sur-Coudenberg

Place Royale; tel: 02 511 78 36; www.eglisesaintjacques.be; Tue–Sat 1–6pm, Sun 9am–6pm; free; tram: 92, 94, bus: 27, 38, 71; map p.135 D/E3

At the heart of the royal district, an earlier incarnation of this church saw the christening of Mary of Burgundy in 1457 and the funeral of Mary's mother, Isabelle, wife of Charles the Bold, in 1465. It was rebuilt as part of the neo-Classical makeover of Place Royale in 1776–87, with a facade in Greco-Roman style, and six Corinthian columns supporting an ornate pediment. Converted to a Temple of Reason and then of Law following the French Revolution, it is surprisingly unadorned inside.

North Brussels and Royal Laeken

Basilique du Sacré Cœur

Parvis de la Basilique 1; tel: 02 425 88 22; www.basilique.be; daily 8am–6pm, winter until 5pm; free; tram: 19, bus: 49, 87

Dominating the northwest skyline, the fifth-largest church and largest Art Deco edifice in the world was inspired by its Parisian counterpart at Montmartre (King Leopold II desired a copy for Brussels) and completed in 1970 after a 66-year construction project. Built entirely of reinforced concrete clad in enamelled terracotta, it has an austere grandeur. An external viewing gallery (admission charge) just beneath the dome at 52m (170ft) high offers a good vantage point for viewing Brussels and many more distant towns, while two museums within the church contain religious art and artefacts from the 14th century to the present.

Right: Eglise Saint-Jean-Baptiste au Béguinage *(see p.37)*.

Environment

The first thing visitors notice about Brussels, when not tripping on uneven cobblestones or picking their way around construction sites, is its absence of a watery heart. Amsterdam has the Amstel, London the Thames, Paris the Seine... and Brussels a river that dares not show its face, since it was covered and made into a sewer in the 19th century. When it comes to the environment, the city could try harder. There are valiant attempts to clean up the 'capital of Europe', and a new generation is re-inhabiting its long-neglected centre, but the push for a greener, cleaner and less congested Brussels has yet to bear fruit.

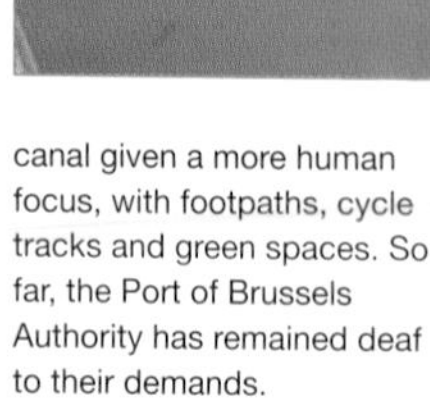

The Senne

The first human settlement in Brussels was on an island in the River Senne. The small, fast-flowing river enabled the city to prosper, permitting transport from the North Sea. Its 103km (64-mile) course flowed from a source near Soignies, southwest of Brussels, to north of Mechelen, where it joined the Scheldt.

Over the centuries, the river became less navigable. Liable to flood or run dry, it was canalised through the city, and progressively used as an open drain. By the late 19th century, it was a health hazard, contaminated by industrial and human waste. The authorities confirmed its role as a public sewer when they made the decision to cover it over: works were completed in 1871. Above the vaulted watercourse, the centre of Brussels was rebuilt with Parisian-style boulevards in place of medieval neighbourhoods. The river's underground course was diverted in the 1930s, and in the 1970s the underground tram route from Rogier to Gare du Midi moved into the space left vacant from the original canalisation.

While many today lament the fate of their city's river, few hope that it will ever be restored. Instead, campaigners want the Brussels–Charleroi canal in the west of the city to be adapted for more leisurely pursuits. Few heavy industries in the city depend on the 14km (9-mile) long urban waterway, which is used principally for transit by industrial barges. At 1,350 tonnes, these vast boats are able to carry the equivalent of 84 container trucks, and represent a green transport solution that everyone welcomes.

Herons, ducks, cormorants, gulls and pike, bream and roach all live in and around the waterway. People tend not to, however, as it is lined with busy roads, industrial units, builders' yards and a waste incinerator. A biofuels production plant and logistics centre are currently at planning stage, both subject to fierce opposition by campaign groups keen to see the banks of the canal given a more human focus, with footpaths, cycle tracks and green spaces. So far, the Port of Brussels Authority has remained deaf to their demands.

Transport

It is a tall order to discourage private car use in a city that in the 1950s was redesigned with speedy underground highways that allow non-stop travel from the periphery to the centre. As a result, although public transport and bike use have grown in recent years, this has not resulted in fewer cars on the road. Two-thirds of commuters travel to Brussels by car, one-third use public transport and 1 percent go by bike. Company vehicles represent a whopping 48 percent of all cars registered in Belgium, a widespread job perk even for employees whose work does not require a vehicle (due to income tax rates among the highest in the world and favourable tax treatment of benefits-in-kind).

Besides congestion and parking problems, not to

Left: the Charleroi canal.

> Brussels organises one of the most radical car-free days during European Mobility Week each September on a Sunday, when all 19 communes of the capital region are off-limits for private vehicle traffic from 9am–7pm, barring special dispensation. See www.dimanchesansvoiture.irisnet.be.

mention Kyoto Protocol commitments to cut CO^2 emissions, Brussels frequently experiences air pollution in the form of ozone from vehicle emissions getting trapped at ground level. Several days a year, the regional authority is obliged to issue public safety announcements that advise at-risk groups to avoid strenuous exercise and outdoor exposure. Calls for a toll-based congestion zone in the centre, the European Quarter and the Gare du Nord business district have yet to be taken seriously.

That is not to say that Brussels has no sense of the need to improve quality of life and reduce traffic-based nuisance. Building permits limit the number of parking spaces that may be incorporated in new office blocks; the public transport network is constantly improving, with trams gaining their own road-space separate from cars; and Cambio, a car-sharing system that uses a chip-and-pin access system, and phone or internet booking, is gaining popularity. All public service workers and many other employees in Brussels also get free annual public transport passes, thanks to a regional subsidy for employers.

Cleanliness

One of the main gripes that foreigners have about Brussels is that its streets are dirty with litter, dog-foul and dumped rubbish, pavements are poorly maintained and graffiti widespread. Official documents may say that Brussels aims to be one of the cleanest cities in Europe, but anyone who spends time here will see that it is still far off target. This is partly the result of the shared responsibility for public cleanliness – a regional authority looks after main roads, household waste collections and recycling, but each of the 19 communes is respectively bound to clean its local streets and empty its public bins.

A certain lack of civic pride among residents is hardly surprising given the local phenomenon of *bruxellisation*, the deliberate neglect of historic buildings by property speculators in order to gain permits for demolition and the construction of new office blocks. At its height in the 1960s and 70s, this tendency is still visible in some quarters, and has blighted Brussels' reputation with heritage organisations.

Below: many workers in Brussels get a free annual transport pass.

Essentials

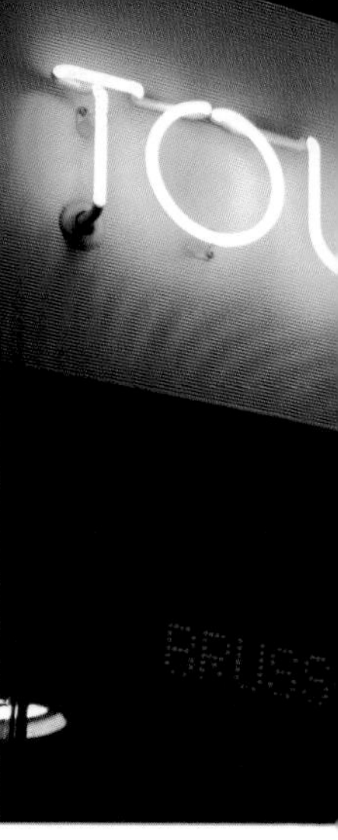

Brussels can seem perplexing and down-at-heel at first sight. Do not be put off – a city of delights is waiting to be explored. Most locals are helpful, and there are so many foreigners in this cosmopolitan capital that you will easily find someone who speaks English. This section contains all the practical information you may need on your trip or before departing. It describes how to use the phone and where to go if you feel ill – the Belgian health service is among the best in Europe, so you will be in safe hands – and lists public holidays, when shops, banks and some restaurants will be closed.

Embassies/Consulates

Australia
Rue Guimard 6–8, 1040 Brussels; tel: 02 286 05 00

Canada
Avenue de Tervuren 2, 1040 Brussels; tel: 02 741 06 11

New Zealand
Square de Meeus 1, 1000 Brussels; tel: 02 512 10 40

Republic of Ireland
Rue Wiertz 50, 1050 Brussels; tel: 02 235 66 76

South Africa
Rue Montoyer 17, 1040 Brussels; tel: 02 285 44 00

UK
Rue d'Arlon 85, 1040 Brussels; tel: 02 287 62 11

US
Boulevard du Régent 27, 1000 Brussels; tel: 02 508 21 11

Emergency Numbers

Ambulance, Fire: 100
Police: 101
Pan-European emergency number (all services): 112

Health

EU NATIONALS

EU nationals who fall ill in Belgium are eligible to receive emergency medical treatment. You will have to pay, but are entitled to claim back 75 percent of the cost of seeing a doctor or dentist and of prescription drugs. You will have to pay part of the costs of hospital treatment. Ambulance travel is not covered.

To receive a refund you need a European Health Insurance Card. For UK citizens, these are available online at www.ehic.org.uk, by picking up a form in a post office or by phoning: 0845 606 2030. Reimbursements are handled in Belgium by Sickness Funds Offices (Mutualités/Ziekenfonds).

Below: police station.

Metric to Imperial Conversions
Metres – Feet 1 = 3.28
Kilometres – Miles 1 = 0.62
Hectares – Acres 1 = 2.47
Kilos – Pounds 1 = 2.2

NORTH AMERICANS

International Association for Medical Assistance to Travellers (IAMAT), 40 Regal Road, Guelph, Ontario, N1K 1B5, Canada; tel: 519 836 0102; www.iamat.org
This non-profit group offers fixed rates for medical treatment. Members receive a passport-sized medical record completed by their doctor and a directory of English-speaking IAMAT doctors who are on call 24 hours a day.

HOSPITALS

CHU Saint-Pierre
Rue Haute 322; tel: 02 535 31 11; www.stpierre-bru.be; metro: Porte de Hal, tram: 3, 4, bus: 27, 48; map p.135 C4

PHARMACIES

Pharmacies are identifiable by a green neon cross sign. Details of duty pharmacies open at night are posted in pharmacy windows, or call 070 66 01 60/visit www.fpb.be.

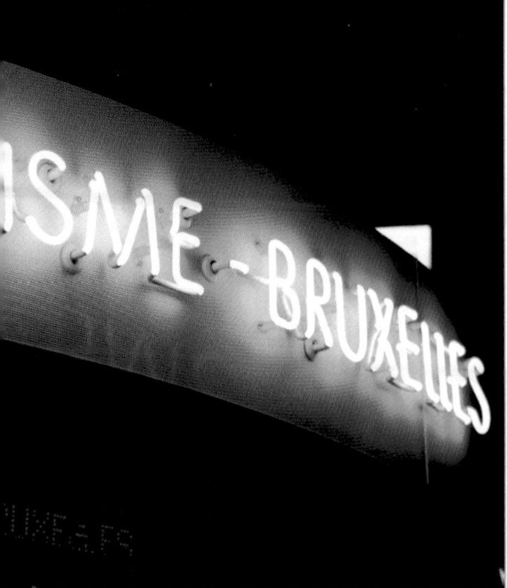

Left: tourist information.

Internet

Dot Spot
Rue du Lombard 83; tel: 02 513 61 03; www.dotspot.be; metro: Gare Centrale, bus: 48, 95; map p.135 D2

2go4 Youth Hostel
Boulevard Emile Jacqmain 99; tel: 02 219 30 19; www.2go4.be; metro: Rogier, tram: 3, 4, bus: 47, 88

Use-it
Rue de l'Ecuyer 24; www.use-it.be; metro: De Brouckère, tram: 3, 4, bus: 63, 71; map p.135 D2

Money

Belgium uses the euro (€), divided into 100 cents. Banknotes *(billets)* come in 5, 10, 20, 50, 100, 200 and 500 euros. Most shops, restaurants and hotels accept credit cards, but few cafés or bars do. Currency exchange website: www.xe.com.

Post

Opening times are 9am–5pm, except in central branches:
De Brouckère: Boulevard Anspach 1; tel: 02 226 97 00; Mon–Fri 8am–6pm, Sat 10.30am–4.30pm; metro: De Brouckère, tram: 3, 4, bus: 63, 71; map p.135 D2
Gare du Midi: tel: 02 524 43 08; Mon–Fri 7am–8pm, Sat 10.30am–4.30pm; metro: Gare du Midi, tram: 3, 4, map p.134 B4
Buy stamps from post offices, and shops selling postcards.

Public Holidays

1 January New Year's Day
1 May Labour Day
21 July National Day
15 August Assumption
1 November All Saints' Day
11 November Armistice Day
25 December Christmas Day

Movable holidays include Easter Monday, Ascension Day and Whit Monday. Holidays falling on a weekend are taken the following Monday.

Telephones

Fixed line numbers in Brussels start 02. You need to use the area code. The code for Belgium is +32. When dialling from abroad, omit the first 0 of the code. For English-language directory enquiries, dial 1405/visit www.infobel.be.

Tourist Information

IN BRUSSELS
Town Hall, Grand'Place; tel: 02 513 89 40; www.brusselsinternational.be; daily 9am–6pm except Sun during winter 10am–2pm, closed 25 Dec, 1 Jan and Sun from Jan–Easter; tram: 3, 4, bus: 48, 95; map p.135 D2
Rue Royale 2; tel: 02 513 89 40; www.brusselsinternational.be; daily 10am–6pm, closed 25 Dec and 1 Jan; map p.135 E3

UK

Belgian Tourist Office Brussels & Wallonia
217 Marsh Wall, London E14 9FJ; tel: 020 7537 1132; www.belgiumtheplaceto.be

Tourism Flanders-Brussels
Flanders House, 1a Cavendish Square, London W1G 0LD; tel: 020 7307 7738; www.visitflanders.co.uk

US

Belgian Tourist Office
220 East 42nd Street, Suite 3402, New York, NY 10017; tel: 212 758 8130; www.visitbelgium.com

Visas

EU nationals require a valid identity card or passport to visit Belgium. Other visitors require a valid passport. No visa is required by visitors from the EU, US, Canada, Australia, New Zealand or Japan. Nationals of other countries may need a visa. If in doubt, check www.diplomatie.be or with the Belgian embassy in your home country. Anyone over the age of 12 must carry ID at all times.

Brussels is generally safe, but pickpockets and thieves are active in stations, street markets and on public transport (especially along the tram axis from Rogier to Midi). Keep your bag secured and avoid carrying obvious laptop bags or other valuables in downtown neighbourhoods after dark.

Fashion

Two decades after a clutch of Belgian designers wowed the world with their distinctive new look, top fashion houses continue to cherry-pick promising graduates from colleges in Antwerp and Brussels. The schools attract talent from around the world, many of whom stay on to make Brussels their base. Rue Dansaert is avant-garde central, developed around influential store Stijl, which stocks clothes by Belgium's top designers; shops in the Avenue Louise district cater for more classic tastes. The following is a pick of the best of Belgian fashion. For accessories, vintage and underwear, *see Shopping, p.114–17.*

Single-Label Stores

Annemie Verbeke
Rue Antoine Dansaert 64; tel: 02 511 21 71; www.annemieverbeke.be; Mon–Sat 11am–6pm; metro: Sainte-Catherine, tram: 3, 4, bus: 47, 88; map p.135 C2
Dressy looks for Flemish fashion girls and other knock-kneed ingénues; fine knitwear and suiting is this designer's forte. Recent success has seen Verbeke open three new stores in Japan.

Azniv Afsar
Rue Léon Lepage 30; tel: 02 649 27 53; www.aznivafsar.be; Mon–Tue by appointment, Wed–Sat 11am–6.30pm; metro: Sainte-Catherine, tram: 3, 4, bus: 47, 88; map p.135 C1
Young Brussels-trained Afsar has inherited the skills of her Armenian weaver grandparents, and makes beautiful garments with an accent on structure and drape. When not designing ready-to-wear for women, she makes theatrical costumes and art.

Chine
Avenue Louise 82–84; tel: 02 512 45 52; www.chinecollection.com; Mon–Sat 10am–6.30pm; metro: Louise, tram: 92, 94, 97
Belgian label known for its slinky dresses and separates for women in colourful silks inspired by the intense colours of the Far East. A second boutique occupies a corner in the Dansaert district, at Rue Van Artevelde 2.

Diane von Furstenberg
Rue du Grand Cerf 11; tel: 02

Left and below: comfy chairs and clothes at Icon *(see p.47)*.

Brussels fashion promotion organisation Modo Bruxellae (www.modobruxellae.be) organises a Parcours des Stylistes ('designers' circuit') every two years in October, with the next edition scheduled for 2010. The weekend-long open-doors event gives behind-the-scenes access to the studios and workshops of local designers.

648 62 24; www.dvf.com; Mon–Sat 10am–6.30pm; metro: Louise, tram: 92, 94; map p.135 D4

The internationally renowned designer known for her signature jersey wrap dress was born in Brussels and recently returned to open a store in the city, selling the classic for every occasion in colour, print, black, and with short, long or three-quarter sleeves.

Escape – Kaat Tilley

Galerie du Roi 6; tel: 02 510 00 12; www.kaattilley.com; Mon–Sat 10.30am–6pm; metro: Gare Centrale, tram: 3, 4, bus: 63, 66, 71; map p.135 D2

Every woman can be a fairy or romantic heroine with a dress by Flemish designer Kaat Tilley. Her day, evening and bridal wear is characterised by crinkly gowns detailed with boned corsets and netting underskirts, all natural fabrics and in shades from ivory to crimson.

Isabelle Baines

Rue du Pépin 48; tel: 02 502 13 73; www.isabellebaines.com; Wed–Sat 10.30am–6pm; metro: Porte de Namur, bus: 71; map p.135 D3

Chic knitwear for sophisticates young and old, male and female, from the finest summer-weight wools to chunky cardies. Superb detailing and colours, and a made-to-measure service available too.

Jean-Paul Knott

Boulevard Barthélemy 20 (Kanal 20 Gallery); tel: 02 514 18 35; www.jeanpaulknott.com; Mon–Fri 10am–6pm, Sat 11am–6pm; metro: Sainte-Catherine or Comte de Flandre, tram: 51, bus: 88; map p.134 C1

Creative director of Cerruti's men's and women's ready-to-wear lines, Brussels designer Knott also produces haute couture under his own name, using minimalist drapes to stunning effect. This space is also a gallery for invited artists.

Maison Martin Margiela Bruxelles

Rue de Flandre 114; tel: 02 223 75 20; www.maisonmartinmargiela.com; Mon–Sat 11am–7pm; metro: Sainte-Catherine, tram: 3, 4, bus: 47, 88; map p.134 C1

Margiela quit the Antwerp Six before their 1986 launchpad show to work for Jean-Paul Gaultier. Developing the deconstructed style launched by Comme des Garçons' Rei Kawakubo, he was Hermès's chief designer from 1998–2004, and now has his own stores all over the world, selling exclusive looks for rock dudes and chicks. This is the Brussels branch, but there are others in Paris, London and New York.

Marie Cabanac

Rue Antoine Dansaert 171; tel: 02 514 78 08; www.mariecabanac.com; Tue–Sat 10.30am–6.30pm; metro:

Left: stylish womenswear at Icon *(see p.47)*.

Above: vintage-style clothing and accessories in Nicolas Woit's store.

Sainte-Catherine, tram: 3, 4, bus: 47, 88; map p.135 C2
A recent relocation for designer Cabanac, whose Ethic Wear label bucks the fashion industry trend for pollution and exploitation by sticking to organic cotton. Her jersey separates for men, women and children are comfy, work well in layers and are identifiable by their overstitched seams.

Mieke Cosyn
Rue Léon Lepage 11–13; tel: 02 512 55 33; www.miekecosyn.com; Tue–Fri 10am–noon, 1.30–5.30pm, Sat 11am–5pm, preferably on appointment; metro: Sainte-Catherine, tram: 3, 4, bus: 88; map p.135 C1
Flemish designer Cosyn makes evening and bridal wear to measure in diaphanous fabrics for modern romantics, based on her small number of adorable designs.

Natan
Avenue Louise 158; tel: 02 647 10 01; www.natan.be; Mon–Sat 10am–6pm; tram: 94, 81, bus: 54
Designer Edouard Vermeulen celebrated 25 years of his Natan house in 2008. A favourite with the royal family, his couture, ready-to-wear and 'Natan +' for larger sizes are perfect for semi-formal to dressy occasions. The above address is the flagship couture store (wedding gowns and evening wear); Natan + is at Rue de Namur 84, and ready-to-wear at Rue de Namur 78.

The principal fashion college in Brussels is La Cambre visual arts school, situated on Avenue Louise near the Bois de la Cambre and founded in 1986 (two years before the 'Antwerp Six', a group of graduates from the Antwerp Fine Arts Academy, caused a storm in London). Places on the five-year fashion course are hotly contested, and the annual graduates' show is the chance to bet on the next big names: each year in June – and tickets sell fast. www.lacambre.be.

Nicolas Woit
Rue Antoine Dansaert 80; tel: 02 503 48 32; www.nicolaswoit.com; Mon–Fri 10.30am–1pm, 2–6.30pm, Sat 10.30am–6.30pm; metro: Sainte-Catherine, tram: 3, 4, bus: 47, 88; map p.135 C2
Woit started out adapting vintage clothing, then turned to designing his own, inspired by 1940s and 50s style. His glamorous evening wear and pretty day wear make every girl feel like a star.

Olivier Strelli
Rue Antoine Dansaert 44; tel: 02 512 09 42; www.strelli.be; Mon–Sat 10am–6.30pm; metro: Sainte-Catherine, tram: 3, 4, bus: 47, 88; map p.135 C2
Colourful, sporty ready-to-wear, shoes, accessories (even bedding) for men and women, designed by Congo-born Strelli, a Belgian success story who also has boutiques in China, France

Right and below: Stijl, the original Flemish trendsetters.

and the UK. A favourite with yummy mummies. Also at Avenue Louise 72.

Multi-Label Stores

Balthazar
Rue du Marché aux Fromages 22; tel: 02 514 23 96; www.balthazar22.com; Mon–Sat 11am–6.30pm; tram: 3, 4, bus: 48, 95
Hippest menswear store in town, with brands including Paul Smith, Comme des Garçons, Filippa K, John Smedley, Essentiel and New York Industrie. Recently opened a second store at Avenue Louise 294, also with womenswear.

Danaqué
Galerie des Princes 2; tel: 02 511 35 33; Tue–Sat 11am–6.30pm; metro: De Brouckère, bus: 63, 66, 71; map p.135 D2
A theatrical selection of womenswear from several brands – many Danish and German but also Belgian – with some lovely gowns and coats and eco-shoes by Trippen. Good for flamboyant women of all ages, sizes and budgets.

Icon
Place du Nouveau Marché aux Grains 5; tel: 02 502 71 51; www.icon-shop.be; Mon–Sat 10.30–6.30pm; metro: Sainte-Catherine, bus: 47, 88; map p.134 C1
Designer Sandrina Fasoli (First Prize Mango Fashion Award 2007) sells her own sexy, demure line (created with duo partner Michaël Manson) and a dozen other womenswear labels – Vanessa Bruno, Humanoid and others – where emphasis is on original cut and fine fabric.

Prive Joke
Rue du Marché au Charbon 76–78; tel: 02 502 63 67; www.privejoke.be; Mon–Sat 11am–7pm, Sun 2–7pm; tram: 3, 4, bus: 48, 95; map p.135 C/D2
Mixed-label streetwear store (Lady Soul, American Vintage, Katherine Hamnett) which also incorporates an in-store boutique of hip label Le Fabuleux Marcel de Bruxelles (www.fabuleuxmarcel.com), inspired by the classic man's vest (*marcel* in French).

Stijl
Rue Antoine Dansaert 74; tel: 02 502 03 13; Mon–Sat 10.30am–6.30pm; tram: 3, 4, bus: 46, 88; map p.135 C2
The shop that launched the neighbourhood – and to some extent Brussels' reputation as a fashion centre to compete with Antwerp. Open nearly 30 years, Sonja Noël's store is the only one in the capital to stock Dries van Noten and Ann Demeulemeester, plus a pick of the best of Belgium's more recent successes: A.F. Vandevorst, Véronique Branquinho, Raf Simons, Tim Van Steenbergen, Sophie d'Hoore and Cathy Pill.

Festivals

Brussels knows better than to bat away charges of 'dull', 'bureaucratic' and 'ugly', due to the EU office blocks that are all most foreigners see of the city on their TV news. Instead, it celebrates the dizzying blend of cultures that live here by inviting artists, composers, musicians and dancers to festivals that seem wildly ambitious for a city of this size. A spirit of curiosity, openness and a fascination for exchanging ideas make such events the cultural equivalent of a global summit, and a lot more fun. This chapter identifies key dates on the city's calendar, but *see also Film, p.50–51; Literature, p.72–3;* and *Music, 86–7*, for more.

March

Ars Musica

www.arsmusica.be

Renowned international composers and performers of contemporary classical music head to Brussels for an intense programme of some 50 concerts, showcasing new works as well as revisiting pioneers like Schönberg and Stockhausen.

May

KunstenFestivaldesArts

www.kfda.be

This fabulous three-week cultural fest offers a voyage of artistic discovery as companies from around the world visit Brussels to present their vision of contemporary theatre, dance, music or visual arts – and quite often a blend of each.

Zinneke Parade

Even-numbered years only; http://zinneke.org

Launched in 2000 when Brussels was European Capital of Culture, this lovely street festival through the city centre is a succession of wild and wonderful costumes, painted faces, floats, street theatre, dance and music, with a cast of thousands – young people, community groups and artists – who have spent months in preparation for the big day. 'Zinneke', or mongrel, is an affectionate designation for the diverse population of Brussels, where almost everyone is of mixed origin (Belgian French, Belgian Flemish, Moroccan, Italian, Turkish...).

June

Couleur Café

Last weekend in June; www.couleurcafe.be

This weekend-long celebration of urban and world music is traditionally held at the Tour & Taxis former customs depot. It's a family-friendly multicultural event with international artists, great food stalls and absolutely no mud.

July

Ommegang

Each first Thursday of July and the preceding Tuesday; www.ommegang.be

This medieval pageant (meaning 'walkabout' in old Flemish) has its roots in a 14th-century religious procession. In 1549, the procession was bumped up a notch to celebrate a visit by Emperor Charles V and his son Philip II. It is this royal visit that is commemorated in today's pageant, which features 1,300 costumed participants playing the roles of emperor, courtier, guildsman or servant. The procession climaxes with a great show of horsemanship, fire-eating and flag-waving on the Grand'Place, for which seats must be booked in advance.

Brosella Folk & Jazz

www.brosella.be

This small jazz and folk festival established in 1977 takes place in the open-air Théâtre de Verdure, near the Atomium. Saturday is devoted to folk music, Sunday jazz. It's fun and, even better, absolutely free.

Fête Nationale

21 July is Belgium's National Day (and a public holiday), which recalls the day Leopold I was crowned first King of the Belgians. It is

Left: medieval pageantry at the Ommegang festival.

The week of Carnaval (with Mardi Gras) at the start of Lent is the occasion for a major party in Belgium. Children have fancy-dress parties at school before they break up for the Carnaval week off, and many towns (although not Brussels) hold large folkloric festivals. The biggest are in Binche and Stavelot in Wallonia and Aalst in Flanders. The costumed parades are irreverent, quite drunken and rooted in ancient traditions of feasting before the fast.

celebrated with a serious military parade and fly-past before the royal family and anyone else who can get near the Palais Royal, but extends with livelier fire service and army demonstrations, food stands and fairground rides along Rue de la Régence to the Palais de Justice, and culminates at night with a fireworks spectacular.

August

Flower Carpet

Three days in mid-August around the 15 August holiday, even-numbered years only; www.flowercarpet.be

As if the Grand'Place weren't already an eyeful, every two years a vast carpet of begonias is laid out on the cobbles of the square, according to an elaborate new design for each edition. The town hall balcony is opened to allow viewing from a good vantage point.

Feeërieën

Last week of August; www.feeerieen.be

Dance with the fairies to mark the end of summer at a five-night free music festival in the Parc de Bruxelles, organised by the Ancienne Belgique rock music venue.

Meiboom Procession

Each 9 August; www.meyboom.be

In a tradition dating back to 1308, a medieval order of crossbowmen and companions commemorate the victory of troops from Brussels over those of Leuven with a procession that culminates with the planting of a tree at the junction of Rue des Sables and Rue de Marais. An ancient folkloric event with giants, burly men speaking Brussels dialect and one very large sapling.

Below: the Grand' Place Flower Carpet.

Film

In art as in life, Belgians are a self-deprecating bunch on a perpetual identity quest, characteristics that set them apart from their French neighbours, whose self-confident, stylish cinema has long eclipsed the local offering. The home film industry is small but of high quality, with a reputation for gritty social realism and quirky satire. Foreign visitors are spoilt, as films are always shown in their original version (never dubbed) with subtitles in French and Dutch. Programmes are dominated by Hollywood and French releases, but it is worth seeking out Belgian films for an insight into the national psyche.

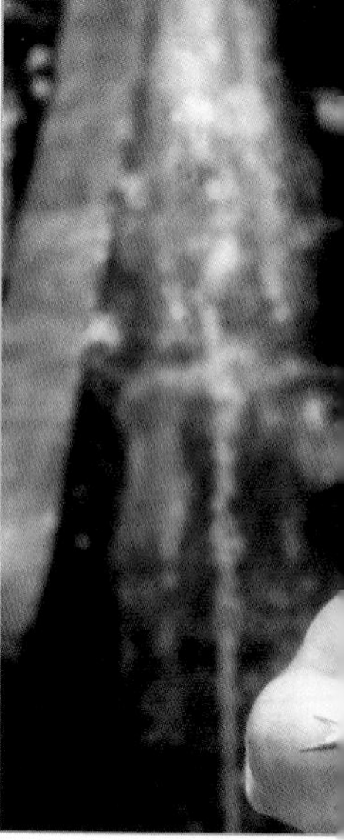

Belgian Film

One of the pioneers of the moving image was a professor of experimental physics from Ghent. In 1836, Joseph Plateau developed a stroboscopic device called the 'phenakistiscope', enabling a sequence of images to be viewed at speed. The illusion of motion through the projection of stroboscopic photographs would lead, in 1895, to the Lumière brothers' invention of cinema.

Since the art was invented, local filmmakers have done little to help the national tourist board. Early pioneer Henri Storck (1907–99) produced gritty documentaries such as *Misère au Borinage* (1933), a silent short showing the exploitation of coal-miners in Wallonia. Storck's unflinching gaze on the most downtrodden in society would be picked up by subsequent generations of filmmakers, among them Chantal Akerman (b. 1950), whose study of three days in the life of a single mother and part-time prostitute, *Jeanne Dielman, 23 Quai du Commerce, 1080 Bruxelles* (1975), received international acclaim.

Above: *L'Enfant*, winner of a Palme d'Or at Cannes.

In a similar vein, brothers Jean-Pierre and Luc Dardenne (b. 1951 and 1954) depict characters on the margins of society confronted with a moral dilemma. Tough portraits of modern Belgium, their pictures have won the top prize at Cannes twice in recent years – *Rosetta* (1999) and *L'Enfant* (2005). Their success marked a turning point in international recognition for Belgian film.

In contrast, Flemish director and conceptual artist Jan Bucquoy (b. 1945) is irreverent and anarchic; his *The Sexual Life of the Belgians* (1994) and *Camping Cosmos* (1996) are both more nuanced than may first appear. Dominique Deruddere's satire on the pursuit of stardom, *Iedereen beroemd!* (2000) is similarly cynical. Gérard Corbiau (b. 1941) has had more mainstream success, with Baroque costume dramas *Farinelli* (1994) and *Le Roi danse* (2000).

Perhaps the most memorable – if disturbing – Belgian film of recent years, combining parody of celebrity culture

Left: *Le Roi danse.*

The Cinémathèque Royale de Belgique (www.cinematheque.be) was founded in 1938 to collect films with aesthetic, technical or historical value. Its collection is among the largest in the world. In 1962, curator Jacques Ledoux founded the Musée du Cinéma to allow filmgoers to benefit from the collection. *See also Museums and Galleries, p.80.*

and social realism, is mockumentary *C'est arrivé près de chez vous* (1992), a modern *Clockwork Orange* in which a camera crew shadows a serial killer, played by the superb Benoît Poelvoorde, and directed by Rémy Belvaux and André Bonzel.

Belgium's best-known export is undoubtedly Jean-Claude Van Damme, the 'muscles from Brussels'. Younger talents include Natacha Régnier and Cécile de France.

Festivals

Anima
www.animatv.be
Animation film festival in late February showing shorts and feature-length movies.

Brussels Film Festival
www.fffb.be
European film festival, showing exclusively the directors' first or second movies. Late June to early July.

Brussels International Fantastic Film Festival (BIFF)
www.bifff.org
Internationally recognised sci-fi, fantasy and horror festival. Two weeks each April.

Festival du Court Métrage de Bruxelles
www.courtmetrage.be
Festival of short films; 10 days each late April–late May.

Cinemas

Actor's Studio
Petite Rue des Bouchers 16; tel: 02 512 16 96; www.actorsstudio.cinenews.be; metro: De Brouckère, tram: 3, 4, bus: 63, 71; map p.135 D2
Cosy multi-screen cinema in the heart of the Ilôt Sacré that shows second-run and minority-interest pictures.

Argos
Rue du Chantier 13; tel: 02 229 00 03; www.argosarts.org; metro: Yser, tram: 51, bus: 47, 88
Video art gallery with screening, exhibitions, lectures and performances.

Cinéma Arenberg
Galerie de la Reine 26; tel: 02 512 80 63; www.arenberg.be; metro: De Brouckère, tram: 3, 4, bus: 63, 71; map p.135 D2
Principal cinema for first-run art-house and non-commercial foreign-language movies.

Kinepolis
Boulevard du Centenaire 20; tel: 02 474 26 03; www.kinepolis.com; metro: Heysel, tram: 23, 51, bus: 84, 88; map p.130 C2
Charmless multiplex, but one of the few cinemas in Brussels to screen Flemish films.

Musée du Cinéma
Rue Baron Horta 9; tel: 02 551 19 19; www.cinematheque.be; metro: Parc, tram: 92, 94, bus: 38, 71; map p.135 E3
Screening rooms and a museum attached to the Cinémathèque. Daily projections at 6.15pm and 8.15pm show classic or art-house pictures, and other treasures from the national archive. There is also a twice-weekly silent movie with live piano accompaniment.

Nova
Rue d'Arenberg 3; tel: 02 511 24 77; www.nova-cinema.org; metro: De Brouckère, tram: 3, 4, bus: 63, 71; map p.135 D2
Alternative cinema for subversive, challenging and avant-garde film, run on a shoestring by volunteers. The downstairs bar also hosts exhibitions, DJ nights and discussions.

UGC Toison d'Or
Avenue de la Toison d'Or 8; tel: 0900 10 440; www.ugc.be; metro: Porte de Namur, bus: 54, 71; map p.135 D4
Tolerable city-centre multiplex in uptown shopping centre which caters well to an international audience.

Food and Drink

Anyone who enjoys their food will feel at home in Belgium, where the national pastime is to enjoy a hearty meal with friends or family, complete with wine or beer. Thanks to the strong emphasis on well-prepared dishes made with seasonal ingredients, it is hard to eat poorly or pay over the odds away from obvious tourist traps. The variety of dishes is enormous, thanks to Brussels' location midway between the North Sea coast and Ardennes forest, and amidst productive farmland. Whatever your tastes, food is sure to be one of the highlights of your trip, so make sure to sample local specialities.

Above: *moules-frites* (mussels and fries) with mayonnaise, Belgium's most famous dish.

Belgian Cuisine

Home from the 14th–16th centuries to the Burgundian dynasty, Belgium witnessed some of the most lavish banquets in recorded history. At the same time, the peasant feasts depicted in paintings by Brueghel provide evidence that eating, drinking and conviviality have a long history as the centre of social life across the social spectrum.

French cuisine has strongly influenced local tastes, but even in this small country, regional cuisines are noticeably distinct: Flemish food includes fish and seafood, eel, chicken and vegetables, often in light, creamy sauces; Walloon dishes are richer and meatier, using mushrooms, game and wildfowl – wild boar, venison, pheasant, rabbit; and Brussels' working-class roots explain the tradition of *stoemp* (mash made with different vegetables, served with sausage), *boulettes-tomates* (meatballs in tomato sauce), and offal, which is increasingly rare on menus, but worth seeking out if you are a fan.

The following typical dishes are widely available: ***Waterzooï*** – a Ghent stew of fish, potatoes, carrots, onions and more in a thin, creamy soup-like sauce. More commonly made with chicken these days, which is cheaper. ***Moules-frites*** – the classic pot of mussels with fries on the side. Mussels are bred in Zeeland, the Netherlands, and cooked in a thin stock of celery and onion, plus white wine, garlic, or other variations on the theme. Fries come with mayonnaise on the side. When the new sea-

Left: Godiva, one of Belgium's most renowned chocolatiers.

The characteristics of Belgian beers are highly dependent on local conditions. When brewing giant InBev attempted to relocate the production of Hoegaarden, a white beer made with wheat and flavoured with coriander spice and Curaçao orange zest, to its factory in Jupille near Liège (home of Jupiler), the beer lost crucial characteristics and grew browner. Plans to close the Hoegaarden site were shelved, and the village known for its *witbier* since the Middle Ages retained its brewery.

son begins in August (mussels are in season as long as the month has an 'r' in its name), the quality of the year's crop makes the national news, with much focus on the price per kilo.
Frites – fries, fried twice for the unique Belgian consistency. Eat from a roadside kiosk or van *(frietkot)*, accompanied with one of many sauce options, usually based on mayonnaise.
Chicon gratin – Belgian endives rolled in a slice of ham and baked in a white sauce topped with cheese.
Croquettes de crevettes – shrimp croquettes: a popular starter. The more of the tiny North Sea grey shrimps there are in the bechamel sauce, deep-fried in breadcrumbs, the better. Served with a deep-fried parsley garnish.
Carbonnades flamandes – rich beef stew, where chunks of meat are cooked for hours in beer.
Maatjes – raw herring, sold on seafood stalls and fishmongers and eaten as they come with chopped raw onions: the Belgian sushi.
Anguilles au vert – eels in green sauce: the subtly flavoured eel is cooked in butter, sorrel (for acidity), spinach (for bitterness), chervil and other green herbs (every chef has his own recipe). Known in Brussels dialect as 'poelink', after the Dutch *paling in 't groen*.
Asperges – asparagus: the large white stalks are in season for two months from April, produced mainly in Antwerp and Limburg provinces. Served as a starter with a sauce of crushed hard-boiled egg, parsley, whisked melted butter and a dash of lemon juice.
Filet américain – the Belgian name for steak tartare: ground raw beef with raw egg, capers, onion and pepper. Make sure it's the prepared-at-the-table variety, rather than the sandwich-filler paste that Belgians love in their lunchtime baguette.

Chocolate

For sweet delights, as well as a variety of fruit tarts and gateaux, Belgians are proud of producing some of the best chocolate in the world (producers adhere strictly to the principle of using cocoa butter and no other vegetable fat). It was in Brussels in 1912 that Jean Neuhaus invented the praline, a sculpted shell with a different filling. A mixed selection of pralines is sold by weight, packaged prettily and for protection in a *ballotin*, a rigid box designed by Neuhaus's wife. The Neuhaus store in Galerie de la Reine still boasts one of the finest window displays in the city.

Beer

Beers are treated with almost the same reverence as wine, and the variety of brews is remarkable. Like wine, in fact, many Belgian beers complete their last stage of fermentation in corked bottles. Until 1900, every village had its own brewery; today there are just over 100. Leuven is the industrial beer capital of Belgium, home to the world's largest brewing company, **Inbev**, which makes Stella Artois, Hoegaarden, Leffe and Jupiler, and which

The large population of foreigners in Brussels means that food from around the world gets a good showing on the local restaurant scene, often offering the best value for money. The best-established of foreign cuisines are those from Greece (grilled meat and ribs), Portugal (baked fish dishes), Italy (pizza and pasta), Vietnam (noodles and rice) and Lebanon (pitta bread with kebabs and salads). Some neighbourhood Spanish cafés serve tasty Sunday lunches, and there are a few Moroccan restaurants specialising in couscous and tajines made with beef or lamb and topped with spicy sauces.

in 2008 snapped up iconic US brewer Anheuser Busch.

Lambic beers are wild beers, so called because they have no yeast added, and their fermentation involves exposure to wild yeast. Many have a sour, apple-like taste, but fruit may have been added to these to impart a distinctive flavour.

Kriek, a cherry beer, comes in a round glass (and can be served hot), while **Framboise** is a pale-pink raspberry brew served in a tall-stemmed glass.

White beer *(blanche)* is cloudy and generally light and youthful in flavour, like the coriander-based Hoegaarden, which is brewed east of Brussels. It often comes with a slice of lemon.

Trappist is a term for beers brewed in an abbey or under the control of Trappist monks. Only six breweries in Belgium (plus one in the Netherlands) bear the authentic Trappist label: Chimay, Orval, Rochefort, Westmalle, Westvleteren, Achel. Among their beers, Tripel denotes a very strong beer that was served to the abbot and other important personages; the monks drank the Dubbel, while the peasants (i.e. everyone else) had only a watery version.

Bières d'abbaye (abbey beers) are produced commercially but using traditional Trappist methods. Grimbergen is one local example.

Kwak (a strong, light-coloured beer) is served in a glass with a spherical base that sits in a wooden stand in order to remain upright. The 1.5-litre glass and its stand are so valuable that customers must often give up a shoe to ensure they don't run off with the merchandise.

One of the strongest beers is the appropriately named **Delirium Tremens**, which can take you by surprise if you're not used to it – though if you see pink elephants, they are on the label and not in your head. Another powerful but delicious beer is **Corsendonck Agnus Dei**.

Gueuze is a Brussels speciality made by combining five or six lambics to produce a cider-like sweet concoction; **Loburg**, a Brussels-brewed light-coloured beer drunk from a vase-like receptacle; **Rodenbach**, a red beer with a sharp apple taste; and **Bourgogne des Flandres**, a flavourful red beer.

Shops

CHOCOLATE AND CAKES

Dandoy

Rue au Beurre 31; tel: 02 511 03 26; www.biscuiteriedandoy.be; Mon–Sat 8.30am–6.30pm, Sun and holidays 10.30am–6.30pm; tram: 3, 4, bus: 48, 95; map p.135 D2

Baudelaire used to shop for his gingerbread at this traditional biscuit-maker's store off the Grand' Place, founded in 1858, and creator of the original spicy *speculoos* biscuit. A tearoom in the rear allows you to sample the nib-

Above: mouthwatering gateaux on display.

bles before buying a bag to take home.

Frederic Blondeel

Quai aux Briques 24; tel: 02 502 21 31; www.frederic-blondeel.com; 10am–6.30pm; metro: Sainte-Catherine, bus: 47, 88; map p.135 C1

Blondeel produces pralines and chocolate spreads in West Flanders, and sells in Knokke and Brussels, where a tearoom within the store serves hot drinks, biscuits and chocolates, as well as home-made ice cream in the summer.

Marcolini

Rue des Minimes 1; tel: 02 514 12 06; www.marcolini.be; Sun–Thur 10am–7pm, Fri–Sat 10am–8pm; tram: 92, 94, bus: 27, 95; map p.135 D3

Award-winning Pierre Marcolini travels the world to select the best cocoa beans on Earth, and specialises in *crus d'origine* bars and bite-size designer pralines in unusual flavours. For decadent connoisseurs.

Wittamer

Place du Grand Sablon 6 and 12–13; tel: 02 512 37 42; www.wittamer.be; Mon 10am–6pm, Tue–Sat 10am–7pm, Sun 10am–6.30pm, patisserie opens earlier; tram: 92, 94, bus: 27, 95; map p.135 D3

The original master in top-quality handmade pralines (he taught Marcolini) with fantastic window displays and seasonal specialities. The pastry shop a few doors up does to-die-for sorbets, gateaux and hot chocolate. Sit in its upstairs tearoom and ride the chocolate high.

Left: Maredsous, a well-known *bière d'abbaye*.

BEER

Beer Mania

Chaussée de Wavre 174–176; tel: 02 512 17 88; www.beermania.be; shop: Mon–Sat 11am–8pm, also Sun in Dec; metro: Porte de Namur; map p.135 E1

Worth walking to – about 10 minutes from Porte de Namur through the Matonge – this go-to address stocks 400 Belgian beers including many rarities, and 100 types of glass (no self-respecting beer-drinker would drink from the wrong glass). The bar is open until 9pm and also serves snacks.

Brasserie Cantillon – Musée Bruxellois de la Gueuze

Rue Gheude 56; tel: 02 521 49 28; www.cantillon.be; Mon–Fri 9am–5pm, Sat 10am–5pm; metro: Clemenceau, bus: 46; map p.134 B3

Brussels' sole surviving brewery (and museum) near the Gare du Midi uses exclusively organic grain and sells its gueuze and lambic on site, as well as through other vendors.

SEE ALSO MUSEUMS AND GALLERIES, P.77

De Bier Tempel

Rue du Marché aux Herbes 56; tel: 02 502 19 06; daily 10am–7pm; tram: 3, 4, bus: 48, 95; map p.135 D2

Just off the Grand'Place and so rather swamped with tourists, but the knowledgeable staff satisfy connoisseurs too. Gift sets, glasses, T-shirts and other paraphernalia are a little overpriced, and the more common beers can invariably be found cheaper elsewhere.

Genever, Belgian gin, is a juniper-flavoured spirit invented around 1580 in the Netherlands, where British troops fighting against the Spanish in the Thirty Years War appreciated the 'Dutch courage' they were given. Containing an unfermented and unfiltered mash of malted grain, mainly barley, genever has more body and a grainier flavour than English-style gin, which was developed after 17th-century Flemish distillers began trading in London. At the start of the 19th century, there was a genever brewery in every town, but few remain today, although many bars do still serve it. To drink it, lean forward at the bar at a right angle and sip from that position. Once you have drunk the meniscus, pick up the glass and down the rest.

Gay and Lesbian

Belgium became the second country in the world, after the Netherlands, to legalise same-sex marriage, in January 2003. The following year, it extended the right to foreign couples, as long as one partner has lived in Belgium for at least three months. Gay adoption was legalised in 2006. Although not known for having a large gay community, Brussels is a very tolerant place and there is plenty going on, both on-scene and off. The scene is close-knit – some say cliquey – and concentrated around Rue du Marché au Charbon near the Bourse. Lesbians are very poorly served, however, except by the Tels Quels association.

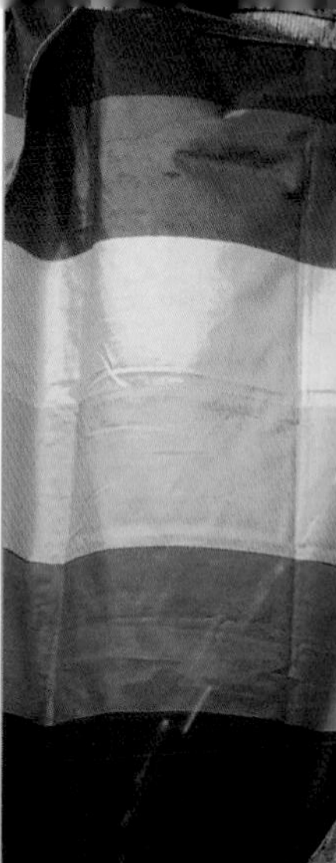

Bars

Le Belgica

Rue du Marché au Charbon 32; www.lebelgica.be; Thur–Sat 10pm–3am, Sun 8pm–3am; tram: 3, 4, bus: 48, 95; map p.135 C/D2

Traditional brown café that is the heart of Brussels' gay scene, frequented by clubbers, intellectuals and everything in between. Women and gay-friendly visitors are also made to feel welcome. DJs on Fri and Sat.

Le Duquesnoy

Rue Duquesnoy 12; tel: 02 502 38 83; www.duquesnoy.com; daily 9pm–3am, Sun from 3pm with admission charge; metro: Gare Centrale, bus: 48, 95; map p135 D2

Leather bar for hardcore action, men-only and with a more mature clientele. Dress code is strictly leather, rubber, latex, uniform or naked.

Le Plattesteen

Rue du Marché au Charbon 41; tel: 02 512 82 03; daily 10am–midnight, food midday–3pm, 6–10pm; tram: 3, 4, bus: 48, 95; map p.135 C/D2

At the heart of the gay quarter, this café-brasserie is the unofficial daytime HQ for the gay community (and a broader public), with a large streetside terrace and reasonable menu of hearty Belgian dishes.

Clubs

Bitchy Butch

Barrio Bar, Place de la Chapelle 6; www.bitchybutch.be; second Sat of the month from 11pm; bus: 27, 48; map p.135 D3

Monthly party in a small bar in Marolles where it gets pretty hot as the night wears on.

La Demence

Fuse, Rue Blaes 208; tel: 02 511 97 89; www.lademence.com; monthly, 10pm–midday; metro: Porte de Hal, tram: 3, 4, bus: 27, 48; map p.135 C4

Many gay visitors organise their weekend visit around this famous monthly night at Fuse. It takes place on a Friday night or the night before a public holiday, but check website for precise dates. With punters from the Netherlands, France and Germany, and all the nationalities in Brussels, you can be sure of 24 hours of Euroboy hedonism.

SEE ALSO NIGHTLIFE, P.88

Shows

Chez Maman

Rue des Grands Carmes 7; www.chezmaman.be; Thur–Sat

Right: the gay scene centres on rue du Marché au Charbon.

Left: the Manneken-Pis decked out for Gay Pride.

Sunday is a big gay party day in Brussels, with several afternoon 'tea dances'. Check the regular gay venues, but also straight club Le You *(see p.89)*, which has an early-evening gay party, and the clubby lounge bar Smouss Café *(see p.90)*.

midnight–dawn; tram: 3, 4, bus: 48, 95; map p.135 C2
Famous transvestite shows attended by a wide (including straight) audience.

Shops

Boris Boy
Rue du Midi 9; www.borisboy.com; Mon–Sat 12.15–7pm, Sun 4–6pm; metro: Anneessens, tram: 3, 4, bus: 48, 95; map p.135 C3
Men's shop with leather and rubber wear, toys, underwear and other accessories.

Eva Luna
Rue du Bailli 41; tel: 02 647 46 45; www.evaluna.be; Mon 1–6.30pm, Tue–Sat 10.30am–2pm, 2.30–6.30pm; tram: 81, 94, bus: 54
Tasteful women's sex shop (straight and gay), with a limited but stylish choice of appliances, and where staff are trained sex therapists.

Lady Paname
Rue des Grands Carmes 5; tel: 02 514 30 35; www.lady-paname.be; Mon–Sat 11.30am–7pm, Sun 3–7pm; metro: Anneessens, tram: 3, 4, bus: 48, 95; map p.135 C2
Charming erotica shop for women with underwear, bodycare products, accessories, toys and books.

Information

English-speaking Gay Group (EGG)
www.geocities.com/eggbrussels
This group organises monthly Sunday afternoon music-free parties for English-speaking gays and lesbians.

International Lesbian and Gay Association (ILGA)
Rue de la Charité 17; tel: 02 502 24 71; www.ilga.org
Lobby organisation representing 560 groups from 90 countries and based in Brussels principally to work with the EU institutions.

Rainbow House
Rue du Marché au Charbon 42; tel: 02 503 59 90; www.rainbowhouse.be; Wed–Thur 6.30–10.30pm, Fri–Sat 6.30pm–midnight, Sun 3–6.30pm; tram: 3, 4, bus: 48, 95; map p.135 C/D2
Information and community centre for both French- and Dutch-speaking gay, lesbian and bi associations, with bar and meeting rooms.

Tels Quels
Rue du Marché au Charbon 81; tel: 02 512 45 87; www.telsquels.be; Mon–Fri from 9am, Sat–Sun from 2pm; café tel: 02 512 32 34, daily 5pm–2am, Fri–Sat until 4am; tram: 3, 4, bus: 48, 95; map p.135 C/D2
Cultural centre by day, café by night – and probably the best women's venue in town. Girls' conversation nights are held each Mon, 7–9.30pm, and there are monthly cultural events for lesbians.

Festivals

Belgian Lesbian and Gay Pride
www.blgp.be
Held each year in May, this small but colourful parade has become more festive than political since the adoption of laws legalising gay marriage and adoption.

Gay and Lesbian Festival
www.fglb.org
For 10 days each year in January at Le Botanique, this long-established festival includes exhibitions, theatre, talks and performances.

Pink Screens Film Festival
www.pinkscreens.org
The 'alternative gender film festival' takes place over 10 days each October in art-house dive Cinema Nova.

Gay and Lesbian Online
www.lesbigaybrussels.be
www.brusselsgay.be
www.gaybelgium.be

History

c.AD 600

According to legend, St Géry builds a residence and chapel on an island in the Senne.

966

First documented reference to Brussels, as Bruocsella (village in the swamp).

979

Considered the city's official foundation; Charles, Duke of Lower Lorraine, occupies a castle built on St-Géry island at Bruocsella.

1005

The Counts of Louvain (Leuven), later Dukes of Brabant, inherit the settlement.

11th and 12th centuries

Brussels grows in prosperity, thanks to its position on the trade route between Bruges and Cologne.

c.1100

The city's first defensive wall is built.

1225

Construction begins on the Gothic cathedral dedicated to St Michael and St Gudula.

1229

Duke Henry of Brabant grants Brussels its first town charter.

1302–6

Revolt by craftsmen and tradesmen against the aristocratic government fails, though the plebeians win some concessions.

1357

Construction of the city's second defensive wall, now dismantled, which followed the course of today's inner ring road, the *petite ceinture* (little belt).

1402

Construction begins on the Gothic town hall (Hôtel de Ville) in the Grand'Place.

1421

A popular uprising leads to more just government, with local powers divided between the patrician families and the crafts guilds and other workers.

1425

Pope Martin V founds the university at Leuven, which develops into a European centre of jurisprudence.

1430

Brussels and the Duchy of Brabant come under the rule of Philip the Good, Duke of Burgundy, who already controls Flanders. The Burgundian Empire begins a cultural golden age; by 1459 Brussels is the empire's capital. Textile industries are the economic mainstay.

1477

Mary of Burgundy grants permission to dig the Willebroek Canal, which gives Brussels access to the sea by way of the Scheldt. Mary marries Maximilian I of Austria. The Low Countries come under the sway of the Habsburg dynasty.

1522

Two Lutheran preachers are burnt at the stake in Brussels; their martyrdom strengthens the forces of the Reformation in the city.

1531

Brussels becomes the capital of the Habsburg Low Countries.

1566

Protestant iconoclasts ransack churches across the Low Countries. Catholic Spain sends the Duke of Alba to suppress the movement. His reign of terror forces thousands of Protestants to emigrate.

1568

Counts Egmont and Hoorn, who had tried to moderate the religious intolerance of Spanish rule, are beheaded.

1579

Seven northern provinces of the Low Countries declare independence.

1585
The southern part of the Low Countries recognises Philip II as its sovereign.

1648
By the Treaty of Westphalia, Belgium remains under Spanish control.

1695
French army of Louis XIV bombards the Grand'Place.

1701–13
The War of the Spanish Succession turns Belgium into a battlefield. Under the 1715 Treaty of Utrecht, the present-day territory of Belgium passes under the authority of the Austrian Holy Roman Emperor Charles VI and his Habsburg successors.

1794
French revolutionaries annex Belgium, which remains under French control until the defeat of Napoleon Bonaparte.

1815
Wellington and Blücher defeat Napoleon at the Battle of Waterloo. Holland and Belgium form the Kingdom of the Netherlands under William I of Orange.

1830–1
Belgium revolts against the rule of the House of Orange, and the country achieves independence under King of the Belgians, Leopold I.

1835
Inauguration of the first Continental railway, between Brussels and Mechelen.

1871
Construction of the grand boulevards through the Lower City; the polluted River Senne is covered.

1885
Congo Free State acquired by Belgium.

1914–18
German troops invade Belgium and occupy Brussels during World War I.

1940–4
Nazi Germany invades Belgium during World War II; Belgian government seeks exile in London. In 1944, the Nazis send King Leopold III to Germany; the Allies liberate Belgium, entering Brussels on 3 September.

1948
A customs union is agreed between Belgium, Netherlands and Luxembourg (Benelux).

1951
King Baudouin I ascends the throne after the abdication of Leopold III.

1957
Belgium joins the European Economic Community.

1959
Brussels becomes headquarters of the European Commission.

1967
Brussels becomes headquarters of Nato.

1977
Establishment of three federal regions in Belgium: Flanders, Wallonia and Brussels.

1993
King Baudouin I is succeeded by his brother, Albert II.

1994
A new constitution completes Belgium's transition to a federal state, with three language communities (Flemish, French and German), and considerable powers devolved to its three regions.

2002
The Belgian franc is replaced by the euro.

2007
Political parties fail to form a government for nine months after elections, due to disagreement between French- and Dutch-speakers on further devolution.

2008
Flemish Christian Democrat Yves Leterme becomes prime minister of a fragile five-party government.

Hotels

Brussels' hotel scene has evolved dramatically in the past 10 years. A decade ago, accommodation was pitched squarely at the staid executive market, with a surfeit of charmless but comfortable rooms, or traditional grand hotels rather fraying around the edges. That changed with the advent of high-speed rail links from nearby European capitals and the resulting influx of city-trippers. Today, although 75 percent of rooms in the city still meet four- or five-star standards, a new breed of stylishly designed mid-market hotels are giving the big guns a serious run for their money.

Grand'Place

Amigo

Rue de l'Amigo 1–3; tel: 02 547 47 47; www.hotelamigo.com; €€€€; tram: 4, 32, 55 (Bourse), bus: 48, 95, metro: Bourse; map p.135 D2

Rooms and service are top-notch in this renowned luxury hotel, where antique furniture, flagstone flooring and Flemish paintings give a Spanish Renaissance air to what is actually a 1950s construction. Tucked discreetly behind the Hôtel de Ville, a minute from the Grand'Place. Some rooms rather small.

Above: one of Amigo's luxury suites.

Le Dixseptième

Rue de la Madeleine 25; tel: 02 517 17 17; www.ledixseptieme.be; €€; metro: Gare Centrale, bus: 63, 66, 71; map p.135 D2

A hotel in two parts: the historic house on the street – residence of the Spanish ambassador in the 17th century – has large, romantic rooms with oak beams, creaky floorboards and antique furnishings, while the modern building beyond the inner courtyard has smaller, well-appointed rooms, some with terrace and kitchen facilities.

Floris Arlequin Grand'Place

Rue de la Fourche 17–19; tel: 02 514 16 15; www.florishotels.com; €€; metro: De Brouckère, tram: 4, 32, 55, bus: 38, 66, 71; map p.135 D2

Nestling in the heart of the historic Ilôt Sacré in a small shopping arcade (which it shares with the Actor's Studio cinema), this modern hotel has rooms which have been recently redecorated in smart neutrals, and a top-floor breakfast room with an unexpectedly good view of the Grand'Place.

La Madeleine

Rue de la Montagne 22; tel: 02 513 29 73; www.hotel-la-madeleine.be; €€; metro: Gare Centrale, bus: 63, 66, 71; map p.135 D2

Price ranges, which are given as a guide only, are for a standard double room with bathroom, including service, tax and breakfast:

€	under €100
€€	€100–200
€€€	€200–300
€€€€	over €300

Left: roof terrace at Amigo, just behind the Grand'Place.

Bed and Brussels (www.bnb-brussels.be) is a useful website of private homes that offer bed and breakfast accommodation, often at a very reasonable price compared to hotels (if 24-hour room service is not a priority for you). Pick your star rating, location or type of lodging and it will search out a choice of options to suit.

A friendly, simple, centrally located hotel with a 15th-century facade and a wide choice of room options, including many singles: with sink; with sink and shower, or with full en suite. Compact but functional, and decorated in lemon with green bamboo furniture, rooms at the rear have no view but are quieter; the front overlooks Place Agora with its craft stalls, buskers and pavement cafés.

The Moon

Rue de la Montagne 4bis; tel: 02 508 15 80; www.memon-hotels.be; €; metro: Gare Centrale, bus: 63, 66, 71; map p.135 D2

Excellent quality-price ratio at this hotel above a café near the Grand'Place, where the 18 rooms have modern decor, laminate flooring, shower and WC; several overlook Place Agora. The first choice for many budget-conscious frequent visitors (including for business) to Brussels.

Royal Windsor

Rue Duquesnoy 5; tel: 02 505 55 55; www.royalwindsorbrussels.com; €€€€; metro: Gare Centrale, bus: 48, 95; map p.135 D2

An upmarket address that prides itself on its British-style formal service and top-notch decor, although it has added a contemporary twist by commissioning Brussels fashion designers to decorate a number of the 250 rooms. All are superbly equipped and furnished (great bathrooms), if not enormous. As well as a smart restaurant and English-style pub, the hotel is unique in Brussels in having its own nightclub, Duke's (Thur–Sun 11pm–dawn).

Saint-Michel

Grand'Place 15; tel: 02 511 09 56; www.hotelsaintmichel.be; €; tram: 4, 32, 55 (Bourse), bus: 48, 95; map p.135 D2

A room with a view – over

Below: the chic interior of the Royal Windsor, which has its own bar and nightclub.

what many believe to be the most beautiful square in Europe – is yours for a surprisingly modest price in this simple hotel with the to-die-for address. Not all rooms have views, however, so you pay for what you get.

Lower City

Brussels Marriott
Rue Auguste Orts 3–7; tel: 02 516 90 90; www.marriottbrussels.com; €€; tram: 4, 32, 55 (Bourse), bus: 46, 48, 95; map p.135 C2
Five years ago, the Marriott group snapped up this prime real estate opposite the Bourse (stock exchange), gutted the building and created a perfect abode midway between hip Saint-Géry and the Grand'Place. Standard rooms are not enormous, but all have super-cosy bedding and are furnished to the highest spec. Breakfast is all-you-can-eat hot and cold buffet.

The Dominican
Rue Léopold 9; tel: 02 203 08 08; www.thedominican.be; €€€; metro: De Brouckère, tram: 4, 32, 55, bus: 63, 66, 71; map p.135 D2
Bang on trend in its design and facilities (rain shower, free Wi-fi), this former Dominican convent behind the opera house has upped the ante on the Brussels hotel scene since it opened in late 2007. Its 150 rooms (all non-smoking) are decorated in muted coffee tones and set around an inner courtyard.

A la Grande Cloche
Place Rouppe 10; tel: 02 512 61 40; www.hotelgrandecloche.com; €; metro: Anneessens, tram: 4, 32, 55, bus: 48, 95; map p.135 C3
Century-old hotel just outside the prime tourist zone, but still entirely walkable (and facing Comme Chez Soi, possibly the best restaurant in town). The clean, well-kept rooms on five floors are adequate if not modernised and have rather antiquated plumbing.

Hooy Kaye Lodge
Quai aux Pierres de Taille 22; tel: 02 218 44 40; www.hooykayelodge.com; €€; metro: Yser or Sainte-Catherine, tram: 81, bus: 47, 88; map p.134 C1
Delightful small guesthouse (three rooms) in a 17th-century house behind the KVS (Flemish theatre), an up-and-coming hip area. Period fireplaces, ceiling beams and antique furnishings are given pride of place in the pared-down chic modern decor, reminiscent of a Dutch interior. There's even a small garden. A gem.

Hotel Orts
Rue Auguste Orts 38–40; tel: 02 517 07 00; www.hotelorts.com; €€; tram: 4, 32, 55, bus: 46, 48, 95; map p.135 C2
This relative newcomer to the Brussels hotel scene is rapidly gaining favour for its stylish dark-hued rooms, great location and good value. Situated above a café-restaurant on the Rue Orts/Rue Dansaert junction, the 13 colour-themed rooms are chocolate, grey, red or blue, all with spanking new fittings.

La Légende
Rue du Lombard 35; tel: 02 512 82 90; www.hotellalegende.com; €; tram: 4, 32, 55, bus: 48, 95; map p.135 D2
Established 50 years ago by the same family that runs it today, this started out as a hotel above a café frequented by philatelists. They grew in the 1990s to this larger property bang in the centre of town, accessed via a traditional coach entrance, and with rooms arranged around a central courtyard. Choice of accommodation from standard single (small but all en suite) to a self-catering apartment for two.

Price ranges, which are given as a guide only, are for a standard double room with bathroom, including service, tax and breakfast:

€	under €100
€€	€100–200
€€€	€200–300
€€€€	over €300

Maison Noble
Rue Marcq 10; tel: 02 219 23 39; www.maison-noble.eu; €€; metro: Sainte-Catherine, tram: 81, bus: 47, 88; map p.134 C1
A welcoming gay couple let three freshly decorated rooms – all fully en suite and with free Wi-fi – in their elegant 1826 home in the quiet Béguinage district. On the ground floor, the breakfast room is lit through a colourful stained-glass window. Pick the room you fancy and you could be staying in a friend's house. Guests may also use the gym and steam room in the basement.

Métropole
Place de Brouckère 31; tel: 02 217 23 00; www.metropolehotel.com; €€€; metro: De Brouckère, tram: 4, 32, 55; map p.135 D1
Possibly the best-known hotel in Brussels, with a famous pavement café and Art Nouveau bar, this large hotel is absolutely gorgeous, dripping with history and a firm favourite with music and entertainment personalities. Rooms along the 9km (5 miles) of corridors vary in decor and style; some have large historic murals, others are more country-style or chandeliered and glitzy.

Noga
Rue du Béguinage 38; tel: 02 218 67 63; www.nogahotel.com; €; metro: Sainte-Catherine, bus: 47, 88; map p.135 C1

Above: Le Plaza's opulent theatre, used for shows, dinners and conferences.

Comfortable family-run hotel in a backstreet near the Béguinage, with an eclectic collection of nautical-themed curios and antiques, and a light-filled breakfast room on the top floor. Not all of the 19 rooms are en suite, and some are rather more spacious than others.

Pacific

Rue Antoine Dansaert 57; tel: 02 213 00 80; www.hotelcafe pacific.com; €€; tram: 4, 32, 55 (Bourse), bus: 48, 95; map p.135 C2

A much-loved former fleapit of a café-hotel has been reborn as if from the pages of an interiors mag, adorned by Brussels accessories queen Mia Zia, and with 12 rooms over five floors in the hip Dansaert district. Rooms have snippets of poetry and art on the walls, and free Wi-fi is included.

Quoted rates include tax and generally breakfast too, which is usually of the continental variety – bread and pastries, cold meats and cheese, fruit, yoghurt and cereals. Cooked breakfast is served only in larger hotels.

Le Plaza

Boulevard Adolphe Max 118–126; tel: 02 278 01 00; www.leplaza-brussels.be; €€€; metro: Rogier, tram: 4, 32, 55, bus: 61; map p.135 D1

A grand 1930s hotel that offers the last word in traditional luxury, entirely renovated in the 1990s with no expense spared in furnishing and fittings. It even has its own theatre, now a protected monument in its own right, which is used for corporate events and fashion shows.

Sheraton Brussels

Place Rogier 3; tel: 02 224 31 11; www.sheraton.com/ brussels; €€€; metro: Rogier, tram: 4, 32, 55, bus: 61

Although located on a busy intersection, this large hotel is peaceful inside and has a great pool (and fitness centre) on the top floor with a panoramic view and loungers on the terrace. Rooms are spacious with wide, comfortable beds; several floors are devoted to business travellers and offer videoconferencing facilities; others have family-friendly rooms with video games and toys.

Sleep Well Youth Hostel

Rue du Damier 23; tel: 02 218 50 50; www.sleepwell.be; €; metro: Rogier, tram: 4, 32, 55; map p.135 D1

Friendly modern hostel – or, more aptly, 'youth hotel' – in a quiet road parallel to the pedestrianised shopping street Rue Neuve. With comic strip murals and a games room, it's bright and fun. Hostel rooms have shared showers and bathroom (all rooms have sinks), and there are singles and twins, as well as dorms (up to 8 beds) and an 11am–3pm lockout. Alternatively, the 'Sleep Well Star' rooms have private facilities for a touch more cash.

Price ranges, which are given as a guide only, are for a standard double room with bathroom, including service, tax and breakfast:

€	under €100
€€	€100–200
€€€	€200–300
€€€€	over €300

Above: at the Pacific hotel in Rue Dansaert *(see p.63)*, each room has its own 'personality'.

La Vieille Lanterne
Rue des Grands Carmes 29; tel: 02 512 74 94; www.lavieille lanterne.be; €; tram: 4, 32, 55 (Anneessens), bus: 48, 95; map p.135 C3
Six small but spotless rooms above a souvenir shop, all with a view of the Manneken-Pis. Decor is somewhat rustic and facilities are limited – breakfast is served in your room – but the welcome is friendly and the central location an advantage, for such a moderate price (which includes breakfast).

Welcome
Quai au Bois-à-Brûler 23; tel: 02 219 95 46; www.brussels hotel.travel; €€; metro: Sainte-Catherine, bus: 47, 88; map p.135 C1
A perennial favourite on the former fish market, where the decoration transforms a Brussels stay into the unexpectedly exotic: each of the 15 rooms is decorated in the style of a different country or region: India, Tahiti, Silk Road, Bali, Marrakesh, Istanbul... most have air conditioning, and the welcome is personal and warm.

Le White Room
Rue Locquenghienstraat 45; tel: 02 538 59 95; www.lewhite room.be; €; metro: Sainte-Catherine, bus: 88; map p.134 C1
A stylish small bed and breakfast with just one room to let in a designer loft apartment. Guests may take breakfast when they like and are made to feel they are the personal guest of the owner, who will give an insider's view on the hottest places to eat, drink, shop and visit.

Marolles

Be Manos
23 Square de l'Aviation; tel: 02 520 65 65; www.bemanos.com; €€€€; metro: Gare du Midi, tram: (Lemonnier) 4, 56, 81, 82; map p.134 B3
A one-off, fabulous new hotel that's all black and silver inside, with designer features and a calming water feature in the interior courtyard. Owned by the same family as the two excellent Manos hotels in the Louise district, and with the same attention to top-quality personal service.

Brussels hotels do most of their business during the week, and many – particularly at the top end – offer excellent deals at weekends. Push for a reduction or a room upgrade if you are visiting at the weekend or during August. Even at other times, the published rates are very often negotiable.

Brueghel Youth Hostel
Heilige Geeststraat 2; tel: 02 511 04 36; www.jeugdherbergen.be; €; metro: Gare Centrale, bus: 27, 48; map p.135 D3
This Flemish youth hostel enjoys an excellent location near the Sablon, with 125 beds in 48 rooms, 22 of which have two beds and four are singles. There's a 1am curfew, though, so if you want to party late don't come back before 7am, when it reopens.

Galia
Place du Jeu de Balle 15–16; tel: 02 502 42 43; www.hotel galia.com; €; metro: Porte de Hal, bus: 27, 48; map p.135 C4
Perfect for early risers and

Right: Be Manos.

knick-knack hunters, this clean, simple hotel occupies a prime location on the sunny side of the flea market's cobbled square, beside the Art Deco public baths. Rooms (for singles up to four people) have double-glazing and solid doors to protect against early disturbance, and each has a WC and shower or bath.

Upper City

Congrès

Rue du Congrès 38–42; tel: 02 217 18 90; www.hoteldu congres.be; €€; metro: Madou, bus: 29, 63; map p.135 E2

Smart neutral furnishings complement the original features retained in this fine town house, located in an unjustly overlooked, elegant part of the city – quiet at night and peopled mainly by Belgian civil servants by day.

Hilton Brussels

Boulevard de Waterloo 38; tel: 02 504 11 11; www.brussels.hilton.com; €€€; metro: Louise, tram: 92, 94, 97; map p.135 D4

The uptown Hilton commands the best views in town, from a landmark tower that teeters over the city from the chic Boulevard de Waterloo. Service and rooms are of suitably international standard (though basic rooms are not large), and house restaurant La Maison du Bœuf is unfailingly good. Some rooms have views over the sweet Parc d'Egmont behind.

NH Hotel du Grand Sablon

Rue Bodenbroek 2–4; tel: 02 518 11 00; www.nh-hotels.com; €€; tram: 92, 94, bus: 27, 95; map p.135 D3

With a superb location facing south on the Place du Grand Sablon, this hotel has a grand entrance and marble lobby area, and comfortable rooms in Italian style, with Louis XIV chairs, velvet headboards and marble bathrooms. Now part of the NH chain, which has several addresses in Brussels, there are very good deals on certain rooms if you book early.

Louise Quarter and South Brussels

L'Art de la Fugue

Rue de Suède 38; tel: 02 513 84 47; www.lartdelafugue.com; €; metro: Gare du Midi or Porte de Hal, tram: 32, 81, bus: 27; map p.134 B4

Bed and breakfast run by a dynamic male duo who've renovated an old house to interiors magazine spec with a mixture of flea market finds and objects brought back from their travels. The three large en suite rooms are decorated in individual and luxurious style. Discounts for multiple-night stays.

> Complimentary tea and coffee is not standard in Brussels hotel rooms, so enquire ahead if this is important for you. The same goes for free internet access; even many pricier hotels do not include this.

Les Bluets

Rue Berckmans 124; tel: 02 534 39 83; www.geocities.com/les_bluets; €; metro: Hôtel des Monnaies, tram: 92, 97

Ten rooms in this characterful home of a family with Colombian roots and a decor to match, including a plant-stuffed conservatory with tropical bird. Some rooms are immense with extra bed options for kids, most have antique beds (and mattresses), and others are tiny but charming. There's a no-noise rule after 10pm, which is handy, as room partitions are not the thickest.

De Boeck's
Rue Veydt 40; tel: 02 537 40 33; www.hotel-deboecks.be; €€; tram: 92, 97
A hotel established in the 18th century with down-at-heel charm occupies a quiet street near Avenue Louise. The large rooms and high ceilings typical of Brussels homes are furnished in slightly outmoded style, but at least one is big enough to accommodate a family of five (on request).

Bristol Stephanie
Avenue Louise 91–93; tel: 02 543 33 11; www.bristol.be; €€€€; tram: 94, bus: 54
Nordic-influenced modern hotel on the smart Avenue Louise, which is discreet and comfortable with indulgent service and facilities, and check-out possible up to 4pm. Its heated indoor pool is a major plus-point.

Conrad Brussels
Avenue Louise 71; tel: 02 542 42 42; www.conradbrussels.com; €€€€; metro: Louise, tram: 92, 94, 97; map p.135 D1
Limousines ferrying heads of state and and their retinues to EU and Nato meetings regularly block the traffic outside this prestigious hotel where the suites are the stuff of legend. Guests have access to the plush branch of the Aspria health club (with pool) located below the hotel, and an ice-rink in the courtyard in winter.

Manos Premier
Chaussée de Charleroi 100–106; tel: 02 537 96 82; www.manoshotel.com; €€€€; tram: 92, 97
The original establishment of this three-hotel chain, covered in ivy and home to the fashionable lounge-bar and restaurant Kolya. A luxury address, with lofty rooms decorated like an elegant Parisian apartment and offering a welcome change from the style of international chain hotels. Refreshingly, too, Manos hotels all provide free internet access, which many of Brussels' swishest hotels, inexcusably, do not.

Manos Stéphanie
Chaussée de Charleroi 28; tel: 02 539 02 50; www.manoshotel.com; €€€; tram: 92, 97
The Manos hotels really punch above their weight in terms of quality of rooms. Although not cheap, the family-run establishments offer a sumptuous experience Louis XIV-style, with red-and-gold furnishings in the rooms and lashings of marble downstairs. There's a courtyard garden and terrace, and service is personal and attentive.

Les Tourelles
Avenue Winston Churchill 135; tel: 02 344 95 73; www.lestourelles.be; €; tram: 23, 24, bus: 60
Chalet-style villa in the leafy suburb of Uccle provides a calm escape from the city bustle, but is connected thanks to a well-served tram route. With warm, country-style decor and quiet service, it feels rather like a visit to the home of your favourite French great-aunt.

Below: Nordic-influenced Bristol Stephanie.

Price ranges, which are given as a guide only, are for a standard double room with bathroom, including service, tax and breakfast:

€	under €100
€€	€100–200
€€€	€200–300
€€€€	over €300

Warwick Barsey
Avenue Louise 381–383; tel: 02 649 98 00; www.warwickbarsey.com; €€€€; tram: 94, bus: 38, 60
Ever since French stylist Jacques Garcia (Hôtel Costes, Paris, among others) did a makeover of this hotel up the park end of Avenue Louise, its bar and restaurant have become the hang-out *du jour* of smart young Belgians. The rooms and lobby are decorated in his trademark theatrical style, part-Napoleon III, part-contemporary, with dark tones, gilt and lashings of opulence.

White Hotel
Avenue Louise 212; tel: 02 644 29 29; www.thewhitehotel.be; €€; tram: 81, 94, bus: 54
This hotel-meets-art-gallery was one of the first boutique hotels in Brussels. Pieces of art were commissioned from contemporary artists for each room, where they are set off by pure white decor, minimalist fittings and floor-to-ceiling windows. A hip but affordable choice, with free Wi-fi in-room.

Above: ornate furniture and fittings at the Warwick Barsey.

European Quarter and the Cinquantenaire

Derby

Avenue de Tervuren 24; tel: 02 733 08 19; www.hotel-derby.be; €; metro: Mérode, tram: 81, bus: 22, 27

Very good-value hotel above the Tavern Aurige in the relaxed but well-connected Mérode area, with rooms for one to four people, all en suite and many with balconies. Good for access to the museums at the Cinquantenaire, as well as for all metro connections to the city centre, this hotel is a good alternative to the more business-focused EU-quarter hotels.

Leopold

Rue du Luxembourg 35; tel: 02 511 18 28; www.hotel-leopold.be; €€€; station: Gare du Luxembourg, bus: 12, 22, 54; map p.136 A3

An upmarket, independent hotel that has long been renowned for its superb restaurant. The hotel has over 100 rooms and seven apartments; the former are not enormous (prices reflect the hotel's proximity to the European Parliament), but all have been freshly renovated and are air-conditioned.

Martin's Central Park

Boulevard Charlemagne 80; tel: 02 230 85 55; www.martinshotels.com; €€€; metro: Schuman, bus: 22, 60; map p.136 B2

A recent change of ownership saw this seven-storey modern hotel substantially refurbished and upgraded, with room categories renamed 'cosy', 'charming', 'great' and 'exceptional'. Each room has a desk with fax, many have a jacuzzi bath and those on higher floors have attractive arched windows. Pass on the overpriced buffet breakfast, however.

> The local telephone numbers provided include the Brussels area code '02', which must be dialled even from a landline within the zone. When dialling from abroad, omit the '0'.

Monty

Boulevard Brand Whitlock 101; tel: 02 734 56 36; www.monty-hotel.be; €€; tram: 23, 24, 25, bus: 27, 28, 80

Surprisingly good-priced, stylish hotel located on the outer edge of this district but well served by public transport. Rooms and common

Above: colourful murals at Hotel Bloom!

areas celebrate the best of contemporary design behind a grandiose 1930s facade. The service and facilities – free Wi-fi, bike loan for guests, complimentary tea and coffee – are popular with regular visitors to Brussels, so book early.

A central online booking service is offered by the Brussels tourist office at the website www.brures.com. Alternatively, and useful for comparing rates, Resotel offers a similar service at www.belgiumhospitality.com. It can track last-minute offers and shows available rates for a defined date, many below the stated rack rate (eg five-star hotels at under €150 a double room). Its calendar of busy periods is a useful indicator of high demand for rooms.

Renaissance

Rue du Parnasse 19; tel: 02 505 29 29; www.marriott.com/brubr; €€€; station: Gare du Luxembourg, bus: 12, 22, 54; map p.136 A4

Its location right near the European Parliament ensures a permanent bustle of lobbyists and PR men hosting political events in this modern, plush hotel, which has serviced apartments as well as a wide range of rooms and suites. Good restaurant and on-site independent gym.

Price ranges, which are given as a guide only, are for a standard double room with bathroom, including service, tax and breakfast:

€	under €100
€€	€100–200
€€€	€200–300
€€€€	over €300

Silken Berlaymont Brussels

Boulevard Charlemagne 11–19; tel: 02 231 09 09; www.hotelsilkenberlaymont.com; €€€; metro: Schuman, bus: 22, 60; map p.136 B2

Artistic black-and-white photography in all the rooms and common areas give this sleek hotel behind the Berlaymont the feel of a comfortable bachelor pad. Right next door to a large media centre, so lots of journalists hang out in the downstairs coffee bar and nearby pubs.

Sofitel Brussels Europe

Place Jourdan 1; tel: 02 235 51 00; www.sofitel-brussels-europe.com; €€€€; bus: 59, 60, 80; map p.136 B4

Sleek and contemporary newcomer in the EU district, with pale, bright rooms and all the upscale add-ons you'd expect, including bathrobes and slippers, and with a rooftop terrace for fine weather. It's right next door to a major EU meeting venue, so gets busy except at weekends or in August, when rates dip. But no free Wi-fi. And how much breakfast can you eat to get €25 worth? Eat out.

Stanhope

Rue du Commerce 9; tel: 02 506 91 11; www.stanhope.be; €€€; metro: Trône, bus: 27, 38, 95; map p.135 E3

A former Dominican convent has been transformed into a refined lodging inspired by the

Right: Sofitel Brussels Europe.

tyle of an English stately ome (Viscount Linley provided some of the furniture). Certain rooms are tiny, so plash out on the Goodwood Suite the other side of the ear garden which is a delight of chintz on two floors. The dining room has fabulous Chinese silk wall coverings.

North Brussels and Royal Laeken

Albert

Rue Royale Sainte-Marie 27–29; tel: 02 217 93 91; www.hotelalbert.be; €; tram: 92, 94, bus: 65, 66

Modest place with a friendly welcome opposite cultural venue Les Halles de Schaerbeek and near several good-value restaurants (Turkish, Belgian and a fancy Italian). Simple rooms and facilities, but the staff go out of their way to accommodate guests' needs, and the tram stops just round the corner.

Hotel Bloom!

Rue Royale 250; tel: 02 220 66 11; www.hotelbloom.com; €€; tram: 92, 94, bus: 61; map p.135 E1

This recent, welcome new addition to the Brussels hotel scene is funky but as smart as they come, with pure white rooms and furniture, and colourful murals by young artists. In-room internet access and coffee is included, and weekend rates are in the lower price category. Recommended.

> Beware the cost of taking a taxi to and from the airport, since local bureaucracy and turf wars mean you effectively pay for a return trip. This is because Brussels taxis may not pick up passengers from taxi ranks in Zaventem (where the airport is); and Zaventem taxis may not pick up passengers in Brussels. The driver is thus obliged to travel one way with no fare. Better to take an overground train or airport bus 12 from the airport, and then a cab from one of the city stations, if required. Journeys times are normally under half an hour.

Around Brussels

Le 1815

Route du Lion 367–369, Waterloo; tel: 02 387 01 60; www.le1815.com; €€; TEC bus: W or 365a (direct from Bruxelles-Midi station, journey time 1 hour)

Dating from rather later than the Battle of Waterloo, this hotel's rooms are named after generals who fought there, and their portraits grace the walls, which is both fun and rather kitsch, like some of the colourful decor. There's not a lot of competition for business this close to the battlefield tourist attraction, but the attached Italian restaurant is not bad at all. Pick a room at the back if you are sensitive to noise.

Château du Lac Genval

Avenue du Lac 87, 1332 Genval; tel: 02 655 71 11; www.martinshotels.com; €€€€; rail station: Genval

A country retreat overlooking a pretty lake in the smart Brussels green-belt town of Genval, 22km (13½ miles) away. Some rooms are more recently decorated than others and have considerably more style; make sure to ask for one with a view of the lake, too. The on-site gym is good, though you pay heavily for the privilege.

Kasteel Gravenhof

Alsembergsesteenweg 676, 1653 Dworp; tel: 02 380 44 99; www.gravenhof.be; €€; exit 20 on E19 Brussels–Charleroi motorway

A moated and turreted 17th-century château 15km (10 miles) from Brussels was substantially remodelled in the 19th century and today has 26 stylish modern rooms, each with a view of the grounds and/or lake.

Language

Brussels is officially bilingual, with public signs and announcements in both French and Dutch. Around 75 percent of the local population speaks French, 15 percent are Flemish and speak Dutch, and the rest are foreign residents, most of whom use French as lingua franca. English is increasingly used in advertising and business, as it is considered a 'neutral' language. Many people are happy to speak English to visitors, although efforts to speak one of the local languages are appreciated. Historically, the city was entirely Flemish, but following independence in 1830 French came to dominate all spheres of life.

General

Yes Oui *Ja*
No Non *Nee*
Please S'il vous plaît *Alstublieft*
Thank you (very much) Merci (beaucoup) *Dank u (wel)*
Excuse me Excusez-moi *Excuseer*
You're welcome Je vous en prie *Graag gedaan*
Hello Bonjour *Dag*
Goodbye Au revoir *Tot ziens*
Do you speak English? Parlez-vous anglais? *Spreekt u Engels?*
I don't understand Je ne comprends pas *Ik begrijp het niet*
I'm sorry Pardon *Sorry*
I don't know Je ne sais pas *Ik weet het niet*
My name is... Je m'appelle... *Ik heet...*

In Dutch, 'hard' consonants such as t, k, s and p are pronounced almost the same as in English, but sometimes softer. Other pronunciations differ as follows: j = y, v = f, je = yer, tje = ch, ee = ay, oo = o, ij = eay, a = u.

I am English/American Je suis anglais(e)/ américain(e) *Ik ben Engelsman/Engelse/Amerikaan*
When? Quand? *Wanneer?*
At what time? A quelle heure? *Hoe laat?*
today aujourd'hui *vandaag*
yesterday/tomorrow hier/ demain *gisteren/morgen*
now/later maintenant/plus tard *nu/later*
this morning ce matin *vanmorgen*
this afternoon cet après-midi *deze namiddag/vanmiddag*
this evening ce soir *vanavond*
day/week jour/semaine *dag/week*
month/year mois/an *maand/jaar*
left/right gauche/droite *links/rechts*

On Arrival

Where is there a bus stop/ tram stop? Où se trouve l'arrêt de bus/tram? *Waar is er een bushalte/ tramhalte?*
railway station gare *station*
I want a ticket to... Je voudrais un billet pour... *Ik wil graag een kaartje naar...*
single (one way) aller simpl *enkele reis*
return (round-trip) aller retour *heen en terug*
I'd like a single/double roon Je voudrais une chambre simple/double *Il wil een eenpersoonskamer/ tweepersoonskamer*
What is the charge per night? Ça coûte combier par nuit? *Hoeveel is het per nacht?*

Emergencies

Help! Au secours! *Help!*
Call a doctor/an ambulanc Appelez un médecin/ ambulance *Bel een dokter/een ziekenwagen*
Call the police/fire brigade Appelez la police/ les pompiers *Bel de politie/brandweer*
Where's the nearest hospital? Où est l'hôpital le plus proche? *Waar is he dichtstbijzijnde ziekenhuis?*
I am sick Je suis malade *Ik ben ziek*
I have lost my passport/ money/bag J'ai perdu mon passeport/argent/sa *Ik heb mijn paspoort/geld. tas verloren*

Shopping

How much is it? C'est combien? *Hoeveel is/kost het?*
Have you got...? Avez-vous...? *Hebt u...?*
enough assez *genoeg*
too much trop *te veel*
a piece un morceau *een stuk*
each la pièce *per stuk*
Do you take credit cards? Est-ce que vous acceptez les cartes de crédit? *Aanvaardt u kredietkaarten?*
Is there a bank near here? Il y a une banque près d'ici? *Is er hier een bank in de buurt?*
department store le grand magasin *het warenhuis*
market le marché *de markt*
supermarket le supermarché *de supermarkt*
postcard la carte postale *de briefkaart*
stamp le timbre *de postzegel*

Sightseeing

Where is...? Où se trouve...? *Waar is hier...?*
tourist information office l'office de tourisme *de toeristische dienst*
museum le musée *het museum*
church l'église *de kerk*
exhibition l'exposition *de tentoonstelling*
open/closed ouvert/fermé *open/gesloten*
free gratuit *gratis*

Dining Out

breakfast le petit déjeuner *het ontbijt*
lunch le déjeuner *de lunch/het middageten*
dinner le dîner *het diner/avondeten*
meal le repas *de maaltijd*
first course l'entrée *het voorgerecht*
main course le plat principal *het hoofdgerecht*
the bill l'addition *de rekening*
I am a vegetarian Je suis végétarien(ne) *Ik ben vegetariër*
I'd like to order Je voudrais commander *Ik wil bestellen/zou graag bestellen*
Enjoy your meal! Bon appétit! *Eet smaakelijk!*

Days of the Week

Sunday dimanche *Zondag*
Monday lundi *Maandag*
Tuesday mardi *Dinsdag*

Left: multilingual street signs.

Wednesday mercredi *Woensdag*
Thursday jeudi *Donderdag*
Friday vendredi *Vrijdag*
Saturday samedi *Zaterdag*

Numbers

0 zéro *nul*
1 un(e) *een*
2 deux *twee*
3 trois *drie*
4 quatre *vier*
5 cinq *vijf*
6 six *zes*
7 sept *zeven*
8 huit *acht*
9 neuf *negen*
10 dix *tien*
11 onze *elf*
12 douze *twaalf*
13 treize *dertien*
14 quatorze *veertien*
15 quinze *vijftien*
16 seize *zestien*
17 dix-sept *zeventien*
18 dix-huit *achttien*
19 dix-neuf *negentien*
20 vingt *twintig*
21 vingt et un *een en twintig*
30 trente *dertig*
40 quarante *veertig*
50 cinquante *vijftig*
60 soixante *zestig*
70 septante *zeventig*
80 quatre-vingt *tachtig*
90 nonante *negentig*
100 cent *honderd*
1,000 mille *duizend*

Below: the *menu du jour*.

Literature

The literary form most associated with Brussels – and a major cultural export – is the *bande dessinée* (comic strip) tradition. The Smurfs, Lucky Luke and Tintin were all dreamt up by Belgian illustrators, enjoying enormous success following World War II. For other writers, the bilingual nature of Brussels has to some extent impeded their visibility, as they are claimed by either French- or Dutch-speakers, but rarely both. In the past, several foreign writers and dissidents have sought refuge in Brussels, including Karl Marx. This section highlights local literature and lists the best bookshops in town.

Above: one of the city's comic murals; the *Adventures of Tintin.*

Comic Strips

One of the earliest albums published in Belgium was Hergé's *The Adventures of Tintin* (1929), including the story *Tintin in the Land of the Soviets*. Hergé, who founded *Le Journal de Tintin*, a weekly magazine (1946–93) which published *Blake and Mortimer* and *Alix* as well as the Tintin stories, pioneered the *ligne claire* style, which uses strong, regular lines without emphasis or shading to accentuate certain elements; the stories are similarly straightforward.

A keen rivalry existed between the Tintin weekly and *Spirou*, the most successful weekly magazine of the 'Ninth Art', launched in 1938. Artists associated with Spirou include Jijé, André Franquin (Gaston Lagaffe and Marsupilami), Morris (Lucky Luke) and Peyo (The Smurfs). Their style, the 'Marcinelle school', evokes a greater sense of movement. *Spirou* is still published today, selling 100,000 copies a week.

A series of large wall murals dotted around the city centre celebrates the comic-strip heroes; their locations are shown on a map available from the tourist office.

Other Literature

Authors who sought refuge in Brussels in the 19th century, particularly from France, include Victor Hugo and Baudelaire, and Karl Marx, who conceived and wrote the *Communist Manifesto* (1848) with Friedrich Engels during his Brussels period. On a brief visit during their torrid affair, French poet Verlaine shot and injured Rimbaud during an argument, for which Verlaine was jailed for two years.

Charlotte and Emily Brontë were not political refugees, but lived in Brussels from 1842–3; Charlotte's *The Professor* and *Villette* are both inspired by her experiences in the city.

Prolific crime writer Georges Simenon (1903–89) hailed from Liège, but set

Left: Tropismes bookshop.

A large book sale and fair, the Foire du Livre de Bruxelles, takes place each year in March and features readings and signings by international and local authors; www.flb.be. Passa Porta, a multilingual literary festival, takes place every two years; www.passaporta.be.

several Inspector Maigret detective stories in Brussels, including *Le Suspect* (The Suspect, set in Schaerbeek) and *Le Locataire* (The Tenant).

The first woman admitted to the Académie Française, Marguerite Yourcenar (1903–87) was born in Brussels to a Belgian mother and French father. Engravings at the Rue aux Laines entrance to the Parc d'Egmont commemorate her novels, of which several, including *Alexis* (1929) and *Memoirs of Hadrian* (1951), have been translated into English.

Bruges-born Hugo Claus (1929–2008) is a key figure in 20th-century Belgian literature, and his *Sorrow of Belgium* is a must for anyone interested in the history of the country.

Brussels novelist Amélie Nothomb (b. 1967) has enjoyed enormous success in France and worldwide with her rather dark studies of human nature – see *Stupeur et Tremblements* (Fear and Trembling; 1999). Most recently, US-based Flemish cognitive psychologist Paul Verhaeghen (b. 1967) made literary waves with his sweeping *Omega Minor*, about deceit, betrayal and particle physics in the wake of the Holocaust, which he also translated from Dutch into English.

Bookshops

BANDE DESSINÉE

Multi BD

Boulevard Anspach 122–124; tel: 02 513 72 35; www.multibd.com; Mon–Sat 10.30am–7pm, Sun 12.30–6.30pm; tram: 3, 4, bus: 48, 95; map p.135 C2

Specialists in the genre.

GENERAL

Nicola's Bookshop

Rue de Stassart 106; tel: 02 513 94 00; www.nicolasbookshop.com; Tue–Sat 10.30am–6.30pm, Thur until 7.30pm; metro: Louise, tram: 92, 94, 97; map p.135 D4

Friendly English-language bookshop specialising in world literature, with a tea-room serving English and Irish teas and cakes.

Passa Porta

Rue Dansaert 46; tel: 02 502 94 60; www.passaporta.be; Tue–Sat 11am–7pm, Sun noon–6pm; metro: Sainte-Catherine, bus: 47, 88; map p.135 C2

A multilingual (mainly French and Dutch) bookshop run by the Passa Porta literary organisation, which also puts on readings, exhibitions and hosts writers-in-residence.

Sterling Books

Rue du Fossé aux Loups 38; tel: 02 223 62 23; www.sterlingbooks.be; Mon–Sat 10am–7pm, Sun noon–6.30pm; metro: De Brouckère, tram: 3, 4, bus: 63, 66, 71; map p.135 D1

Independent English bookshop open since 1997; provides a good personal service, with mass-market titles and classics downstairs and non-fiction upstairs.

Tropismes

Galerie des Princes 11; tel: 02 512 88 52; www.tropismes.be; Mon 1–6.30pm, Tue–Thur 10am–6.30pm, Fri 10am–8pm, Sat 10.30am–6.30pm, Sun 1.30–6.30pm; metro: De Brouckère, tram: 3, 4, bus: 63, 66, 71; map p.135 D2

A beautiful French literature store, with passionate and knowledgeable staff.

Waterstone's

Boulevard Adolphe Max 71–75; tel: 02 219 27 08; http://users.skynet.be/waterstones; Mon–Sat 9am–7pm, Sun 10.30–6pm; metro: Rogier, tram: 3, 4, bus: 61; map p.135 D1

Well-stocked branch of the UK chain, with a large magazine section, DVDs and audio books, and non-fiction and study books upstairs.

Markets

The charmingly mongrel nature of Brussels is most visible in its street markets, where all the nationalities who inhabit the city mingle to pick over antiques, bric-a-brac or the best foods from each immigrant community – dried fruit and olives from North Africa, hams from Italy, Alpine cheeses, Ardennes dried sausage and fast-food trucks serving Vietnamese spring rolls or a pot of hot snails. The shops may be closed on Sundays, but that doesn't stop everyone doing all their grocery shopping that day. Everyone has their favourite market, usually dependent on the nearby café they prefer for coffee or lunch after shopping.

Above: plants and flowers at the Grand'Place Flower Market; organic garlic for sale in Place de la Monnaie.

Christmas Market
Streets around Grand'Place, Bourse and Sainte-Catherine; tel: 02 279 25 20; www.plaisirsdhiver.be; late Nov–late Dec noon–9pm approx, earlier closing 24 Dec and 31 Jan; tram: 3, 4 (Bourse); bus: 48, 95; map p.135 D2
Traditional European Christmas market, with small wooden cabins selling Christmas specialities from Belgium and other countries. Ice-rink, big wheel, merry-go-rounds and lots and lots of mulled wine.

Be extra careful to keep a close guard on wallets and handbags when you visit street markets. Pickpockets are adept at walking close beside unsuspecting shoppers and sliding a hand into their bag while the owner is distracted.

Grand'Place Flower and Plant Market
Mar–Oct Tue–Wed, Fri–Sun 8am–6pm; tram: 3, 4, bus: 48, 95; map p.135 D2
Colourful focal point on the Grand'Place, although you won't find any bargains.

Marché Abattoirs
Rue Ropsy-Chaudron; tel: 02 521 54 19; Fri–Sun 7am–1pm; metro: Clemenceau, bus: 46; map p.134 A2
Like the (nearby) Marché du Midi, but piled even higher and sold even cheaper, and with a large fresh meat section in the abattoir buildings. Also lots of plumbing parts and other bric-a-brac, new and old.

Marché du Midi
Between Boulevard du Midi and Gare du Midi rail station; tel: 02 536 02 11; Sun 6am–1.30pm; metro: Gare du Midi, tram: 3, 4, 81, bus: 27, 49, 50; map p.134 B4
The largest, and definitely the best-known, this souk-like Sunday market has everything from food, homeware and clothing to fresh flowers and an excellent houseplants section. A bike market selling cycles of dubious provenance takes place on the car park of

Left: festive fun at the Christmas Market.

Many stallholders offer the chance to sample the produce before you buy, and Belgians take full use of this option – from a snippet of spicy sausage or cheese, or a garlicky olive, to a sliver of melon or orange. There are also some great food-and-drink stands for impromptu dining – wine-tasting at Châtelain, snails at Saint-Gilles, Moroccan pastries and mint tea at Midi, and oysters and white wine at Sainte-Catherine.

nearby Boulevard du Midi, south of the railway bridge.

Organic Market
Place de la Monnaie; tel: 02 279 25 20; Wed 9am–2pm; metro: De Brouckère, tram: 3, 4; bus: 38, 66, 71; map p.135 D2
Organic produce, local and imported fresh foods, and breads and cheeses from the Ardennes.

Parvis Saint Gilles
Tel: 02 536 02 11; Tue–Sun 6am–1pm; metro: Parvis de Saint-Gilles, tram: 3, 4, 51, bus: 48
The stalls at this market vary daily but are best at the weekend, especially Sunday, when the eclectic local population (Spanish, Portuguese, Poles, Belgian artists with baby in sling) turns out for organic veg, Swiss cheeses, savoury and sweet home-made tarts, clothing, plants and fresh fish.

Place du Châtelain
Wed 2pm–7.30pm; tel: 02 515 63 07; tram: 81, bus: 54
Afternoon and early evening market for the discerning *bobos* (bohemians) who inhabit the Châtelain neighbourhood, with a good variety of stalls where small-scale producers sell tasty cheeses, quiches, bread and wines. There are also stalls selling jewellery and clothing. Popular on sunny evenings for after-work drinks in the café Le Châtelain.

Place Flagey
Avenue Général de Gaulle and Place Sainte-Croix; tel: 02 515 63 07; Sat–Sun 7am–1pm; tram: 81, bus: 38, 60, 71
Bohemian families and eurocrats rub shoulders at this popular weekend market for general produce, flowers, cheeses and more, in the streets bordering the Ixelles ponds.

Place Jourdan
Tel: 02 627 23 35; Sun 8am–1pm; bus: 34, 60, 80; map p.136 B4
On weekdays a car park and congested square prized mainly for its superlative *frites* stand, this square goes full-colour for its Sunday market, frequented by all the European nationals who live around here.

Place Sante-Catherine
Tel: 02 279 25 20; daily 7am–5pm; metro: Sainte-Catherine, bus: 47, 88; map p.135 C1
Small, attractive market with a few stalls selling general produce and flowers, and with an oyster bar on Saturday.

Sablon Antiques Market
Place du Grand Sablon; tel: 02 279 25 20; www.sablonantiquesmarket.com; Sat 9am–6pm, Sun 9am–2pm; metro: Louise, tram: 92, 94, bus: 27, 48, 95; map p.135 D3
Where the Belgian bourgeoisie likes to see and be seen of a weekend morning before moving on to aperitifs or lunch in the nearby cafés and restaurants. Stalls are strong on Art Nouveau and Deco silverware and glassware, and original artworks.

Vieux Marché
Place du Jeu de Balle; tel: 02 279 25 20; www.marcheauxpuces.org; daily 7am–2pm; metro: Louise or Porte de Hal, tram: 3, 4, 92, bus: 27, 48; map p.135 C4
The original and best flea market, with everything from antiques to tat on a picturesque cobbled square lined with cafés. Tourist prices apply at weekends, so be sure to haggle.

Museums and Galleries

A medieval scholar's study, a traditional brewery and a luxurious Art Deco home are just a few of the many fascinating museums in Brussels that no visitor should neglect to explore. The choice is so varied, from major institutions with world-class collections to obscure and bizarre places run almost as a hobby, that this section is unable to do justice to them all. Admission charges are very reasonable, but a Brussels Card offers the best deal, giving free access to 26 museums for one, two or three days.

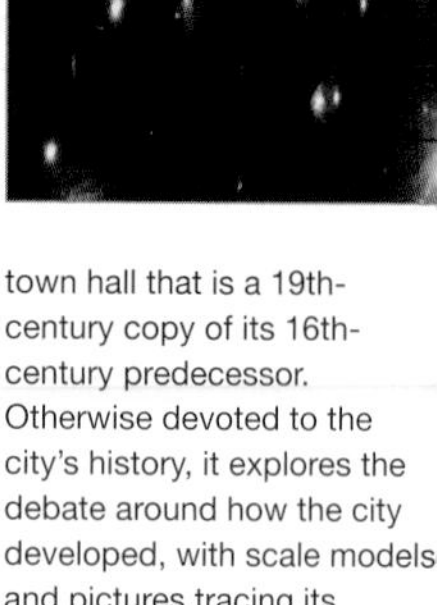

Grand'Place

Maison des Brasseurs

Grand'Place 10; tel: 02 511 49 87; www.beerparadise.be; daily 10am–5pm; admission charge; metro: Bourse, Gare Centrale; tram: 3, 4; bus: 38, 71, 95; map p.135 D2

The art of beer-making from the 18th century to the present is presented in this House of Belgian Brewers on the Grand'Place. Study the latest innovations in brewing technology, learn how water, malt, hops and yeast are combined to produce beer, and be rewarded at the end with a glass of the in-house brew.

Below: poster at the Centre Belge de la Bande Dessinée.

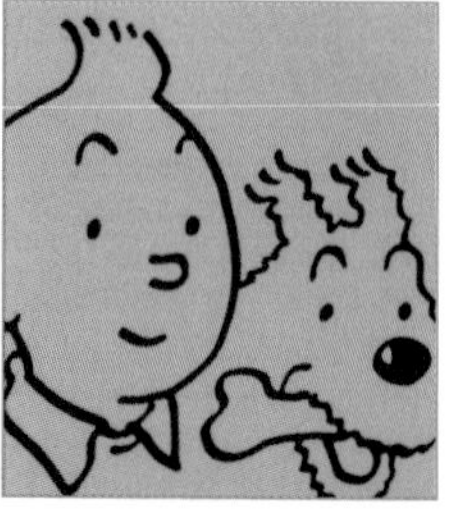

Musée du Costume et de la Dentelle

Rue de la Violette 12; tel: 02 213 44 50; Mon–Tue and Thur–Fri 10am–12.30pm, 1.30pm–5pm, Sat–Sun 2–5pm; admission charge; metro: De Brouckère, bus: 48, 95; map p.135 D2

Brussels grew rich on the skill of its weavers and needleworkers; lacemakers soon joined in and its fortune was assured, as the population laboured to adorn the richest families in Europe. This museum, in two 18th-century houses, displays fashions from the 17th century to the present, plus regular temporary exhibitions.

Musée de la Ville de Bruxelles – Maison du Roi

Grand'Place; tel: 02 279 43 50; Tue–Sun 10am–5pm; admission charge; metro: Bourse, Gare Centrale, tram: 3, 4, bus: 38, 71, 95; map p.135 D2

The costume collection of the Manneken-Pis (760 outfits from the 18th century to the present) is on display in this ornate edifice opposite the town hall that is a 19th-century copy of its 16th-century predecessor. Otherwise devoted to the city's history, it explores the debate around how the city developed, with scale models and pictures tracing its growth through the ages.

Lower City

Centre Belge de la Bande Dessinée

Rue des Sables 20; tel: 02 219 19 80; www.cbbd.be; Tue–Sun 10am–6pm; admission charge; metro: Botanique, Gare Centrale, tram: 92, 94, bus: 58, 61; map p.135 D1

Tintin and his creator Hergé are given full acknowledgement in this temple to Belgian comic-strip art (other heroes include The Smurfs and Lucky Luke) in a restored Art Nouveau draper's warehouse designed by Victor Horta. The centre presents a history of the Belgian style, celebrated for its *ligne claire* (clean line), samples of fantasy, satire and other genres, and the story of how an album takes shape, from concept to bookstore. The

Left: Maison des Brasseurs.

ground floor is accessible free of charge for an appreciation of the architecture.

Maison d'Erasme

Rue du Chapitre 31; tel: 02 521 13 83; www.erasmushouse.museum; Tue–Sun 10am–5pm; admission charge; metro: Saint-Guidon, tram: 56, bus: 46, 49

Dutch humanist and scholar Erasmus (*c.*1469–1536) spent just six months in this house in 1521, but the preserved Gothic building and peaceful garden, provide a glimpse into what medieval Brussels must have been like when this neighbourhood was still countryside. Rooms are furnished in the style of the period and decorated with paintings by Bosch, Dürer and Holbein. Nearby, the Anderlecht Béguinage (admission price included in the ticket), a convent founded in 1252, is now a museum. Erasmus House is located in the Anderlecht area, west of the Lower City, but is easy to reach by metro.

Musée Belge de la Franc-maçonnerie

Rue de Laeken 79; tel: 02 223 06 04; www.mason.be; Thur 2–5pm except public holidays; admission charge; metro: Yser, Sainte-Catherine, De Brouckère, tram: 3, 4, bus: 47, 88; map p.135 D1

A rare insight into the secretive world of freemasonry, through an exhibition of objects, documents and books dating from the 18th century. The order grew powerful in Belgium as a philanthropic association that stood in opposition to the grip of the Catholic Church on education and political institutions.

The Brussels Card is a one-, two- or three-day pass that gives free entry to 26 museums, free use of public transport and other discounts. Price: 24-hour card €20; 48-hour card €28; 72-hour card €33. It can be purchased online at www.brusselsinternational.be, in tourist offices and in some museums. The card comes with a free guidebook that can be downloaded at www.brusselscard.be.

Brasserie Cantillon – Musée Bruxellois de la Gueuze

Rue Gheude 56; tel: 02 521 49 28; www.cantillon.be; Mon–Fri 9am–5pm, Sat 10am–5pm; admission charge; metro: Clemenceau, bus: 46; map p.134 B3

This sole surviving authentic Brussels brewery – Cantillon – is also a museum dedicated to the art of producing lambic, gueuze, faro and kriek beer. Located in an unprepossessing street, the brewery is unchanged since it was established in 1900. Visitors get to observe the enthusiastic Van Roy family going about the business of brewing, bottling, cleaning the copper vats or making fruit beers in summer, and are rewarded with a glass of gueuze at the end of the visit.

Musée des Egouts

Pavillon de l'Octroi, Porte d'Anderlecht; tel: 02 500 70 30; Tue–Fri 10am–5pm; admission charge; tram: 81, 82, bus: 46; map p.134 B3

Brussels buried its river below ground in 1869, and it has long served as its sewer system. Until 2006, when a treatment plant was built, 75 percent of Brussels' sewage flowed directly into the waterway. As well as explaining how the system works, it is also possible to visit a 50m (165ft) section of the sewer network. Guided visits with sewer-workers are available on request.

Scientastic

Bourse metro station, Boulevard Anspach; tel: 02 732 13 36; www.scientastic.be; Mon, Tue and Thur, Fri 10.30am–5.30pm, Wed, Sat–Sun 2–5.30pm; admission charge; metro: Bourse, tram: 3, 4, bus: 38, 71, 95; map p.135 C2

A real hit with children, this interactive science museum in the Bourse metro station reveals the magic in the real

world, offering dozens of experiences to test sensory perception, illusions and explain the fascinating phenomena that surround us in daily life.
SEE ALSO CHILDREN, P.34

Marolles

Musée Juif de Belgique
Rue des Minimes 21; tel: 02 512 19 63; www.mjb-jmb.org; Sun–Fri 10am–5pm; admission charge; metro: Louise, tram: 92, 94, bus: 27, 48, 95; map p.135 D3
Housing a permanent collection of Jewish cultural and religious artefacts from a former synagogue in the commune of Molenbeek, this museum also hosts regular temporary exhibitions on Jewish life and art.

La Porte de Hal
Boulevard du Midi; tel: 02 534 15 18; www.mrah.be; Tue–Fri 9.30am–5pm, Sat–Sun and public holidays 10am–5pm; admission charge; metro: Porte de Hal; tram: 3, 4; bus: 27, 48; map p.135 C4
The freshly scrubbed-up Porte de Hal reopened in 2008 as a museum of the history of Brussels. Pass under the chain-mail entrance curtain and mount the stone staircase of the former city gate (and, more recently, prison) to discover scale models, virtual reconstructions, artworks and weaponry, guildsmen's chains, a floor devoted to children's activities for budding knights and ladies, and thematic temporary exhibitions.
SEE ALSO ARCHITECTURE, P.24

Upper City

BELvue Museum
Place des Palais 7; tel: 070 22 04 92; www.musbellevue.be; Tue–Sun, June–Sept 10am–6pm, Oct–May 10am–5pm; admission charge; metro: Parc, Trône, tram: 92, 94; bus: 21, 27, 38; map p.135 E3
Belgium is a young stripling of a country, born in 1830, and with strong pressure to fracture the nation still further, it's anyone's guess how much longer it can survive. Discover its history in the elegant salons of the Bellevue mansion adjoining the royal palace.

Bibliotheque Royale de Belgique
Mont des Arts; tel: 02 519 53 11; www.kbr.be; Mon–Sat 9am–7pm, July–Aug until 5pm; admission charge; metro: Gare Centrale, tram: 92, 94, bus: 27, 38, 71; map p.135 D3
Principally a study and research institution, the national library and archives frequently displays part of its valuable collection in temporary exhibitions, such as the illuminated manuscripts collected by the Dukes of Burgundy in the 15th century. The remains of a 15th-century chapel, part of the earlier Nassau mansion, are contained within the library, which was built in the 1950s, and there are also museums of francophone literature and printing.

Good Museum Cafés

Musées Royaux des Beaux-Arts *(see p.80)*: MuseumCafé and MuseumBrasserie. Musée des Instruments de Musique *(see p.80)*: a café-restaurant with a view. Atomium *(see p.25)*: a café-restaurant in the top ball offering a bird's-eye view. Musée du Cinquantenaire *(see p.82)*: the smart Midi Cinquante brasserie has a view over the park.

Below: the Musée Bruxellois de la Gueuze in the Brasserie Cantillon *(see p.77)*.

Above: the Palais des Beaux-Arts (Bozar) complex (*see p.80*) hosts superb exhibitions and concerts.

Coudenberg

7 Place des Palais; tel: 02 545 08 00; www.coudenberg.com; Tue–Sun, June–Sept 10am–6pm, Oct–May 10am–5pm; admission charge; metro: Parc, Trône, tram: 92, 94, bus: 21, 27, 38; map p.135 E3

Entered via the BELvue Museum *(see left)*, this subterranean visit reveals the vestiges of the former Brussels palace, right beneath Place Royale. Occupied since the 11th century, it was remodelled in 1459 for Philip the Good, Duke of Burgundy, and later occupied by Holy Roman Emperor Charles V. It was destroyed by fire in 1731, after which the whole neighbourhood was redeveloped in its current form. The full extent of this once majestic residence has only been discovered in recent years as excavations have revealed remains of the great hall, chapel and other buildings.

Musée du XVIII Siècle

Place du Musée 1; tel: 02 519 53 11; www.kbr.be; Sat 1–5pm; admission charge; tram 92, 94, bus 27, 38, 71; map p.135 D2

Charles de Lorraine, governor of the Austrian Netherlands from 1744–80, was interested in the new discoveries in science, art and the occult of his time. His former apartments comprise richly decorated salons containing an eclectic collection of musical and scientific instruments, and other curios that evoke the style of his period, assembled from museums and private collections.

Musée Magritte

Place Royale, due to open in 2009; www.fine-arts-museum.be; admission charge; tram: 92, 94, bus: 27, 38, 71; map p.135 D3

Not open at the time of writing, this new showcase for 150 works by Surrealist master René Magritte will open in 2009 in a renovated wing of the Musées Royaux des Beaux-Arts on Place Royale. The largest Magritte museum in the world, it will show the artist's work over three floors in chronological order, with the earliest at the top, and arranged thematically within floors (Magritte and Communism, his 'cow' period...). Besides the familiar paintings, visitors will also be able to view quirky amateur films that Magritte made with friends.

Most museums in Brussels (like many shops) are closed on a Monday, but the following are open:
Autoworld *(see p.82)*
Brasserie Cantillon – Musée Bruxellois de la Gueuze *(see p.77)*
Maison des Brasseurs *(see p.76)*
Musée du Costume et de la Dentelle *(see p.76)*
Musée David et Alice van Buuren *(see p.81)*
Musée Juif de Belgique *(see p.78)*
Bibliotheque Royale de Belgique *(see p.78)*
Scientastic *(see p.77)*

Musée Charlier

Avenue des Arts 16; tel: 02 220 26 90; www.charliermuseum.be; Tue–Fri noon–5pm except public holidays and July; admission charge; metro: Madou, bus: 29, 63, 65; map p135 E2

A wealthy 19th-century arts patron had the interior of his mansion redesigned in 1890 by Art Nouveau architect Victor Horta, and on his death bequeathed the house to sculptor Guillaume Charlier, whose work he admired. The mansion now displays painting from the late 19th-century Belgian School, as well as furniture, tapestries, porcelain and silverware. It frequently hosts lunchtime lectures and concerts (during which the museum is closed).

Musée du Cinéma

Rue Baron Horta 9; tel: 02 551 19 19; www.cinematheque.be; 5.30pm–end of film screening; admission charge; metro: Gare Centrale, tram: 92, 94, bus: 27, 38, 71; map p135 E2

Attached to the national film archives (that Martin Scorsese spoke up for when a funding crisis threatened their work a few years ago), this museum traces the inventions that led to the discovery of cinematography, with interactive exhibits, a documentation centre, bar and projection rooms.

SEE ALSO FILM, P.51

Musée des Instruments de Musique (MIM)

Montagne de la Cour 2; tel: 02 545 01 30; www.mim.fgov.be; Tue–Fri 9.30am–5pm, Sat–Sun 10am–5pm; admission charge; tram: 92, 94, bus: 27, 38, 71; map p.135 D3

Behind the fabulous restored ironwork-and-glass facade of an Art Nouveau former department store, this museum contains 7,000 musical instruments from around the world – plus a section devoted to Adolphe Sax, Belgian inventor of the saxophone. A clever use of headphones and infrared signals allows visitors to hear the instruments being played as they move around the space.

Musées Royaux des Beaux-Arts

Rue de la Régence 3; tel: 02 508 32 11; www.fine-arts-museum.be; Tue–Sun 10am–5pm; admission charge; tram: 92, 94, bus: 27, 38, 71; map p135 D3

Belgium's principal art museum is split into two: Ancient Art, for works from the 15th–18th centuries, and Modern Art, which shows 19th- and 20th-century art. The distinction is helpful, as it is impossible to do justice to both in one visit. Many of the works are by artists who lived in what is now Belgium, and the roster is impressive. In the Ancient section, the work is arranged chronologically and starts with the golden era of the Flemish Primitives: artists like Jan Van Eyck, Hans Memling, Rogier van der Weyden and Hieronymus Bosch, who perfected oil painting to create jewel-hued panels on commission during the heyday of Burgundian rule. The 16th century in the Southern Netherlands is exemplified in the work of Pieter Brueghel the Elder and Younger, and the 17th by the output of Peter Paul Rubens's prolific Antwerp studio, and his pupil Antoon Van Dyck. In the Modern section, works by 19th-century artists occupy a neo-Classical building, while the 20th-century gallery is built in concentric form and part-underground. Local Surrealist Paul Delvaux, James Ensor and the Flemish Expressionists, and Cobra movement founder Pierre Alechinsky are represented, and there are several pieces by witty conceptualist Marcel Broodthaers, including his iconic pot of mussels.

Best Museums for Art

Musées Royaux des Beaux-Arts *(see above)*
Wiels *(see p.82)*
Musée d'Ixelles *(see p.81)*

Palais des Beaux-Arts – Bozar

Rue Ravenstein 23; tel: 02 507 82 00; www.bozar.be; Tue–Sun 10am–6pm; admission charge; metro: Gare Centrale, tram: 92, 94, bus: 38, 71; map p.135 D/E3

This extensive arts complex designed by Art Nouveau master Victor Horta opened as a multidisciplinary cultural centre in 1928. Besides a concert hall and theatres, including Le Rideau de Bruxelles its suite of exhibition halls host major temporary exhibitions. It sits almost below ground level on the edge of the upper and lower towns, and has floors on eight levels, although this is barely perceptible from inside.

SEE ALSO THEATRE AND DANCE, P.121

Louise Quarter and South Brussels

Musée Constantin Meunier

Rue de l'Abbaye 59; tel: 02 648 44 49; www.fine-arts-museum.be; Tue–Fri 10am–noon, 1–5pm; free; tram: 94, bus: 38, 60

The house where Realist sculptor and painter Constantin Meunier (1831–1905) lived and worked was purchased for the nation in 1935. Hundreds of the artist's sculptures, paintings and drawings evoke the tough living conditions in Belgium during the industrial era.

Best Museums for History
Musée de la Ville de Bruxelles – Maison du Roi *(see p.76)*
Maison d'Erasme *(see p.77)*
Musée du Cinquantenaire *(see p.82)*

Musée David et Alice van Buuren
Avenue Léo Errera 41; tel: 02 343 48 51; www.museumvanbuuren.com; Wed–Mon 2–5.30pm; admission charge; tram: 23, 24, bus: 60
A beautifully preserved Art Deco house built by a wealthy Dutch banker and his wife, who were keen art collectors. Don the shoe-covers and explore a real home decorated in the splendour of the period, with rare furniture and carpets. The gardens constitute a visit in their own right.
SEE ALSO PARKS AND GARDENS, P.96

Below: *The Justice of Emperor Otto* (*c.*1475) by Dirk Bouts is housed in the Musées Royaux des Beaux-Arts.

Musée des Enfants
Rue du Bourgmestre 15; tel: 02 640 01 07; www.museedesenfants.be; Wed, Sat, Sun 2.30–5pm, daily during school holidays; admission charge; tram: 23, 24, 25; bus: 71
Immensely popular museum designed for kids aged 4–12 years, but younger ones enjoy it too.
SEE ALSO CHILDREN, P.34

Musée Horta
Rue Américaine 25; tel: 02 543 04 90; www.hortamuseum.be; Tue–Sun 2–5.30pm except public holidays; admission charge; tram: 81, 92, 97, bus: 54, 60
The Unesco World Heritage List describes this pair of houses and two others designed by Victor Horta in Brussels as 'representing the highest expression of the influential Art Nouveau style in art and architecture'. From the street, the architect's former home and studio is almost indistinguishable from the other houses on the street, but inside it is a jaw-dropping time-capsule. Horta (1861–1947), who occupied the property until 1919, commissioned the fixtures and fittings, stained glass and original furniture, that it still contains today. Exhibits of his best-known architectural achievements, blueprints and his personal archive are also on display.
SEE ALSO ART NOUVEAU, P.26

Musée d'Ixelles
Rue Jean Van Volsem 71; tel: 02 515 64 22; www.ixelles.be; Tue–Sun 11.30am–5pm; free except for temporary exhibitions; tram: 81, bus: 38, 60, 71
A local museum with a fine collection of 19th- and 20th-century paintings, in particular from the *fin de siècle* period. Works by Picasso, Magritte, Toulouse-Lautrec, Berthe Morisot as well as Belgian artists Paul Delvaux

and Constant Permeke attest to the long-standing affluence and artistic character of Ixelles. Temporary exhibitions are a particular draw, and every Sunday art historians are on hand to help visitors appreciate the collection.

Wiels

Avenue Van Volxem 354; tel: 02 347 30 33; www.wiels.org; Wed–Sat noon–7pm, Fri until 10pm, Sun 11am–5pm; admission charge; tram: 82, 97, bus: 49, 50

Brussels' new (and first) contemporary art museum, in an Art Deco former brewery, is intended as a shot in the arm to the rather dilapidated lower quarter of Forest commune. It shows six temporary exhibitions a year over several floors in a bare concrete space that still bears traces of its original function.

European Quarter and the Cinquantenaire

Autoworld

Parc du Cinquantenaire 11; tel: 02 736 41 65; www.autoworld.be; Apr–Sept daily 10am–6pm, Oct–Mar Mon–Fri 10am–5pm, Sat–Sun 10am–6pm; admission charge; metro: Mérode; tram: 81, bus: 27, 60, 80; map p.136 C3

Not many people know that Belgium had a major car industry before World War II, developing the Minerva, FN, Imperia and Nagant. Or that the first person to break the 100kmh (62mph) barrier, in 1899 with electric car 'Jamais Contente', was Belgian racing driver Camille Jenatzy. The arching glass-and-steel structure that hosted the Belgian motor show from 1902–34 now houses a collection of 450 vehicles, including pre-World War I motors, a 1911 Model T Ford, the low-slung Citroën model 7 from the 1930s and Modernist Soviet Bloc Tatras.

Musée Antoine Wiertz

62 Rue Vautier; tel: 02 648 17 18; www.fine-arts-museum.be; Tue–Fri 10am–noon, 1–5pm, Sat–Sun by appointment; free; bus: 21, 27, 54; map p.136 A4

Best Museums for Science

Muséum des Sciences Naturelles *(see p.83)*
Scientastic *(see p.77)*
Musée Royal de l'Armée et de l'Histoire Militaire *(see p.83)*

The former home and studio of artist Antoine Wiertz (1806–65), who rather fancied himself as a latter-day Rubens, and created vast tableaux on mythological and religious themes, with hints of the macabre and erotic. Controversial in his day, Wiertz left his house and works to the state.

Musée du Cinquantenaire

Parc du Cinquantenaire 10; tel: 02 741 72 11; www.kmkg-mrah.be; Tue–Sun 9.30am–5pm; admission charge; metro: Mérode, tram: 81, bus: 27, 60, 80; map p.136 C3

The largest of Brussels' Royal Museums of Art and History has a huge collection of art and artefacts from the major civilisations (bar sub-Saharan Africa, which has a dedicated

Below: the exquisite Art Nouveau staircase in the Musée Horta *(see p.81)*.

Above: intricate ironwork on the Musée Royal de l'Armée et de l'Histoire Militaire.

museum in Tervuren *(see page 21)*. The four main sections cover national archaeology, antiquity, non-European civilisations and European decorative arts, with highlights including a 5th-century Syrian mosaic and a bronze sculpture of the African-born Roman emperor Septimius Severus. The section devoted to non-European civilisations is rich in Incan, Mayan and Aztec artefacts, plus a refurbished hall of Islamic art. The European decorative arts collection includes furniture, altarpieces and medieval tapestries, ceramics, interiors by Art Nouveau architects and a section devoted to film and photography. Audio guides to several sections are included in the admission charge. In the park outside the building (near the mosque) is the

Musée Royal de l'Armée et de l'Histoire Militaire

Parc du Cinquantenaire 3, tel: 02 737 78 11; www.klm-mra.be; Tue–Sun 9am–noon, 1–4.45pm, except some public holidays; free; metro: Mérode, tram: 81, bus: 27, 60, 80; map p.136 C3

A large collection of weaponry and armour dating from the Middle Ages, and a vast aviation hall with some 80 aircraft, including a rare Fairey Battle and Blenheim, make this an odds-on Dad's favourite. The building (due to be refurbished when they find the funding) is magnificent on its own account, with lofty halls typical of the hubris that characterised Belgian public works during the reign of Leopold II. One of the best panoramas in Brussels can be enjoyed from the top of the Cinquantenaire arch, accessed via a lift from within the museum.

Muséum des Sciences Naturelles

Rue Vautier 29; tel: 02 627 42 38; www.sciencesnaturelles.be; Tue–Fri 9.30am–4.45pm, Sat–Sun 10am–6pm; admission charge; metro: Maelbeek, Trone, bus: 34, 80; map p.136 A4

Thirty fossilised iguanodon skeletons at least 120 million years old are displayed in the stunningly refurbished dinosaur hall of this popular museum. Discovered down a mineshaft in Bernissart, southern Belgium, in the late 19th century, the iguanodons have revealed their secrets gradually: only recently has it become accepted that they walked on their hind feet with their bodies in a horizontal position, using their forefeet for extra support and feeding. There is plenty to keep families occupied for hours: an exhibit on the evolution of man and the history of the last Ice Age in the region, the whale hall, a section on the polar regions, the insect gallery, vivarium, shell gallery with tropical aquarium, and a large collection of minerals, not to mention a lovely shop with a fascinating array of toy animals, cuddly and otherwise.

SEE ALSO CHILDREN, P.34

Musée du Transport Urbain Bruxellois (Tram Museum)

Avenue de Tervuren 364 B;

tel: 02 515 31 08; www.tram museumbrussels.be; late Mar–early Oct Sat–Sun and public holidays 1.30–7pm; admission charge; tram: 39, 44, bus: 36, 42
Closed until the end of 2008 for restoration, this 1897 tram depot opposite Woluwe Park houses a collection of buses, trams, trolleybuses and taxis which have ferried Brussels inhabitants around for the past 150 years. The volunteer-run operation also operates rides on vintage trams from April to October on Sundays and public holidays from 2–6pm, to Tervuren and the Cinquantenaire.

Pavillon Horta-Lambeaux
(Tue–Sun, Oct–Apr 2.30–3.30pm, May–Sept 2.30–4.30pm, except public holidays; admission charge; map p136 C3), a small temple designed by Victor Horta to house *Les Passions Humaines*, a monumental – and somewhat risqué – frieze on the theme of human happiness, sin and death, by Antwerp sculptor Jef Lambeaux (1852–1908).

North Brussels and Royal Laeken

Musées d'Extrême-Orient – Pavillon Chinois, Tour Japonaise and Musée d'Art Japonais
Avenue Van Praet 44; tel: 02 268 16 08; www.kmkg-mrah.be; Tue–Fri 9.30am–5pm, Sat–Sun 10am–5pm; admission charge; tram: 4, 19, 23, bus: 53; map p.131 E2
Following the Universal Exhibition of Paris in 1900, King Leopold II commissioned two exotic 'follies' for the edge of his royal estate in Laeken. The Chinese Pavilion was built 1901–10 and its external wood panelling and entry pavilion were sculpted in Shanghai. It contains rare Chinese porcelain, among other riches. The entry pavilion to the Japanese Tower was purchased at the exhibition in Paris by a French architect hired by the king and decorated by artists from Yokohama. A museum of Japanese art next to the Chinese pavilion shows art from the Edo period (17th–19th century).

Musée René Magritte
Rue Esseghem 135; tel: 02 428 26 26; www.magritte museum.be; Wed–Sun 10am–6pm; admission charge; metro: Belgica, tram: 51, 94, bus: 49, 53; map p.132 B1
A train appears to be entering through the fireplace in one room of this otherwise ordinary suburban house, where

Above: Musée Royale de l'Afrique Centrale in Tervuren.

René Magritte (1898–1967) lived and worked from 1930–54. A large collection of personal objects record his time here, along with a small number of artworks and a section devoted to the Belgian proponents of Surrealism. (The museum may be renamed in 2009 to avoid confusion with the forthcoming Musée Magritte on Place Royale, *see p.79*.)

Around Brussels

Fondation Folon
Ferme du Château de La Hulpe, Drève de la Ramée 6A, 1310 La Hulpe; tel: 02 653 34 56; www.fondationfolon.be; Tue–Sun 10am–6pm; admission charge; TEC bus 366 (departs Place Flagey) to Etangs Solvay, then a 1.2km walk

Jean-Michel Folon (1934–2005) was an illustrator, engraver and sculptor (and later Unicef ambassador), whose poetic watercolours garnered worldwide commissions for poster campaigns, particularly for peace and humanitarian organisations. Although he lived most of his life abroad, the artist left some 500 works to the Folon Foundation, which shows its collection in a delightfully whimsical visit with sound-effects, video and poetry. The farm has a good café too.

Left: Musée René Magritte.

Musée Royale de l'Afrique Centrale
Leuvensesteenweg 13, Tervuren; tel: 02 769 52 11; www.africamuseum.be; Tue–Fri 10am–5pm, Sat–Sun 10am–6pm; admission charge; tram: 44

With a collection largely composed of the spoils of colonial rule in the Congo, this museum has worked hard to craft a reputation acceptable to modern visitors. Leopold had the vast neo-Classical edifice built to house his growing collection, obtained from forays into the 'Dark Continent' by emissaries such as Henry Morton Stanley, whose archives are among the exhibits. Others are ethnographic objects from Central Africa, maps and geological samples. Renovation work is ongoing to update exhibition halls and promote a better understanding of modern Africa. The museum sits in an extensive formal park adjoined to a large arboretum of exotic tree species.

Commercial Galleries

Aliceday, Rue des Fabriques 1bis; tel: 02 646 31 53; www.aliceday.be; Tue–Sat 10am–6pm

Baronian Francey, Rue Isidore Verheyden 2; tel: 02 512 92 95; www.baronianfrancey.com; Tue–Sat noon–6pm

CCNOA (Centre for Contemporary Non-Objective Art), Boulevard Barthélémy 5; tel: 02 502 69 12; www.ccnoa.org; Thur–Sun 2–6pm

Jozsa Gallery, Rue Saint-Georges 24; tel: 02 640 06 71; www.jozsagallery.com; Thur–Sat noon–6pm

Locuslux Gallery, Rue du Vieux Marché aux Grains; tel: 02 512 13 11; www.locuslux.com; Thur–Fri 2–7pm, Sat 11–7pm

Meessen De Clercq, Rue de l'Abbaye 2; tel: 02 644 34 54; www.meessendeclercq.be; Tue–Sat 11am–6pm

Pascal Polar, Chaussée de Charleroi 108; tel: 02 537 81 36; www.pascalpolar.be; Tue–Sat 2–7pm

Taché-Levy, Rue Tenbosch 74; tel: 02 344 23 68; www.tache-levy.com; Tue–Fri 11am–6.30pm, Sat noon–6pm

Think.21, Rue du Mail 21; tel: 02 537 81 03; www.think21gallery.com; Tue–Sat noon–6.30pm

Music

One of the best things about Brussels is its rich cultural scene, which remains affordable thanks to generous public funding and an eclectic range of venues, all within easy reach of the centre and public transport. Two excellent concert halls, Bozar and Flagey, have undergone major renovations in recent years, and their acoustics are state-of-the-art. For rock gigs, mid-sized venues like the Ancienne Belgique and Le Botanique are popular with international acts who want to reconnect with their fans. In fact, many bands choose to start their tours in Belgium because the local audience is so appreciative.

Classical

Brussels has superb venues suited to both symphony and chamber music. The Belgian National Orchestra (www.nob.be), based at Bozar, specialises in 19th- and 20th-century works and film scores. The Brussels Philharmonic (www.brusselsphilharmonic.be), based at Flagey, started out as a radio orchestra and still works closely with media organisations. La Monnaie has a reputation for modern stagings of the repertoire and the orchestra frequently performs concerts outside the opera.

Several venues hold lunchtime concerts, offering an affordable way to see professional musicians in an informal setting. The Conservatoire Royale and Eglise des Minimes are excellent for chamber music; the amateur choir and orchestra of the latter present the cantatas of JS Bach.

Each year in April, the Ars Musica festival at Flagey (www.arsmusica.be) attracts top artists and a hip local crowd, who appreciate the crossover of new music with with jazz, pop and electronica. Local ensembles to look out for include Ictus and Bl!ndman.

VENUES

Bozar
Rue Ravenstein 23; tel: 02 507 82 00; www.bozar.be; tickets Sept–June Mon–Sat 11am–7pm, July–Aug Mon–Fri 11am–5pm; metro: Gare Centrale, tram: 92, 94, bus: 38, 71; map p.135 D3

Conservatoire Royale de Bruxelles
Rue de la Régence 30; tel: 02 500 87 23; www.conservatoire.be; tram: 92, 94, bus: 27, 95; map p.135 D4

Eglise des Minimes
Rue des Minimes 62; tel: 010 22 32 30; www.minimes.net; tram: 92, 94, bus: 27, 95; map p.135 D4

Flagey
Place Sainte-Croix; tel: 02 641 10 20; www.flagey.be; box office Tue–Sat 11am–10pm, Sun 3–10pm, Mon 5–10pm; tram: 81, bus: 38, 60, 71

La Monnaie
Place de la Monnaie; tel: 070 23 39 39; www.lamonnaie.be; box office (Rue Leopold 23) Tue–Sat 11am–6pm; metro: De Brouckère, tram: 3, 4, bus: 65, 66, 71; map p.135 D2

Contemporary

Brussels gave the world one of the famous troubadours of the 20th century, singer-songwriter Jacques Brel (1929–78), whose cabaret classics *Ne me quitte pas* and *Amsterdam* are haunting tearjerkers. The **Fondation Jacques Brel** (Place de la Vieille Halle aux Blés 11; tel: 02 511 10 20; www.jacquesbrel.be) hosts exhibitions of the singer's life.

Left: the Jazz Station.

Left: Le Botanique.

Brel's spirit lives on to some extent in Brussels-based Fleming Arno (Hintjens), an ageing rebel singer whose live appearances never fail to lift a crowd. Vaya Con Dios, a gypsy-influenced pop band had enormous success in the 1980s and '90s, and pop diva Lara Fabian was born in Brussels (but acquired Canadian citizenship in 1994). Successful Belgian acts from outside Brussels include dEUS, Daan, Hooverphonic, Girls in Hawaii, Ozark Henry and 2 many DJs. The largest venue is Forest National, followed by the Cirque Royal; bands who prefer more intimate gigs go to Ancienne Belgique or Le Botanique; the VK Club is more alternative and the Beurschouwburg for world and art-house events.

Each May, the Queen Elisabeth Competition (www.cmireb.be) tests the talent of promising young singers, pianists or violinists, depending on the year. Musicians from around the world compete to become one of the 12 finalists, and the final week of concerts is broadcast live from Bozar *(see left)*. The contestants' performance, if good, can buy them a place on the international concert and recording circuit for years.

VENUES

Ancienne Belgique
Boulevard Anspach 110; tel: 02 548 24 24; www.abconcerts.be; Mon–Fri 11am–6pm and during concerts; tram: 3, 4, bus: 48, 95; map p.135 C2

Beursschouwburg
Rue Auguste Orts 20–28; tel: 02 550 03 50; www.beursschouwburg.be; Mon–Fri 10am–6pm and during concerts; metro: Bourse; tram: 3, 4, bus: 47, 88; map p.135 C2

Le Botanique
Rue Royale 236; tel: 02 218 37 32; www.botanique.be; metro: Botanique, tram: 92, 94, bus: 38, 58, 61; map p.135 E1

Cirque Royal
Rue de l'Enseignement 81; tel: 02 218 20 15; www.botanique.be; Mon–Sat 10.30am–6pm and during concerts; metro: Madou, bus: 63, 65, 66; map p.135 E2

Forest National
Avenue Victor Rousseau 208; tel: 0900 00 991; www.forestnational.be; tram: 32, 82, 97, bus: 48, 50, 54

VK Club
Rue de l'Ecole 76; tel: 02 414 29 07; www.vkconcerts.be; metro: Ribaucourt or Comte de Flandre

Jazz

Belgian gypsy jazz guitarist Django Reinhardt (1910–53) is one of the most celebrated jazz musicians of all time. He drew world-class jazzmen to the city, which continues to spawn prominent acts. Brussels-born Toots Thielemans (b. 1922) has been acclaimed as the best jazz harmonica-player of the 20th century. He performed the scores of *Breakfast at Tiffany's*, *Midnight Cowboy* and *Bagdad Café*. Guitarist Philip Catherine (b. 1942) played with Charlie Mingus and Chet Baker, and can regularly be seen in Brussels, as can Bruges pianist and avant-garde jazz composer Kris Defoort (b. 1959). Also look out for the Brussels Jazz Orchestra, Aka Moon and Mâäk's Spirit. Big names tend to perform at classical venues, but the jazz bar scene is eclectic and accessible.

VENUES

Jazz Station
Chaussée de Louvain 193; tel: 02 733 13 78; www.jazzstation.be; Wed–Sat 11am–7pm and during concerts; bus: 29, 59, 63; map p.136 B1

The Music Village
Rue des Pierres 50; tel: 02 513 13 45; www.themusicvillage.com; Mon–Sat 7pm–1am; tram: 3, 4, bus: 48, 95; map p.135 C2

Sounds Jazz Club
Rue de la Tulipe 28; tel: 02 512 92 50; www.soundsjazzclub.be; Mon–Sat 8pm–4am; bus: 54, 71, 95; map p.135 E4

Nightlife

The Brussels party scene attracts clubbers from all over Europe. It is quite alternative, and not exclusive, in attitude or in cost. Locals tend to dress down to dress up, and most are content with hanging out in one of the many bars that stay open late into the night. But sometimes you just have to boogie, and that is where this section comes in, detailing clubs and bars where you can count on a good DJ and a dance floor. Most are gay-friendly, but for dedicated gay bars and club nights *see Gay and Lesbian, p.56–7*. For bars and live music venues, *see Bars and Cafés, p.28–33*, and *Music, p.86–7*.

Clubs

Dirty Dancing @ Mirano

Chaussée de Louvain 38; tel: 02 227 39 48; www.mirano.be; admission charge; Sept–June Sat 11pm–6am; metro: Madou; map p.136 A2

One of the biggest clubs occupies a former cinema with many retro features. Its main night is Dirty Dancing each Saturday, when the sounds are electro, techno and house, and door staff are very selective. The same venue also hosts **@7**, a networking club-cum-disco, each Thursday (7pm–1am), where the focus is more social than business.

Fuse

Rue Blaes 208; tel: 02 511 97 89; www.fuse.be; admission charge; Sat 11pm–7am; metro: Porte de Hal, bus: 27, 48, tram: 4, 55; map p.135 C4

The church of the techno god, a long-established venue that has played host over the years to all the top DJs, and despite being rather monochrome and impersonal inside, is a true place of pilgrimage (clubbers arrive on coaches from the Netherlands and Germany). Cheap admission before midnight. A monthly gay night is also a major draw.

SEE ALSO GAY AND LESBIAN, P.56

Jeux d'Hiver

Chemin du Croquet 1, Bois de la Cambre; tel: 02 649 08 64; www.jeuxdhiver.be; admission charge; Thur–Sat from 10pm; tram: 23, 24, 94

The preferred hangout of the Brussels francophone *beau monde*: suburban rich kids who come to strut their preppy style in this club in the woods. There's a strict no street- or sportswear dress code and a selective door policy, but once in, it's hedonism all the way with a soundtrack of hits from the '60s to the present.

Louise Gallery

Galerie Louise Level -1, Avenue de la Toison d'Or; www.louisegallery.com; Fri–Sun from 10pm; admission charge; metro: Louise, tram: 92, 94, 97; map p.135 D4

In the bowels of the glitzy Louise shopping arcade, fresh-faced young wannabes pre-book tables for their mates to feel like the celebs they hope to meet. Pricey

Above: the Event Hall at the Louise Gallery.

Left: Brussels' club scene attracts top name DJs.

Website www.noctis.com gives pretty good up-to-the-minute listings for nightlife throughout Belgium.

entrance and drinks, but good sounds guaranteed – sometimes with added foam.

Le You

Rue Duquesnoy 18; tel: 02 639 14 00; www.leyou.be; Thur 11pm–5am, Fri 11.30pm–6am, Sun 8pm–2am; admission charge; metro: Gare Centrale, bus: 71; map p.135 D2

Veteran Belgian DJ Olivier Gosseries spins house, funk and R'n'B in a dazzling fuchsia decor for a glammed-up young bunch. Sunday is gay night and starts early. Admission price includes one drink.

Dance Bars and DJs

Bazaar

Rue des Capucins 63; tel: 02 511 26 00; www.bazaarresto.be; disco Fri–Sat 11pm–4am; free; bus: 27, 48

A good address for an all-in-one night out: an atmospheric restaurant upstairs and a dance floor in the vaulted basement – part of an old Capuchin monastery – where diners of all nationalities wind down with an unpretentious boogie to pop, rock and R'n'B.

Le Corbeau

Rue Saint-Michel 18; tel: 02 219 52 46; www.lecorbeau.be; Mon–Thur 10am–1am, Fri–Sat 10am–4am; metro: De Brouckère, tram: 4, 55, 56; map p.135 D1

The strangest place: a traditional café-brasserie by day, but on Friday and Saturday nights all hell breaks loose, with a DJ playing uplifting pop for students, EU interns and anyone else prepared to contemplate dancing on a table.

Dali's Bar

Petite Rue des Bouchers 35; www.myspace.com/dalisbar; Thur–Sat 10pm–5am; free; metro: De Brouckère, tram: 3, 4; map p.135 D2

Backpackers and young dance-heads have been coming to this hardcore electro bar for years, down a

Below: Bazaar – a dining and clubbing experience all in one venue.

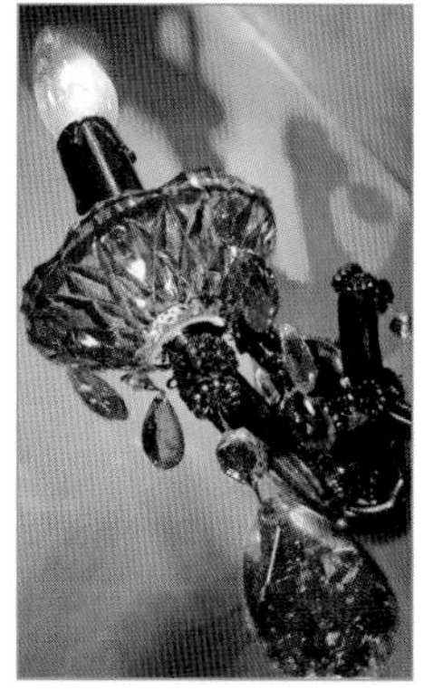

Above: some of the best club nights in Brussels are one-off parties in unusual venues, usually advertised on the internet.

narrow corridor off a narrow alley. With a look inspired by the Surrealist moustachioed master, it is heavy on colour with sounds to match: drum'n'bass, breakbeat, house, groove.

Havana Club

Rue de l'Epée 4; tel: 02 502 12 24; www.havana-brussels.com; restaurant Wed 7pm–3am, Thur 7pm–4am, Fri–Sat 7pm–7am, Sun 2pm–late; admission charge; metro: Louise, bus: 27, 48; map p.134 D4

The warmth of summer all year round is guaranteed at this steamy Cuban-inspired house at the foot of the Palais de Justice lift. Popular with the international crowd, it does good Latino food and cocktails, and has a DJ and live percussion on Friday and Saturday nights, playing Latin, pop and dance music.

Recyclart

Rue des Ursulines 25; tel: 02 502 57 34; www.recyclart.be, check website for details; admission charge/free; metro: Gare Centrale, tram: 4, 55, bus: 48, 95; map p.135 C3

Edgy arts venue in a working station, with workshops, a bar, exhibition space and, on some nights, indie and dance parties, when the ticket office and subways are transformed into dance floor and concert hall, with bands or DJs playing space disco, hip-hop and electro cold wave for urban warriors, artists and skate kids – sometimes for free.

Smouss Café

Rue du Marché au Charbon 112; tel: 0476 288 540; www.smousscafe.be; free; Thur–Fri 4.30pm–late, Sat 6pm–late; metro: Anneessens, bus: 48, 95; map p.135 C/D2

Cocktail lounge with resident DJs in the heart of the hip Saint-Jacques quarter.

La Tentation

Rue de Laeken 28; tel: 02 223 22 75; www.latentation.org; metro: De Brouckère, tram: 3, 4, bus: 47, 88; admission charge; map p.135 D1

Sunday nights are salsa night in this Galician cultural centre, where a free dance class at 6pm is followed by

Below: try your luck at the Grand Casino.

Many of the best nights in Brussels are one-off parties organised by promoters in unusual venues – old industrial spaces, canal barges, the Atomium, or elsewhere. Check flyers posted in toilets of bars around Saint-Géry and Rue du Marché au Charbon, or check the top party websites: Anarchic hosts regular parties in an old hangar alongside the canal: www.anarchic.be. Crazy Pump encourages bad-taste retro dress from the '70s and '80s – wear oversized shades and wristbands: www.myspace.com/crazypump. Bulex is a legend on the scene, popular with a hip, alternative crowd, and hosts a party each first Sat of the month: www.bulexasbl.be. It often teams up with Nemo, New Electronic Music Organisation, www.underground adventures.be. The Backstage is a regular fashion-inspired night with catwalk shows, held at ballrooms or other glitzy joints: www.thebackstage.be.

a DJ session spinning salsa, merengue and *bachata* for energetic dancing into the night, with all levels welcome. Other nights there are tango and flamenco classes, folk dancing and traditional instruments, and live bands.

The Wax Club

Boulevard Anspach 66; tel: 02 787 82 26; www.thewax club.com; Wed–Sat from 9pm; free; metro: De Brouckère, tram: 3, 4, bus: 63, 66, 71; map p.135 D2

As far from the black box nightclub concept as you could hope to get, this colourful small lounge-style dance bar occupies the first floor, with massive windows offering a view of the city's busiest street. Resident and guest DJs play electro and house tunes.

Casinos

Grand Casino

Rue Duquesnoy 12–14; tel: 02 289 11 30; www.grandcasino brussels.be; daily noon–5am; free; metro: Gare Centrale, bus: 48, 71, 95; map p.135 D3

A couple of years back Brussels got its own casino, which holds regular poker tournaments in addition to the classic blackjack and roulette. Open to over-21s, the main floor has gaming tables and some 200 slot machines, as well as dining area and cocktail bars. Upstairs is more exclusive, with eight further tables, a club and restaurant.

Night Transport

BUSES

Local transport company STIB runs an evening schedule on trams and buses up to around midnight; night buses all start at De Brouckère from 00.15 and the last services leave between 2.30–2.45am, so from 3–5am there is no service. See website for routes and timetables: www.stib.be.

TAXIS

Official Brussels cabs are identifiable from the official sign on their roof. Four firms operate: Taxis Bleus, Taxis Verts, Taxis Oranges and Autolux, the first two of which are most common.

Taxis Bleus, tel: 02 268 00 00
Taxis Verts, tel: 02 349 49 49
Taxis Oranges, tel: 02 349 43 43
Autolux, tel: 02 411 12 21

They can also be hailed in the street. Prices are fixed and indicated clearly inside the cab.

SEE ALSO TRANSPORT, P.125

Below: the long road home after a big night out.

Pampering

In health and beauty as in many other domains, Brussels is the perfect meeting ground of the beauty-conscious Mediterranean cultures and a more Germanic focus on health. Every woman has her preferred *esthéticienne*, operating alone or in a small parlour and serving as both confidante and beautician, and men are not shy to book a facial or wax treatment. In saunas, unisex nudity is standard, although the growing international population of Brussels has prompted at least one to offer a swimsuit-permitted area, too. This section covers beauticians, spas, saunas and shops.

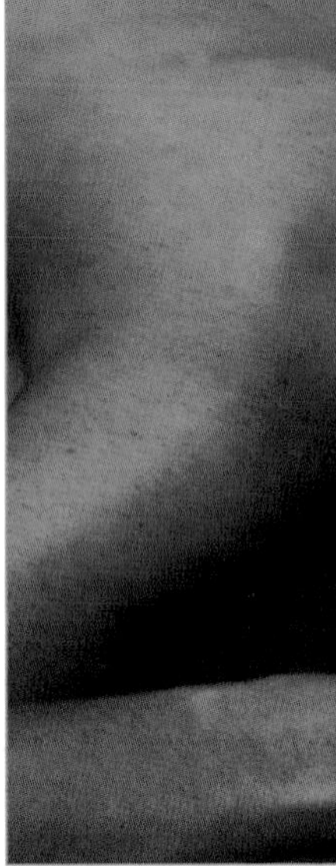

Beauty Treatments

L'Institut de la Reine

Galerie de Reine 21; tel: 02 513 75 15; www.institutdelareine.be; Mon noon–6.30pm, Tue, Wed and Fri 9am–6.30pm, Thur 9am–8pm, Sat 10am–6pm; metro: De Brouckère, tram: 3, 4, bus: 38, 63, 66; map p.136 D2

Small spa and beauty centre in the town centre, but not overpriced for all that. It uses algae-based products from the French Seaderm range for facials, massage and bath therapy.

Karen Sammon

Rue Franklin 147; tel: 02 742 02 38; www.karensammon.be; Mon and Thur 10am–3pm, Tue and Fri 10am–9pm, Sat 9am–1pm, Wed by appointment only; metro: Schuman, bus: 21, 79; map p.136 C2

Skincare specialist Sammon is Irish but has lived in Belgium for 20 years. She uses Dermalogica products for superb facials for men and women, and offers bronzing and waxing too. Book in advance for evening or weekend appointments.

Tao Center

Rue du Noyer 223; tel: 0473 93 63 59; www.taocenter.be; Tue–Sat 9am–6.30pm by appointment only; bus: 21, 61, 79; map p.136 C2

You need to book ahead for the house speciality – a foot-bath with essential oils followed by medical treatment of nails, hard skin and calluses. Also does reflexology treatments and massage.

Wax Zone

Rue du Tabellion 16–18; tel: 02 537 37 70; www.wax-zone.com; Mon 11.30am–7.30pm, Tue–Sat 9.30am–7.30pm; tram: 81, bus: 54

Small chain of waxing salons offering good-value hair removal with no appointment required. Besides this Châtelain branch, others are in Stockel, Montgomery and Waterloo. Regular clients get reductions.

Spas and Saunas

Serendip Spa

Place Stephanie 18; tel: 02 503 55 04; www.serendipspa.com; Mon–Sat 10am–8pm, Sun 10am–6pm; metro: Louise, tram: 94

Serene and stylish Asian-inspired centre that uses all-organic products for facial

and full-body massages and offers personalised yoga and meditation sessions. Clients can choose the gender of their masseur.

Thermae Grimbergen

Wolvertemsesteenweg 74, Grimbergen; tel: 02 270 81 96; www.thermaegrimbergen.be; daily 10.30am–11pm, Fri–Sat until midnight; De Lijn bus: 230 or 231 from Gare du Nord, alight at Grimbergen Stelplaats, then a 300m walk

A well-appointed sauna near the pretty village of Grimbergen, north of Brussels, with a section for swimsuit-wearers as well as a nudist area (towels and robes obligatory). Both have a variety of saunas and steam rooms, an outdoor pool and hot tubs, and the emphasis is on health and

Left: Serendip Spa.

Cosmetics and Treatment Shops

Cosmeticary

Rue Auguste Orts 11B; tel: 02 346 89 62; www.cosmeticary.com; Mon–Sat 10.30am–6.30pm; tram: 3, 4, bus: 48, 95; map p.135 C2

Superb cosmetics store with a small but excellent collection of make-up, perfume and skincare brands (Terry, Stella McCartney, Dermalogica, Dr Hauschka), and knowledgeable staff who will happily advise on how to apply make-up to best effect. Great wrapping for gifts, too. (Also at Galerie du Roi 23.)

Desmecht

Place Sainte-Catherine 10; tel: 02 511 29 59; www.desmecht.com; Tue–Fri 9.30am–6pm, Sat 9.30am–5pm; metro: Sainte-Catherine, bus: 47, 88; map p.135 C1

Fab traditional herbalist that as well as supplying top chefs with exotic spices, provides over-the-counter advice on natural solutions to every beauty, health or household-cleaning query imaginable. The expert owners (Flemish, with good English) sell herbal infusions, essential oils, toiletries, food products, beehive products and gift ideas.

> Traditional Turkish baths (hammams) can be found in neighbourhoods with a concentration of Turkish or North African residents, such as Anderlecht, Molenbeek and Schaerbeek. With separate opening hours for men and women, they offer a sociable experience that can be a lot cheaper than a sauna.

natural treatments but with no hint of puritanism: the café serves a range of food and drinks including beer.

Thermen Dilbeek

Kattebroekstraat 290, Dilbeek; tel: 02 466 00 88; www.thermendilbeek.be; daily 11am–midnight; bus: 20 from Simonis metro, alight at 'Broek', take Rue Dilbeek then 10-minute walk

Spend an afternoon drifting from sauna to icy plunge barrel, steam room to salt-rub shower, or wallow in one of two small pools at this modern sauna complex on the western edge of Brussels. To wind down, flop on a lounger in the garden. Belgians are very unfussed about mixed nudity: no bathing suits may be worn here, and accompanied children are welcome. Robes and towels can be hired.

Below: Cosmeticary sells a wide range of cosmetics and skincare products.

Parks and Gardens

It is often said that the best of Brussels is hidden from sight, and this is certainly true of its green spaces. The centre of the city has few parks, yet the capital is one of the greenest in Europe. That's partly due to the large 'islands' of private gardens behind houses, their century-old trees protected by local bylaws, but also thanks to the vast Forêt de Soignes on the eastern edge of the city, lush and shady in summer and copper-hued in autumn. There are also numerous out-of-centre parks, in Schaerbeek, Ixelles and Heysel.

Bois de la Cambre
Entrance at south end of Avenue Louise, or along Chaussée de Waterloo; www.boisdelacambre.info; free; tram: 23, 24, 94, bus: 38, 41
The most popular park (or literally, 'wood') in Brussels and the landscaped preliminary to the extensive Forêt de Soignes, of which it used to be a part. Beginning at the end of Avenue Louise and ending at Chaussée de la Hulpe, where the forest begins, the wooded walks, sweeping lawns and lakeside paths are popular with walkers, joggers, cyclists and riders, as well as drummers and picnickers on

Above: Brussels' green spaces are great for kids to explore.

summer weekends. The F1-style road that runs through the further section of the park is closed to traffic at weekends, when rollerbladers and cyclists take over (skates and cycles are for hire at the main intersection, Carrefour des Attelages, from Mar–Oct). A small roller-skating rink is used year-round, opposite the Patinoire café-restaurant, run by the same team as the Bois's chic nightclub, **Jeux d'Hiver**.
SEE ALSO NIGHTLIFE, P.88

Best Cafés in Parks
Patinoire in Bois de la Cambre *(see above)*: a café and more, right by the children's playground.
Brasserie des Etangs in the Etangs Mellaerts *(see p.96)*: a café and brasserie serving good food in an elegant setting.
L'Orangerie du Parc du Palais d'Egmont *(see p.97)*: for lunches inside or outdoors.

Cimetière de Laeken
Parvis Notre-Dame; Tue–Sun 8.30am–4pm; free; metro: Bockstael, tram: 94, bus: 49, 53, 88; map p.131 D4
The Belgian equivalent of Père Lachaise in Paris, this cemetery is the oldest still functioning in Brussels and has been the preferred resting place for royalty, artists and architects since the 19th century. Symbolist painter Fernand Khnopff is buried here, as are 19th-century opera diva Maria Malibran and her husband, the violinist Charles-Auguste de Beriot. The funerary art and ornamentation is in every style imaginable, designed to make an impression and stand out from the rest. Favourite features include a copy of Rodin's sculpture *The Thinker* on the grave of artist and collector Jef Dillen (1878–1935), and a chapel in the shape of a heart, which is something of of pilgrimage site for lovers.

Etangs d'Ixelles
Near Place Flagey, Avenue du Général de Gaulle; free; tram: 81, bus: 38, 60, 71

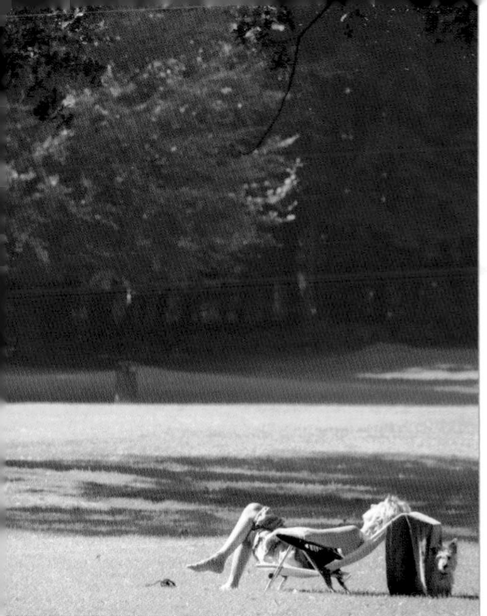

Left: soaking up the sun in the Bois de la Cambre.

Two elongated ponds surrounded by a verdant border make this neighbourhood highly desirable – also due to the beautiful Art Nouveau houses and, more recently, arts venue Flagey and its hip bar, **Café Belga**. The ponds occupy the course of the former River Maelbeek; a third was where Place Flagey now stands, and explains why the cellars of properties in the area are prone to flooding in heavy downpours. At the southern end of the ponds, the attractive (and little-visited) gardens of the Abbaye de la Cambre are accessible: a formal garden surrounding the former Cistercian abbey that extends up a steep slope to the top end of Avenue Louise. A popular weekend market stretches from the square along the side of the ponds.

SEE ALSO BARS AND CAFÉS, P.32; MARKETS, P.75

Forêt de Soignes

Chaussée de la Hulpe/Avenue de la Foresterie; free; www.soignes-zonien.net; tram: 94, 44, bus: 17, 41, 42

Brussels' peerless green space – a vast forest of 4,000 hectares (2,500 acres) stretching from the fringes of the city to Tervuren, created as a royal hunting ground and protected over the centuries (although reduced in size: in 1822, it still covered 12,000 hectares/7,500 acres). For many years it has been cultivated as a homogenous beech forest, with towering trees grown to create a 'cathedral effect', their lower boughs removed, although there are now attempts to introduce diversity of species and encourage wildlife. Wild boar, absent from the forest since 1917, have been spotted here since 2006: visitors are advised to avoid thickets of undergrowth between February and mid-June, when a mother will fiercely protect

Best Parks for Jogging

Bois de la Cambre *(see left)*: the sandy pavement along the road that circuits the lake is about 2km (1¼ miles) round.
Parc de Bruxelles *(see p.96)*: almost flat and with a good geometric shape, wide sandy paths and grassy strips.
Parc du Cinquantenaire *(see p.97)*: very popular, although you have to slip out of the park to get around the museums.

Below: the Abbaye de la Cambre at the Etangs d'Ixelles.

The southern Brussels commune of Watermael-Boitsfort has two **garden cities**, Floréal and Le Logis, built on the English model to meet the urgent need for housing after World War I, and designed to mix city and rural living with small cottage-style houses surrounded by hedges. Very well preserved according to strict rules governing the green spaces and public areas, the streets in Floréal are named after flowers; those in Le Logis have animal names. Visit in the month of April or May to enjoy the heady blossom of the Japanese flowering cherries. Hermann-Debroux is the nearest metro.

Above: the elegant orangery in Parc du Palais d'Egmont.

her young. The network of paths is arranged for cyclists, horse-riders and walkers – and certain ones are reserved for one or the other. It is absolutely safe to visit in daylight hours, but beware of getting lost, as it all looks rather the same.

Musée David et Alice van Buuren

Avenue Léo Errera 41; tel: 02 343 48 51; www.museumvanbuuren.com; Wed–Mon 2–5.30pm; free; admission charge; tram: 23, 24, bus: 60

It is possible to visit just the garden of this Art Deco house, now a delightful museum. The grounds often display art exhibits, and there is a maze, orchard, formal and landscaped gardens, all in a quiet suburban street.

SEE ALSO MUSEUMS AND GALLERIES, P.81

Parc de Bruxelles

Place des Palais; 6am–9pm, free; metro: Parc, tram: 92, 94, bus: 21, 27, 65; map p.135 E2

Hard to believe today, but this neat park with wide avenues and disciplined espalier trees was once a hunting ground for the Dukes of Brabant (known as *de warande*). Located between the royal palace and the Belgian Parliament, and surrounded by neo-Classical white facades, it was here that the Belgian patriots first clashed with Dutch troops in 1830. Now it's a rather more peaceful place, dotted with fountains and statues – many of which make reference to the symbols of freemasonry. It is used by joggers, office workers during lunch hour and – by night – is something of a gay cruising ground. In summer, music venue Ancienne Belgique holds a laid-back festival, **Feeërieën**, over several evenings.

SEE ALSO FESTIVALS, P.49

Below: statue in Parc du Cinquantenaire.

Parc de Woluwe

Junction Avenue de Tervuren/ Boulevard du Souverain; free; tram: 39, 44, bus: 36, 42

For all his faults, Belgians have several reasons to be thankful for what King Leopold II did for their capital, and many of those reasons are green. This extensive hilly park is yet another of his creations and is one of the largest green spaces in Brussels' region. Landscaped 1896–9, it has a rich variety of trees (180 species), artificial ponds, rock gardens and stepping stones and dramatic floodlighting by night. Across the Boulevard du Souverain is the lovely **Etangs Mellaerts** (Mellaerts Ponds) park, with a mini-golf and rowing boats on pedalos for hire in summer, and fishing on the second lake. Between the two green spaces is a railway line converted into a *voie verte* (green way) for pedestrians and cyclists (see the bridge over the Avenue de Tervuren).

Parc du Cinquantenaire

Entrances on Avenue de la Joyeuse Entrée, Avenue des Nerviens; free; metro: Schuman or Mérode, tram: 81, bus: 22, 27, 61; map p.136 C3

A park created, along with the vast museums within it, in 1880 to celebrate Belgium's 50 years of independence. Eight statues around the perimeter symbolise the (then) eight provinces of Belgium (Brabant was subsequently split into two along the Flemish-Walloon border). Dissected by a stretch of the mainly below-ground dual carriageway beneath, it has a formal, rather uninspired layout, but lends itself well to jogging and ball games. The main Brussels mosque is located within the park, as is Victor Horta's Pavillon des Passions Humaines, visits to which are arranged at the Musée du Cinquantenaire.

SEE ALSO MUSEUMS AND GALLERIES, P.82

Parc du Palais d'Egmont

Entrance from Boulevard de Waterloo (side of Hilton), Rue du Cerf or Rue aux Laines; free; metro: Louise/Porte de Namur, tram: 92, 94; map p.135 D4

A real hideaway in the city, tucked behind the Hilton hotel tower on Boulevard de Waterloo, which offers a welcome patch of grass, shade and an elegant orangery converted in a café. It used to be the garden of the Palais d'Egmont next door, now owned by the foreign affairs ministry. The Sablon side of the park has stone engravings from the writings of Marguerite Yourcenar (1903–87).

SEE ALSO LITERATURE, P.73

Parc Josaphat

Avenue des Azalées; free; tram: 23, 24, bus: 65, 66

A lush, landscaped local park built in something of a bowl and surrounded by elegant houses in the residential neighbourhood of Schaerbeek. It allegedly owes its name to a 15th-century pilgrim who returned from the Holy Land and remarked on the area's similarities with the Josaphat valley. The grotto, bandstand, pond and archery field evoke its *fin de siècle* origins, but the population of Moroccans, Turks, Belgians and Eurocrats who visit provide a snapshot of life in 21st-century Brussels. There are playgrounds, a mini-golf and an animal enclosure, and while the refreshments kiosk in the park is adequate, the best ice creams can be found at Cocozza, Avenue des Azalées 8, alongside the park.

Parc Leopold

Junction Rue Belliard/Chaussée d'Etterbeek; free; metro: Maelbeek, bus: 21, 27, 59; map p.136 A/B3

Built on a steep slope, this park offers a pleasant cut-through from the EU Parliament to the Council of Ministers and Commission, so suited lobbyists jostle for space with schoolkids and dog-walkers, all watched over by a beady-eyed heron spying fish in the pond, one of the last remaining in the Maelbeek valley. It is a very learned park: within its boundaries are the **Muséum des Sciences Naturelles** and the former Brussels uni-

Below: Parc du Cinquantenaire's monumental arch.

Above: Parc Tenbosch, the perfect spot for a picnic.

versity science departments and libraries, now a secondary school and EU think tank.
SEE ALSO MUSEUMS AND GALLERIES, P.83

Parc Tenbosch
Rue des Mélèzes/Rue Hector Denis; Oct–Mar 8am–6pm, Apr 8am–7pm, May–Aug 8am–9pm, Sept 8am–8pm; free; bus: 38, 60
A former private garden in the Châtelain district complements the smart boutiques and restaurants of the neighbourhood and is highly prized by locals. Amazingly for its relatively small size, it fits in a synthetic football pitch, fish-pond with waterfall, playground for under-6, and plenty of exotic plants, yet still manages to be full of surprises.

Parc Tournay-Solvay
Chaussée de La Hulpe, Watermael-Boitsfort; free; tel: 02 513 89 40; tram: 94, bus: 17
An unusual folly of a place built by industrialist Ernest Solvay on a steep hill in the green suburb of Watermael-Boitsfort. The hilly domain has much to recommend it, from the former Solvay château, destroyed by fire in 1982 and left to return to nature as a romantic ruin, orchards, sloping lawns, a circular botanical garden, rose garden, sculptures, along with clever perspectives and views.

Serres Royales
Château Royal, Laeken; www.monarchie.be; three weeks in late April–early May each year (dates are announced at the start of the year: check with tourist office); admission charge; tram: 4, 23, bus: 53; map p.131 D2
Not exactly a garden, as the visit is mostly indoors, but kilometres of fuchsias, pelargoniums and rather more exotic plants, which can be viewed (and sniffed) when the royal family open the doors to their greenhouses for a few flower-bedecked weeks in spring. The interlinked network of ironwork glasshouses was built in 1895 by Leopold II to provide a winter garden and house palms and plant species from the Congo, and he left the legacy that they should be opened to the public for a few weeks each year. Many of the plants are now historically significant specimens: orange tree varieties over 200 years old, rare ferns, orchids and camellias (Leopold's favourite flower).

Square du Petit Sablon
Place du Petit Sablon; daily summer 8am–8.40pm, winter until 5.40pm, Apr until 6.40pm,

A fabulous new resource for walkers and cyclists is in the process of being created: the **Promenade Verte** (green path) is a signposted, 60km (37-mile) route linking green spaces in the outer suburbs and entirely encircling the city. It is divided into seven sections of 5–10km (3–6 miles) each, some of which have still to be marked out. See www.promenade-verte.be.

Sept until 7.40pm; free; tram: 92, 94, bus: 27, 95; map p.135 D3

Pretty green square east of the Grand Sablon main square, where the Art Nouveau railings designed by Paul Hankar are punctuated with stone columns topped by bronze statues representing the 48 crafts guilds of Brussels. The large bronze sculpture at the top depicts the Counts of Egmont and Hoorn, who led Protestant resistance to the Spanish in 1568, and were beheaded on the Grand'Place.

Around Brussels

Nationaal Plantentuin (Botanical Garden)

Domein van Bouchout, Nieuwelaan 38, Meise; tel: 02 260 09 70; www.jardinbotanique.be; summer 9.30am–6pm, winter 9.30am–4.30pm; admission charge; bus: 250, 251

A much-renovated 12th-century castle with moat sits amid the large estate to which the botanical garden relocated from its city location (beside Botanique metro) in 1944. The Palais des Plantes glasshouses recreate the conditions of different biospheres (Himalayas, dry desert, damp forest), with a new section on the evolution of plant life on Earth. The 93-hectare (58-acre) estate also contains herb gardens, rose garden, wooded areas, and makes for a long walk. A simple café in the former orangery opens from Easter to October and commands a lovely view over the lake. The Flemish De Lijn buses depart from the North Station and stop right outside.

Tervuren Park

Leuvensesteenweg (entrance by Africa Museum); free; tram: 44

Tervuren is a leafy Flemish town 10km (6 miles) east of Brussels inhabited by diplomats and EU top brass (and Brits, since the British School is located here). Its park is perfect for a Sunday promenade (it is also at the furthest reach of the Forêt de Soignes, so you could walk through one to the other and catch a tram back from here). Although substantially remodelled by King Leopold II when he built the Africa Museum, the long lakes and formal gardens existed centuries earlier. In the early 17th century, they were the site of glittering court balls hosted by Albert and Isabella, who had a palace (now destroyed) in the vicinity. Just beyond the park is the Tervuren arboretum, a dark wooded area of sequoias and other exotic tree species collected from around the world.

Below: the Square du Petit Sablon is dotted with interesting sculptures.

Restaurants

It is often said that everyone eats well in Belgium. It is also true that everyone eats out, and often. As a result there are innumerable good restaurants in Brussels, few of which are aimed solely at tourists. Although no visit to Brussels would be complete without sampling local specialities – mussels, rabbit in cherry beer, or *stoemp* – this international city also does well for foreign cuisine, particularly Lebanese, Japanese, Italian and French regional cooking. This section selects some of the best of a very large choice. For an introduction to the typical local cuisine and beers, *see Food and Drink, p.52–5.*

Grand'Place

BELGIAN

Aux Armes de Bruxelles

Rue des Bouchers 13; tel: 02 511 55 50; www.auxarmesdebruxelles.be; Aug–June Tue–Sun noon–11.15pm; €€; metro: De Brouckère, tram: 3, 4, bus: 63, 66, 71; map p.135 D2

The best establishment in the Ilôt Sacré has no need to set up an ornate seafood display or have its waiters hawk for business on the street, like its neighbours. Discreet and traditional with a beautiful Art Deco interior, it excels in Belgian specialities – seafood gratin, shrimp croquettes (best in Brussels) and steaks. Get a table in the main room and watch the chef prepare *crêpes flambées* in a copper pan.

Above: morning coffee at Arcadi *(see p.102).*

Maison du Cygne

Grand'Place 9; tel: 02 511 82 44; www.lamaisonducygne.be; Mon–Fri noon–2pm, 7–10pm, Sat 7–10pm; €€€; tram: 3, 4, bus: 48, 95; map p.135 D2

Karl Marx and Friedrich Engels hatched their 1848 *Communist Manifesto* at this address when it was a simple tavern. Today it is a gastronomic restaurant resembling an exclusive gentlemen's club, serving French cuisine with a Belgian twist: roast lamb in a parsley crust with *gratin dauphinois* and green beans, or goose liver terrine with Szechuan pepper and fruit chutney. Dress code smart.

't Kelderke

Grand'Place 15; tel: 02 513 73

Prices for an average two-course meal with one glass of house wine:

€	under €25
€€	€25–50
€€€	over €50

Left: upmarket brasserie Belga Queen *(see p.102)*.

44; www.atgp.be; Sun–Wed noon–midnight, Thur–Sat noon–2am; €€; tram: 3, 4, bus: 48, 95; map p.135 D2

It may be on the Grand' Place, but the 'little cellar' is a more than reliable address. It manages to combine good looks – a 17th-century vaulted brick cellar – a lively atmosphere, unpretentious service and tasty Belgian cuisine – including *stœmp*, mussels, *carbonnades*, horse steak – at realistic prices. It's also open practically round the clock.

Vegetarians are not well served in Belgium, especially if they do not eat fish. Although many restaurants will readily prepare a dish of fresh wok-fried or steamed vegetables, this can get rather dull. Better to avoid Belgian cuisine altogether and go for Lebanese, Vietnamese or Indian restaurants, or pizzerias.

Le Taverne du Passage

Galerie de la Reine 30; tel: 02 512 37 31; www.tavernedupassage.com; daily midday–midnight; €€; metro: Gare Centrale, bus: 63, 66, 71; map p.135 D2

Classic address for a leisurely Sunday lunch: the Art Deco interior has not changed in decades, and the liveried waiters have been there almost as long. Sample Belgian specialities like Mechelen asparagus, *waterzooï* or eels in green sauce, and if you like people-watching, sit on the terrace, which is in the historic shopping arcade and therefore sheltered year-round.

Vincent

Rue des Dominicains 8–10; tel: 02 511 26 07; www.restaurantvincent.com; daily noon–2.45pm, 6.30–11.30pm; €€; metro: De Brouckère, tram: 3, 4, bus: 63, 66, 71; map p.135 D2

A perennial favourite, with marine-themed frescoes on tiled walls (the building is a listed Art Deco monument), this old-school brasserie does fish and meat dishes to perfection – learn how by watching the chef flambée and grill steaks in the dining room – as well as Belgian staples. Good fixed-price menus and dish of the day.

LEBANESE

Al Barmaki

Rue des Eperonniers 67; tel: 02 513 08 34; www.albarmaki.be; Mon–Sat 7pm–midnight; €€; metro: Gare Centrale, bus: 48, 95; map p.135 D2

The Middle Eastern tradition for hospitality and fine feasting is upheld in style in this cool oasis, where light filters from filigree brass lamps onto mosaic wall tiles and mirrors. Lebanese cuisine is a good vegetarian option, with fresh hummus, falafel, tabbouleh, aubergine dip and warm pitta bread. Save choosing

Below: old-fashioned tins on disply at Arcadi *(see p.102)*.

The seafood displays on Rue des Bouchers/Petite Rue des Bouchers may look appealing and the waiters are certainly charming, but beware of eating in this famous tourist trap near the Grand'Place. Most of the restaurants are unscrupulous about charging exorbitant prices for water and wine, and will pressure customers to order expensive – and mediocre – seafood platters.

between the dishes and take a mixed platter of meze to share; meat-eaters can always add a skewer of juicy lamb chunks, chicken or spicy sausage.

MEDITERRANEAN

Arcadi

Rue de l'Ecuyer 1bis; tel: 02 511 33 43; daily 7am–11.30pm; €; metro: De Brouckère, tram: 3, 4, bus: 63, 66, 71; map p.135 D2

Perfect pit-stop for a cheap and nourishing lunch or a light meal, serving superb savoury quiches and tarts (many of them vegetarian), salads, pancakes and pasta bakes, using fresh vegetables and a hint of North African spice. Excellent home-made cakes, too. Only downside: it's so popular it can get rather cramped.

Lower City

BELGIAN

Belga Queen

Rue du Fossé-aux-Loups 32; tel: 02 217 21 87; www.belgaqueen.be; daily noon–2pm, 7–10pm; €€€; metro: De Brouckère, tram: 3, 4, bus: 63, 66, 71; map p.135 D2

This 18th-century former bank turned stylish restaurant has a large seating area where the tellers sat, an oyster bar and a cigar lounge downstairs in what was once the vault. Portions are generous and the modern brasserie food good, but the sonorous acoustics make for rather a din, so better for groups than romantic dinners for two. Sittings are at fixed times up to 10pm.

Bij den Boer

Quai aux Briques 60; tel: 02 512 61 22; www.bijdenboer.com; Mon–Sat noon–2.30pm, 6–10.30pm; €€; metro: Sainte-Catherine, bus: 47, 88; map p.135 C1

In an area famous for its fish restaurants, this is one of the best. Unpretentious, so popular with locals, and skilled in preparing the best of the day's catch, without frills and at no-frills prices. Try the local grey shrimps, eels in green sauce or the North Sea bouillabaisse.

Comme Chez Soi

Place Rouppe 23; tel: 02 512 29 21; www.commechezsoi.be; Aug–June Tue–Sat (except Wed lunch) noon–2.15pm, 7–11pm; €€€; tram: 3, 4 (Anneessens), bus: 48, 95; map p.135 C3

Gourmets travel from far and wide to sup in the Art Nouveau dining room of this undisputed (and expensive) top table of Brussels, oblivi-

Below: Belga Queen, complete with life-size horse sculpture.

Above: the Art Nouveau dining room at Comme Chez Soi.

ous of the close-set tables and rather scruffy neighbourhood. The subtle and unforgettable creations inspired by the best French cuisine have a hint of Belgian Surrealism: scallops marinated with yuzu and three peppers with a green bean mousseline sauce; or white truffle and veal risotto. Aficionados ask for a table in the kitchen so they can observe the action.

Fin de Siècle
Rue des Chartreux 9; tel: 02 503 33 53; daily 5pm–1am, café until 3am; €; tram: 3, 4, bus: 47, 88; map p.135 C2
Relaxed and very reasonably priced café-restaurant frequented by groups of friends young and old, in a pretty Belle Epoque dining room with scrubbed wooden tables and stained-glass windows, and a few tables on the pavement for warm weather. The menu has Belgian classics like *stœmp*, rabbit in kriek and ham in mustard sauce, but also salads and pastas. No reservations, so arrive early or take a drink at the bar while you wait to be seated.

Friture René
Place de la Résistance 14, Anderlecht; tel: 02 523 28 76; Mon 11.45am–2.30pm, Wed–Sun noon–2.30pm, 5.30–8.30pm; €€; tram: 81, bus: 46
Although slightly out of the centre in Anderlecht (why not combine with a trip to the Maison d'Erasme, nearby?), this place is a true institution. It was established in 1932 and employs three generations of the same family, who treat customers with a genuine warmth that's sadly rare in Brussels. Come here for top-notch mussels and fries, but also *carbonnades flamandes*, *croquettes de crevettes* and home-made chocolate mousse. No bookings or credit cards.
SEE ALSO MUSEUMS AND GALLERIES, P.77

In 't Spinnekopke
Place du Jardin aux Fleurs 1; tel: 02 511 86 95; www.spinnekopke.be; Mon–Fri noon–3pm, 6–11pm, Sat 6pm–midnight; €€; tram: 3, 4 (Bourse), bus: 46; map p.134 C2
Stoop down from the street into this ancient tavern, with teeny tables and upright wall-benches. Once ensconced in the 'little spider', indulge in kidneys in mustard sauce, *waterzooï*, rabbit in gueuze, snails or steak tartare. The beer-flavoured ice cream (scoops flavoured with kriek, Maredsous and Betchard) is surprisingly tasty.

De Markten
Place du Vieux Marché aux

Prices for an average two-course meal with one glass of house wine:

€	under €25
€€	€25–50
€€€	over €50

> In addition to the restaurants listed here, many bars and cafés in Belgium serve a short menu of satisfying fare for hungry bellies: principally soup, spaghetti Bolognese, omelettes and toasted sandwiches. For a nourishing snack, choose a *portion mixte* of cubes of cheese, salami and pickles.

Grains 5; tel: 02 514 66 04; www.demarkten.be; Mon–Sat 8.30am–midnight, Sun 10am–6pm; €; metro: Sainte-Catherine, bus: 47, 88; map p134 C2

Flemish cultural centre café whose large terrace under plane trees on the square draws an arty Dansaert crowd, many with children. Most popular for drinks and a read of the papers, but the homely canteen staples – soup, salads, ciabattas, lasagne and spaghetti Bolognese – are reasonable. Service can be frosty if you make no effort to speak Dutch, however.

Le Pré Salé

Rue de Flandre 18; tel: 02 513 65 45; Wed–Sun noon–2.30pm, 6.30–10.30pm; €€; metro: Sainte-Catherine, bus: 47, 88; map p.134 C1

One of several great addresses on Rue de Flandre, this one a no-frills, white-tiled room with an open kitchen and long tables, better for a night out with friends rather than a romantic tête-à-tête. The Flemish character of the neighbourhood is echoed in the menu, which is strong on *moules-frites* and other Belgian ways with seafood.

Au Stekerlapatte

Rue des Prêtres 4; tel: 02 512 86 81; www.stekerlapatte.be; Mon–Fri noon–2.30pm, 7pm–midnight, Sat 7pm–midnight; €€; metro: Hôtel des Monnaies or Louise, tram: 92, 94, 97; map p.134 C4

A well-hidden traditional bistro in the Marolles, tucked away in a backstreet behind the Palais de Justice, with an extensive menu of Brussels specialities (fried veal's liver, baked ham and mustard, ribs, steaks and fish), wood-panelled walls and long benches. Good for groups and lively at weekends, plus monthly gigs in an upstairs room.

Viva M'Boma

Rue de Flandre 17; tel: 02 512 15 93; Mon, Tue noon–2.30pm, Thur–Sat noon–2.30pm, 7–10.30pm; €€; metro: Sainte-Catherine, bus: 47, 88; map p.134 C1

'Long live Grandma' (in Brussels dialect) serves flavours of yesteryear in a hip setting. The old working-class inhabitants of central Brussels let no part of an animal go to waste, and so were very creative with offal. Play safe with meatballs in tomato sauce or sample cow's udder carpaccio, juicy sweetbreads, brains or horse steak, all served with panache in sparkling white-tiled rooms (and a quiet suntrap rear courtyard on fine days). Absolutely not for vegetarians.

Below: the best seafood restaurants can be found on the quaysides near Place Sante-Catherine.

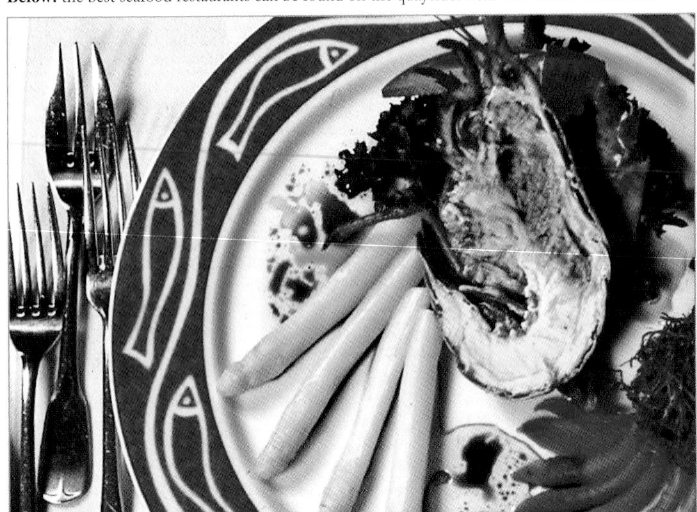

Above: Samouraï is renowned for its exquisite sushi.

FRENCH
Domaine de Lintillac
Rue de Flandre 25; tel: 02 511 51 23; Tue–Sat noon–2pm, 7.30–10pm; €; metro: Sainte-Catherine, bus: 47, 88; map p.134 C1
The cuisine of Southwest France is not recommended for slimmers or veggies – but others are recommended to try the foie gras, cassoulet, *confît de canard* or gizzards at this perfect winter-warmer for hearty appetites, with surprisingly good prices. Candles, bare brick walls and red-check tablecloths make for a cosy, rustic atmosphere in an otherwise fashion-forward neighbourhood.

JAPANESE
Samouraï
Rue du Fossé-aux-Loups 28bis; tel: 02 217 56 39; www.samourai-restaurant.be; Mon, Wed–Sat noon–2pm, 7–9pm, Sun 7–9pm; €€€; metro: De Brouckère, tram: 3, 4, bus: 63, 66, 71; map p.134 D1
The best sushi restaurant in the capital and among the top 10 of all the city's restaurants, this family-run address is to most sushi bars what haute couture is to high-street chic: handcrafted artworks that perfectly balance flavour and texture bear no comparison with their industrially produced imitators. Advance booking advised.

Prices for an average two-course meal with one glass of house wine:
€ under €25
€€ €25–50
€€€ over €50

MOROCCAN
La Kasbah
Rue Antoine Dansaert 20; tel: 02 502 40 26; www.lakasbah.be; daily noon–3pm, 6.30pm–midnight, Fri–Sat until 1am; €€; metro: Sainte-Catherine, tram: 3, 4, bus: 47, 88; map p.134 C2
Despite its large Moroccan population, Brussels has few stylish Moroccan restaurants; in fact, this is the only one. Hung with jewel-coloured lanterns and lit with candles, it is popular with lovers and party-goers in search of a mountain of couscous or steaming *tajine*. End the meal with a juicy baklava cake or a fruit-scented smoke of the waterpipe.

SEAFOOD
Sea Grill
Radisson SAS Royal Hotel; Rue du Fossé-aux-Loups 47; tel: 02 217 92 25; www.seagrill.be; Mon–Fri noon–2pm, 7–10pm, closed public holidays; €€€; metro: De Brouckère, tram: 3, 4, bus: 63, 66, 71; map p.134 D1
Superior fish restaurant in the Scandinavian-owned SAS Radisson Hotel, helmed by charismatic chef Yves Mattagne, who likes to dabble in exotic spices while upholding the best traditions of French gastronomy. Try spicy Norwegian crab, roast turbot with an oyster béarnaise, pressed lobster or any variety of seafood platter.

Marolles

FRENCH
Le Chaff
Place du Jeu de Balle 21; tel: 02 502 58 48; daily, café from 7.30am, food noon–3pm, Sat–Sun until 4pm, Tue–Sat 7–11pm; €€; metro: Porte de Hal, bus: 3, 4, 27, 48; map p.134 C4
This café-bar on the flea market square does tasty lunches – warm salads, soups and other stomach-fillers – and a pricier evening

menu with a French-Mediterranean flavour. Friendly young bohemian types staff the skinny three-storey venue, and Thursday evening is board-game night, so bring your dice and counters. Also regular live jazz concerts.

L'Idiot du Village

Rue Notre-Seigneur 19; tel: 02 502 55 82; Mon–Fri noon–2pm, 6–11pm; €€€; bus: 27, 48; map p.135 D3

Cluttered with flea market bric-a-brac, painted midnight blue and dark red, and with romantic candlelight, this 35-seater is a tucked-away gem with a touch of the Baroque. An appreciative clientele book well ahead to enjoy the de luxe bistro food, with dishes like black pudding tart with rhubarb, stewed rabbit with bacon, and goats' cheese terrine.

FUSION

Soul

Rue de la Samaritaine 20; tel: 02 513 52 13; www.soulresto.com; Wed–Sun 7–10pm; €; bus: 27, 48, 95; map p.135 D3

An exception to the standard sauce-rich Belgian dining experience, this brainchild of two Finnish sisters serves a largely organic menu free of additives, refined sugars, wheat and dairy. There's no compromising on flavour, though: halloumi cheese salad with fried squid, ginger and coriander, sliced filet steak rolled in herbs and sprouts and organic wines will all do wonders for body, mind and spirit.

Prices for an average two-course meal with one glass of house wine:

€	under €25
€€	€25–50
€€€	over €50

SNACK

Le Perroquet

Rue de Watteau 3; tel: 02 512 99 22; daily 11am–1am; €; tram: 92, 94, bus: 27, 95; map p.135 D4

More snack bar than restaurant, this cheap eat in a glorious Art Nouveau corner shop is ideal for a nourishing stuffed pitta bread – hot or cold – salad or pasta. The young staff are rather long-suffering, and space is tight, but between the Sablon and Palais de Justice, and with tables outdoors, there's not a lot to complain about.

Upper City

BELGIAN

Lebeau Soleil

Rue de Rollebeek 25–27; tel: 0479 42 03 82; www.lebeausoleil.be; €; Tue–Sun 9am–7pm; bus: 27, 48, 97; map p.135 D3

Really just for breakfast, lunch or tea, this address on a pretty cobbled street off the Sablon deserves a mention for its unusual other function – as a violin-maker's workshop. The Greek owner combines his two activities with charm and panache, for the open sandwiches, salads and tarts are a delight.

Museum Brasserie

Rue de la Régence 3; tel: 02 508

Below: a little French will come in handy in many restaurants.

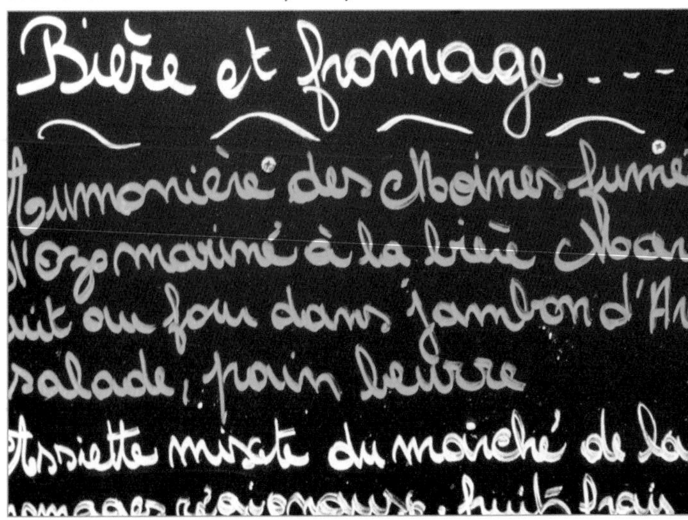

Above: Brussels offers a rich and varied restaurant scene.

5 80; www.museumfood.be; €€; Tue–Sun noon–2.30pm, .30–10.30pm; tram 92, 94, bus 7, 95; map p.135 D3

This seriously good brasserie in the Musées Royaux des Beaux-Arts attracts a local following thanks to the renown of chef Peter Goossens (of Michelin three-starred Hof van Cleve, between Ghent and Kortrijk), an interior designed by Antoine Pinto and a pricing approach aimed at museum-goers who want good food without breaking the bank. Dishes focus on Belgian specialities – tomato soup with meatballs, salmon pâté with eel fillets, steak tartare – but include adventurous concoctions like lobster stew with sweetbreads and chicken breast and veal's head stew with tomato and gherkins.

SEE ALSO MUSEUMS AND GALLERIES, P.80

Den Talurelekker

Rue de l'Enseignement 25; tel: 02 219 30 25; Mon–Fri noon–2pm, 6–10pm; €€; tram: 92, 94, bus: 29, 65, 66; map p.135 E2

The 'plate-licker', as its name suggests, will inspire the same among diners, serving traditional dishes such as meatballs in tomato sauce, kidneys cooked in beer with bacon and onion, veal cutlets and *stœmp*. Popular with local office workers for its homely fare and excellent price-quality ratio, although portions are not enormous.

Au Vieux Saint-Martin

Place du Grand Sablon 38; tel: 02 512 64 71; Tue–Sun noon–midnight; €€; tram: 92, 94, bus: 27, 95; map p.135 D3

This smart bistro is an institution on the Sablon, established in 1968 and the best address for steak tartare (known as *filet américain* in Belgium) in town. For those left cold by the thought of a dish of raw mince, the salad of grey Ostend shrimps is a winner. Service is more attentive on weekdays when it is less crowded: on Sunday mornings, the fur-coat brigade occupies the pavement terrace in force, with a platter of oysters, champagne and a haughty regard for passers-by.

Tax and service charges are included in the bill, and it is customary – unless you are a large group or receive exceptional service – to leave just a nominal tip of loose change, rounding up the bill to the nearest €5 (for two people).

FRENCH

L'Arrière Pays

Rue des Minimes 60; tel: 02 514 77 07; www.arrierepays.be; Tue–Fri, noon–2.30pm, 6–11pm; Sat–Sun, noon–11pm; €; metro: Louise, tram: 92, 94, bus: 27, 95; map p.135 D4

Bucking the Sablon trend for overpriced dining, this rustic-modern bistro does a great line in French provincial stews, salads and sandwiches, served in a warm red dining room or on a pretty pavement terrace outside.

Louise Quarter and South Brussels

BELGIAN

Les Brassins

Rue Keyenveld 36; tel: 02 512 69 99; www.lesbrassins.com; Mon–Fri noon–2.30pm, 5.45pm–midnight, Sat noon–1am, Sun 5.45pm–midnight; €; metro: Louise or Porte de Namur, bus: 54, 71; map p.135 E4

This jolly – and sometimes raucous – bar-brasserie has a very good beer list and a concise menu of Belgian staples and salads. Dependably good and very reasonable, it enjoys a faithful following among locals, students and for pre-cinema dining. No credit cards.

Le Café des Spores

Chaussée d'Alsemberg 103–108; tel: 02 534 13 03; www.cafedesspores.be; Wed–Fri noon–2.30pm, Tue–Sat 6–10pm; €€; tram: 3, 4, 51, bus: 48, 54

A black temple to the earthly delights of fungi and wine, run by an enthusiastic team who tour markets selling speciality mushrooms. Something of an upmarket tapas-cum-wine bar for urbane epicureans, it serves small taster dishes like boiled egg with white truffle, caramelised endives with trompette mushroom or crème brûlée with foie gras and porcini mushroom, and it offers a superb wine list to match.

> One of the best areas for dining out away from the central tourist zone is Châtelain *(see p.14)*, an area inhabited largely by affluent young professionals and which as a result has a concentration of good restaurants in the upper-middle price range. Rue Américaine, Rue du Page and Rue de l'Aqueduc all have good restaurants; and although not on the metro network the area is well connected by tram routes 81, 92, 94 and 97.

Cospaia

Rue Capitaine Crespel 1; tel: 02 513 03 03; www.cospaia.be; Mon–Thur noon–2.30pm, 7–10.30pm, Fri noon–2.30pm, 7–11pm, Sat 7pm–11pm; €€€; metro: Louise, tram: 92, 94, 97; map p.135 D4

A chic hangout for uptown fashionistas with a large first-floor outdoor terrace for watching shoppers on Avenue de la Toison d'Or or staking out the Hilton opposite. The designer black-and-white decor within sets off an equally stylish menu: half-baked tuna with baby spinach leaves, duck breast confit with braised endives and orange sauce; all good, but you pay a premium for the setting.

La Quincaillerie

Rue du Page 45; tel: 02 533 98 33; www.quincaillerie.be;

Below: Café des Spores specialises in all things fungi.

bove: Café des Spores' earthy cuisine is matched by a simple but stylish interior.

lon–Sat noon–2.30pm, 7pm–nidnight, Sun 7pm–midnight; €; tram: 81, 92, bus: 54
spectacular Belle Epoque onmonger's store was con-erted 20 years ago into a tylish brasserie and shellfish ar, with seating downstairs nd around an upper balcony eached via a grand central taircase and lined with vooden drawer cabinets. As efits the hip Châtelain eighbourhood, the menu eatures vegetarian and 'light' ptions as well as brasserie avourites like seafood plat-ers, frogs' legs, steak tartare nd sole meunière.

ouge Tomate

venue Louise 190; tel: 02 647 0 44; www.rougetomate.be; lon–Fri noon–2.30pm, –10.30pm, Sat 7–10.30pm; €€; tram: 81, 94, bus: 54
Dressed in warm white with splashes of red, this suave modern brasserie adheres to principles of nutritional balance and locally sourced, seasonal ingredients – preferring wild fish (crispy John Dory with braised salsify and red sorrel) and quality-label meats (roasted duck breast with cauliflower, broccoli and Brussels sprouts) to industrial produce. A second branch opened in autumn 2008 in New York's Upper East Side.

Prices for an average two-course meal with one glass of house wine:

€	under €25
€€	€25–50
€€€	over €50

FRENCH

Le Fils de Jules

Rue du Page 37; tel: 02 534 00 57; www.filsdejules.be; €€; Tue–Fri noon–2.30pm, Tue–Sun 7–11pm, Sat–Sun until midnight; tram: 81, 92, bus: 54
For unfailingly good cuisine from Gascony, head for this Châtelain establishment, where the sharp decor is a modern version of Art Deco and the food rooted in the rich flavours of the French southwest (goose liver, duck, white beans), the Pyrenees (ewes'-milk cheese risotto) and the Spanish Basque Country (seafood, chorizo).

GREEK

Au Bon Cœur

Rue de Mérode 117; tel: 02 539 22 37; €; metro: Gare du Midi, tram: 81, 82, bus: 49, 50
A simple formula works to a treat at this neighbourhood eaterie in working-class Saint-Gilles. Tuck into a plateful of herb-sprinkled spare ribs, a bowl of fries and, if you fancy, a feta, lettuce and tomato salad on the side. Wash down with retsina or a Stella, watch the football on TV, study the kitsch murals, talk to the in-house parrot and revel in the cosmopolitan character of everyday Brussels. This is the third branch – the first is at nearby Place de Béthléem 9.

Notos

Rue de Livourne 154; tel: 02 513 29 59; www.notos.be; €€€; Tue–Sat noon–2pm, Mon–Sat

7–11pm; tram: 81, 94, bus: 54
Far removed from the ribs-and-meze joints found all over Brussels, this restaurant was founded in 1996 by a Greek sociologist inspired to trace the roots of antiquity in Greek regional cuisine. Try grilled octopus salad, squid in ink with spinach or beef with artichoke aïoli, pea purée and potatoes. Booking advised.

ITALIAN
Mamma Roma
Chaussée de Vleurgat 5; tel: 02 640 42 80; daily noon–midnight, ovens stop at 10pm; €; tram: 81, bus: 38, 60, 71
Slices of pizza with perfect crusty bases are sold by weight in this favourite (but rammed) haunt of students, artists and Italian Eurocrats. Try the potato-and-truffle topping, and hope you can grab a stool, or take out to eat on Place Flagey or by the Ixelles ponds.

JAPANESE
Yamato
Rue Francart 11; tel: 02 502 28 93; Tue, Wed, Fri noon–1.45pm, Tue, Wed, Fri, Sat 6.30–8.45pm; €; metro: Porte de Namur, bus: 54, 71; map p.135 E4
Tiny noodle bar in Saint-Boniface where punters wait on window-seats for a space to become vacant at the bar overlooking the kitchen area. It's worth the wait (which can be long): the gyoza and ramen soups are delicious, and the service friendly and simple. Our only regret is that the limited opening hours and seating mean you practically have to plan your week around eating here.

LEBANESE
Le Mont Liban
Rue de Livourne 30–32; tel: 02 537 71 31; www.montliban.be; €; daily noon–3pm, 7–11pm; tram: 92, 94, 97
Ignore the lap-dancing bars nearby, the hot and cold starters (meze) and meat kebabs are delicious and the service friendly at this address, both in the comfortable, wood-panelled restaurant and the relaxed kitchen café, where the menu is identical. The fish dip with tahini and onions *(tajen)*, tabbouleh salad of mint, parsley and tomato, and lentils with onion are highlights.

SNACK
Exki
Chaussée d'Ixelles 12; tel: 02 502 72 77; www.exki.be; Mon–Sat 8am–10pm; €; metro Porte de Namur, bus: 54, 71, 80 map p.135 E4
A healthy fast-food chain with a wholesome philosophy based on fair-trade and natural ingredients, where you can eat in or take out additive-free salads, wraps, soups, pasta, hot dishes an[d] cakes. In place of the ubiqu[i]tous mayonnaise, vegetable

Prices for an average two-course meal with one glass of house wine:

€	under €25
€€	€25–50
€€€	over €50

Below: Brussels is home to many top-notch restaurants, including several with Michelin stars.

Above: Greek, Turkish and Lebanese restaurants are a good alternative to traditional Belgian ones.

apenades are used for sandwich spreads, and many ingredients are organic. Great for a snack before a movie or while shopping (the pecan-caramel slice is scrumptious). Branches at Rue Neuve 78, Gare du Midi and in La Monnaie opera house, among others.

THAI
Blue Elephant
Chaussée de Waterloo 1120; tel: 02 374 49 62; www.blueelephant.com; Sun–Fri noon–2.30pm, daily 7–10.30pm, Fri–Sat until 11.30pm; €€€; bus: 41
Belgian antiques dealer Karl Steppe and his Thai wife Nooror Somany founded their successful international chain with this restaurant in 1980. The backdrop is like a tropical conservatory, with plants, fountains and dotted with antiques, the dishes are finely spiced and stunningly presented, and the service, although a little slow, is charming. The fixed-price lunch is a bargain.

VEGETARIAN
La Tsampa
Rue de Livourne 109; tel: 02 647 03 67; www.tsampa.be; Mon–Fri noon–7pm; €; tram: 81, 94, bus: 54
If you're fed up with the limited veggie options on menus, this wholefood restaurant at the rear of a Tibetan community-run health-food store is your answer: Asian-inspired and vegan-friendly dishes, many with seaweed and other exotic flavourings, are served from the à la carte menu until 2.30pm, after which options are limited to the dish of the day, or salads, quiches, pizzas and other tasty nibbles, savoury and sweet.

European Quarter and the Cinquantenaire

BELGIAN
La Bonne Humeur
Chaussée de Louvain 244; tel: 02 230 71 69; www.labonnehumeur.be; Thur–Mon noon–2pm, 6.30–9.30pm; €€; bus: 29, 59
Even though well and truly 'discovered', this working-class canteen has remained unchanged in nearly 40 years, with grey formica furniture and *faux* wood panelling – although prices aren't as low as the decor might suggest. Mussels are the speciality, but the *anguilles au vert* (eels in green sauce) are excellent, as are the snails in garlic sauce, horse steak and other 'grandmother's specials', not to mention the *frites*, which are served with almost everything.

Smoking has been forbidden in restaurants in Belgium since January 2007. Bars and cafés do not have to respect the rule, although those that serve food must designate a non-smoking area. This is often more notional than real.

ITALIAN
La Brace
Rue Franklin 1; tel: 02 736 57 73; Mon–Sat noon–3pm, 6–11.30pm; €€; metro: Schuman, bus: 21, 22, 60; map p.136 B2
Lively pizzeria in the shadow of the EU Commission, always packed with a cosmopolitan mix of power brokers who come for fast (if brusque) service and an authentic taste of Italy. The decor has the clichéd taverna look, but don't let that put you off the pizzas, which

For a taste of the world in one city, head to the neighbourhoods where immigrant communities are concentrated. For simple Greek food, that's Place de Bethléem in Saint-Gilles; for Moroccan couscous and tajines, visit Rue de Moscou, also in Saint-Gilles; for Turkish pizza and other Eastern delights, go to Chaussée de Haecht in Schaerbeek (the town side of Avenue Rogier), and for fine regional Italian cuisine head into the EU quarter and Rues Archimède, Franklin and Général Leman, the last off Place Jourdan.

are slightly overpriced but otherwise just so.

MEDITERRANEAN
Au Petit Village
Rue Froissart 87; tel: 02 230 93 88; €; Mon–Fri noon–3pm; metro: Schuman, bus: 60; map p.136 B3
The welcome is warm and the hearty home-cooked food delicious at this lunch-only diner with checked tablecloths and walls covered in paintings and posters. After being seated, visit the kitchen to pick your dish – stuffed Mediterranean vegetables, moussaka, chicken tajine, lentils and lamb stew are regulars – followed with complimentary mint tea and (space permitting) a slice of chocolate tart. Eurocrats book ahead; do likewise.

SNACK
Maison Antoine
Place Jourdan; tel: 02 230 54 56; €; bus: 34, 80, 60; map p.136 B4
Regularly voted the best *fritkot* in the city, this 60-year-old fries business now occupies a modern kiosk, and there is always a queue waiting for a paper *cornet* of fresh twice-fried *frites*, with or without added (industrial) burger, sausage or nuggets. Eat right away, or retire to one of the nearby bars to ea with a chilled beer for the true Brussels experience.

Below: *frites* with mayonnaise – fast food Belgian-style.

North Brussels and Royal Laeken

BELGIAN
L'Âne Vert
Rue Royale Sainte Marie 11; tel: 02 217 26 17; www.anevert.be; Mon–Fri 11.30am–2.30pm, Mon–Sat 6.30–10.30pm; €€; tram: 92, 94, bus: 65, 66
Local institution that celebrates the history of Schaerbeek commune, with photos and old postcards on the wall showing previous burgomasters and historic scenes. A popular spot for lunch and dinner before or after a concert or performance at Les Halles de Schaerbeek opposite, when it serves very good brasserie dishes and excellent desserts (the *tarte tatin* is a particular treat).

Restaurant de l'Atomium – Belgium Taste in the Sky
Square de l'Atomium 1; tel: 02 479 58 50; www.belgiumtaste.be; daily noon–3.30pm, 7.30–11pm; €€; metro: Heysel, tram: 23, 51; map p.130 C2
Book early to be sure of a table, for this restaurant in the top ball of the Atomium has a 360° view of Brussels and a reputation to match. The Belgian cuisine is inspired by fresh, seasonal ingredients and served in generous portions (and includes creative vegetarian options – a rarity). Menus are fixed-price for a minimum three courses. Lunchtime costs total about half those of the evening.
SEE ALSO ARCHITECTURE, P.25

Prices for an average two-course meal with one glass of house wine:
€ under €25
€€ €25–50
€€€ over €50

INTERNATIONAL
Tasso
Tour et Taxis, Avenue du Port 86C; tel: 02 427 74 27; www.tassobxl.be; Mon–Sat 10am–midnight; €€€; metro: Yser or Ribaucourt, bus: 14, 57, 88; map p.133 C3
Good for a special occasion dinner, in the beautiful Tour et Taxis former customs depot by the canal. Decor is luxurious contemporary-industrial – pillars covered in white leather, flooring in concrete and wood, chandeliers – and the menu inspired by Belgo-Italian-world cuisine with contemporary flourishes (and always a sushi option), by a chef who's going places.

Around Brussels

BELGIAN
La Ferme du Hameau du Roy
Chaussée de Bruxelles 70, 1472 Vieux-Genappe; tel: 02 387 15 15; www.fermeduhameauduroy.be; Tue–Sun 7am–7pm; €; TEC bus: 365a from Gare du Midi, alight at Garage Quernette then 1 min walk
This farm bakery and café near the Waterloo battlefield sites is ideal for a warming pick-me-up after a chilly tour of the site. It serves breakfast and lunch in a rustic dining room with an open fire (or, on fine days, in a courtyard garden with view over fields). Savoury quiches and fruit tarts are the highlight, and you'll want to buy several bakery products to take home.

Below: traditionally cooked with onion, celery, garlic and herbs, mussels feature on many menus.

Shopping

After shopping for chocolate, beer and the best of Belgian fashion, you'll want to plan a separate trip to acquire further purchases – a piece of antique lace, Moroccan-inspired pottery, a burlesque outfit or some handmade jewellery. Belgians take pride in their homes and seek out one-off items created by craftspeople, who can still – just – afford city-centre rents. This section highlights stores which offer the best flavour of local creativity and tastes, suitable for gifts or souvenirs large and small. Other sections cover shops for specific items: *see Fashion, p.44–7; Food and Drink, p.52–5; Literature, p.72–3;* and *Pampering, p.92–3.*

Above: all things kitsch and retro can be found in Wasko.

Gifts and General

Senses Art Nouveau
Rue Lebeau 31; tel: 02 502 15 30; www.senses-artnouveau.com; Tue–Sat 11am–6.30pm, Sun 11am–3pm; tram: 92, 94, bus: 27, 48, 95; map p.135 D3
Jewellery, scarves, ties and other mementos inspired by Art Nouveau. The glassware with silver detailing makes an excellent gift or souvenir of a trip to Brussels.

Wasko
Rue Antoine Dansaert 126; tel: 02 502 10 29; www.wasko.be; Tue–Fri 11am–6.30pm, Sat 11am–7pm; metro: Sainte-Catherine, tram: 51, bus: 88; map p.135 C2
Add colour to your life with anything from this haven of carefully chosen kitsch. Items are vintage, retro or hail from regions of the world where bright colours are de rigueur: bags, tablecloths, homeware and lots of stuff for kids.

Whazup
Rue des Chartreux 14; tel: 02 503 47 57; www.whazup.be; Tue–Sat 10.30am–6.30pm; tram: 3, 4, bus: 46, 88; map p.135 C2
Geeks and style-obsessives take note: this place has the latest high-tech gadgets, robots and accessories, inspired by the Japanese fascination for funky playthings for adults.

Lace

Maison F Rubbrecht
Grand'Place 23; tel: 02 512 02 18; Mon–Sat 9am–7pm, Sun 10am–6pm; tram: 3, 4, bus: 48, 95; map p.135 D2
Specialists in handmade lace and restorers of antique lace, the Rubbrecht family maintains Brussels' tradition for lacemaking that dates back to the Middle Ages, when a lace collar signified wealth and status. Although gra-

Rue de Brabant near the Gare du Nord is lined with Turkish shops selling mint tea teapots and glasses – which make excellent cheap gifts – belly-dancing belts, CDs of Turkish music, electrical items, rugs and furniture. Be aware that the parallel street, Rue d'Aershot, is the city's seedy red-light district.

Left: Manufacture Belge de la Dentelle.

cious with tourists in search of an inexpensive, factory-made souvenir, their main business is for larger, hand-made orders.

Manufacture Belge de la Dentelle
Galerie de la Reine 6–8; tel: 02 511 44 77; www.mbd.be; Mon–Sat 9.30am–6pm, Sun 10am–4pm; metro: De Brouckère, tram: 3, 4, bus: 63, 66, 71; map p.135 D2
Established in 1810, and located at this address since 1847, this family-run business stands apart from tourist-trap outlets, with its knowledgeable and attentive service, and no pressure to buy. It can explain the varieties of lace and has many articles in stock – from handkerchiefs to full-length bridal veils.

Interiors and Antiques

Emery & Cie
Rue de l'Hôpital 27; tel: 02 513 58 92; www.emeryetcie.com; Mon–Sat 11am–7pm; bus: 48, 95; map p.135 D3
Wonderful shop between the Grand'Place and Sablon that must be explored to be believed: behind the facade is a fabulous decaying mansion decorated with designer Agnès Emery's Moroccan-inspired fabrics, lamps, pottery, tiles and furniture. The store produces unique paints and tiles (cement and enamelled terracotta) that work well as well in a lofty 19th-century Brussels house as in a Marrakesh *riad*.

Flamant Concept Store
Place du Grand Sablon 36; tel: 02 514 47 07; www.flamant.com; Mon–Thur 10.30am–6.30pm, Fri 10.30am–7pm, Sat 10am–7pm, Sun 10am–6pm; tram: 92, 94, bus: 27, 95; map p.135 D3
Belgian interiors/reproduction company founded by three brothers and now with stores worldwide, its style is a cross between gentleman's club and holiday home in the Hamptons. Also has a restaurant for breakfast, lunch or afternoon tea, as well as private receptions in the evening.

Modes
Rue Blaes 164; tel: 02 512 49 07; www.modes-antique-textiles.com; Tue–Fri 10am–2.30pm, Sat–Sun 10am–3.30pm; metro: Louise, tram: 92,

Below: Brussels is a great place to buy traditional lace and antiques.

A new shopping arcade – the **Galerie Horta** – will open in 2009 in the bowels of the Gare Centrale, in the underground passages built for a tram line that was never completed. It will be accessed from Place de l'Albertine or Rue de la Madeleine. Other shopping malls in Brussels are **Galerie Louise**, a maze of boutiques accessible from Avenue de la Toison d'Or or Avenue Louise, and **City 2**, at the Rogier end of Rue Neuve, a multi-floor mall of high-street stores including the excellent multimedia store FNAC, which also sells concert tickets.

94 (then take lift), bus: 27, 48; map p.135 C4
Just off the flea market, an emporium of antique clothes from the early 20th century – including a large collection of cufflinks, spectacles, hats and other accessories, plus old furnishing fabrics and lace. Collectors from all over Europe keep a keen eye on its stock and snap up their favourites.

Postcards

Plaizier

Rue des Eperonniers 50; tel: 02 513 47 30; www.plaizier.be; Mon–Sat 11am–6pm, Dec Sun too; metro: Gare Centrale, bus: 48, 95; map p.135 D2
Postcard publisher and the best card store in town for non-tourists, with cards showing the unique charm of Brussels past and present, as well as posters, books, illustrations and other gift ideas.

Leatherware

Delvaux

Boulevard de Waterloo 27; tel: 02 513 05 02; www.delvaux.be; Mon–Sat 10am–6.30pm; metro: Porte de Namur, bus: 54, 71; map p.135 D4
This leather goods manufacturer was founded a year before the Belgian state, in 1829. A royal supplier since 1883, its luxurious bags and accessories maintain an edge thanks to creative input from young designers. A second branch, at Galerie de la Reine 31, is also open Sun 2–5.30pm.

S en Ciel

Rue Haute 158; tel: 02 511 77 46; www.s-en-ciel.be; Mon–Fri 1–6pm, Sat 10.30–6pm, Sun 10.30–3pm; metro: Louise, tram: 92, 94 (then take lift by Palais de Justice), bus: 27, 48; map p.135 C4
Behind one of the most beautiful Art Nouveau facades – and window displays – this shop sells traditionally crafted, stiff leather bags, wallets, belts and accessories designed in neat, classical style by a Belgian-US couple.

Floral Design

Daniel Ost

Rue Royale 13; tel: 02 217 29 17; www.danielost.be; Mon–Fri 9am–6.30pm, Sat 9am–5pm; metro: Parc, tram: 92, 94, bus: 29, 63; map p.135 E2
Floral designer Ost works on commission to royalty and the super-rich to create lavish, gravity-defying sculptures for banquets and receptions. They may last just days, but are artworks while they last. His Brussels store has a stunning Art Nouveau facade, and also makes more everyday arrangements.

Jewellery

Christa Reniers

Rue Antoine Dansaert 29; tel: 02 510 06 60; www.christareniers.com; Mon–Sat 10.30am–1pm, 2–6.30pm; metro: De Brouckère or Sainte-Catherine, tram: 3, 4,

Below: Agnès Emery's unique designs at Emery and Cie *(see p.115)*.

bove: head to the Sablon area for antiques, including cutlery.

The antiques district extends southwards from the Sablon, along Rue des Minimes and into the Marolles along Rue Haute and Rue Blaes. Allow time to browse in any number of the larger shops, which group together collections of several dealers and offer an insight into Belgian interiors past and present, notable particularly for their size – the immense furniture requires large rooms with lofty ceilings.

us: 47, 88; map p.135 C2
ike miniature sculptures, eniers's silver and gold ewellery is inspired by rganic shapes from ature, and crafted in er Brussels workshop.

iel mes Bijoux
alerie du Roi 16; tel: 02 514 71 8; www.cielmesbijoux.com; ue–Sat 11am–1.30pm, 2.30–pm; metro: De Brouckère, am: 3, 4, bus: 38, 66, 71; nap p.135 D2
intage haute couture cos-ume jewellery of the most utlandish and decadent var-ety – some are true museum ieces – plus jewellery by ontemporary creators.

es Précieuses
ue Antoine Dansaert 83; el: 02 503 28 98; Tue–Sat 1am–6.30pm; metro: Sainte-atherine, tram: 3, 4, bus: 88; nap p.135 C2
esigner Pili Collado uses eads, buttons, ribbons and lass baubles to make neck-aces that can transform an utfit. The tiny boutique also ells luxury socks, scarves nd Diptyque candles, so mells divine, too.

ccessories

hristophe Coppens
ue Léon Lepage 2; tel: 02 512 7 97; www.christophe coppens.com; Tue–Sat 11am–6pm; metro: Sainte-Catherine, tram: 3, 4, bus: 88; map p.135 C1
Christophe Coppens has a streak of the original Belgian Surrealist. Designing for men and women, his eye-print gloves, scarves and hats are attention-grabbing and fun, his feather-trimmed hats the last word in handmade lux-ury, with the sort of attention to detail that has earned him fans in Japan.

Hoet Design Store
Rue Antoine Dansaert 97; tel: 02 511 04 07; www.hoet.be; Tue–Sat 10.30am–6.30pm; metro: Sainte-Catherine, tram: 3, 4, bus: 88; map p.135 C2
Designer eyewear by the Bruges-based Hoet family brand, which produces more a funky – and colourful – line under the Theo label, as well as sleek furniture and other accessories.

Underwear

Mademoiselle Jean
Rue Antoine Dansaert 100; tel: 02 513 50 69; www. mademoisellejean.com; Tue–Sat 11am–6.30pm; metro: Sainte-Catherine, tram: 3, 4, bus: 88; map p.135 C4
Corsets, accessories and more for the average girl who fancies a bit of burlesque glamour. Risqué but trendy with it.

Underwear
Rue Antoine Dansaert 47; tel: 02 514 27 31; www.dunder wear.be; Mon–Sat 10.30am–6.30pm; metro: De Brouckère, tram: 3, 4, bus: 47, 88; map p.135 C2
Men's and women's designer smalls, beachwear and night-wear, including by Belgian couturiers AF Vandevorst and lingerie brand La Fille d'O.

Below: an upmarket jewellery shop in the Louise Quarter.

Sport

Belgium may not feature highly on the Olympics medal board or in international tournaments outside women's tennis, but any visitor should be aware that the Belgian capital is home to the world's greatest ever cyclist, an original Art Deco football stadium and the world's deepest swimming pool. National cycling and football date back to the 19th century, and some fixtures created before 1900 still survive today, such as the Liège–Bastogne–Liège cycle race, the oldest road race in the world, which first went pro in 1894. This chapter covers three sports with unique local characteristics.

Cycling

Belgium has enjoyed its most important sporting success in cycling. Its champion, Eddy Merckx, is still widely regarded as the greatest cyclist of all time. Born just outside Brussels in 1945, the 'Cannibal' dominated the sport from 1968–74, winning dozens of day-classics and stage races (including the Tour de France five times from 1969–74). Merckx now runs a bike factory in Meise, north of Brussels. The city metro station named in his honour displays the bicycle on which he set the hour-record in 1972.

Competitive cycling is a popular weekend sport in the countryside around Brussels, where clubs of identikit men in Lycra whistle around the lanes in a streak of colour. This pastime and its fans have little in common with the growing army of city cyclists – in fact, many racing cyclists are openly scornful of their urban counterparts, arguing that the town is no place for bikes.

For those who do want to take to two wheels in Brussels, the most pleasant riding is around the leafy eastern and southern suburbs, Forêt de Soignes and Bois de la Cambre (partially closed to cars on weekends). The regional government of Brussels, which is making strenuous efforts to get more people cycling, produces route maps and itineraries (see www.bicycle.irisnet.be).

Dotted around the city, the Cyclocity (www.cyclocity.be) self-service rental bikes are ideal for short hops, but a little heavy for longer rides.

Point Vélo
Gare du Nord, Place du Nord 1; tel: 02 203 85 55; www.recyclo.org; Mon–Fri 11am–6pm; metro: Rogier, tram: 3, 4 (Gare du Nord), bus: 61; map p.133 D4

This small shop associated with non-profit, bike-reconditioning group Cyclo rents lightweight folding bikes, which are perfect for nipping about the city but not ideal for long treks.

Pro Vélo
Rue de Londres 15; tel: 02 502

Below: there are plenty of cycling routes in and around Brussels.

Left: Brussels is home to the world's deepest dive pool.

very Friday evening from early June to late September, –10pm (and weather permitting), in-line skaters have an escorted run through the tunnels and highways of the city, ourtesy of the Brussels Roller Parade. The route changes weekly, but regularly includes a whirl around the Bois de la ambre and up Avenue Louise. Bikes are welcome too, and ller-blades and protection kits can be hired on the night from one hour before departure. See www.belgiumrollers.com.

55; www.provelo.org; r–Oct daily 10am–6pm, v–Mar Mon–Fri 10am–5pm; etro: Porte de Namur, bus: 38,), 71; map p.135 E4

his organisation rents city kes, tandems, electric bikes d folding bikes from the aison des Cyclistes in Rue e Londres. Bikes can also e rented from Easter–Oct, un and public holidays, oon–6pm, in the Bois de la ambre at the Carrefour des telages, and at the same nes in Parc de Woluwe.

E ALSO WALKS AND TOURS, P.127

Diving

For a country with few coral reefs, Belgians are pretty keen on deep-water sports. Several world record holders for the extreme sport of free diving or apnea come from Belgium; they train in former quarries in Wallonia, following a string into the dark water to resurface clutching a depth-marker and gasping for air. In 2005, Belgian Patrick Musimu completed a perilous 'no limits' free dive in the Red Sea to a record-beating depth of 209m (690ft).

The deepest swimming pool in the world is in Brussels. Nemo 33 is a recreational scuba-diving centre 33m (109ft) deep. The drinkable, non-chlorinated water is heated by solar panels, and there's a café and Thai restaurant on-site with views through portholes into the pool. It does not allow free diving, however.

Nemo 33

Rue de Stalle 333; tel: 02 332 33 34; www.nemo33.com; Mon–Fri noon–1.30pm, 7–9pm, Nov–Apr Sat 11am–9pm, Sun 11am–8pm, May–Oct Sat–Sun noon–8pm; admission charge; tram: 4, bus: 48, 50, 98

Times listed above indicate dive times.

Football

The most popular sport in Belgium is football, although local clubs are relative minnows on the international scene today. They do have a reputation for talent-spotting, however, particularly in West Africa, and many foreign players start their careers in Belgium before being snapped up by wealthier clubs. Ironically, this situation came about after Belgium lost a 1995 case in the European Court against Liège player Jean-Marc Bosman. The Bosman ruling opened the way for easier transfers within Europe for foreign players and gave EU players the right to a free transfer at the end of their contract.

Anderlecht – 'les Mauves' – are the country's most successful club and have a demanding fan base. In their glory years during the 1970s and 80s, they won several European competitions.

For a slice of Belgian footballing history, however, join the joyful Saturday crowd watching Union Saint-Gilloise in Forest commune, where the Art Deco stadium recalls the club's pre-World War II glory.

RSC Anderlecht

Stade Constant Vanden Stock, Avenue Théo Verbeeck; tel: 02 522 15 39; www.rsca.be; metro: Saint-Guidon, tram: 81, bus: 46, 75

Union Saint-Gilloise

Stade Joseph Marien, Chaussée de Bruxelles 223; tel: 02 544 03 16; www.rusg.be; tram: 82, 97, bus: 48

Theatre and Dance

Theatre in Brussels reflects the linguistic landscape of the city: a large number of French-language theatres present the full repertoire from French classics to contemporary and avant-garde drama, as well as foreign works in translation. The Flemish scene is smaller, and tends to favour experimental theatre, frequently incorporating dance, visual arts and a liberal use of English. Dance, in contrast, has no need of translation, which may explain its strength, both locally and as a foreign export.

Theatre

With both the French and Flemish communities subsidising their operations (although not by enormous amounts), Brussels' theatrical scene is rich and diverse. Cultural operators embrace the international dimension of their city, and welcome foreign artists and companies for short and long stays.

Two names stand out among Belgian playwrights: Symbolist and Catholic Church-baiter **Maurice Maeterlinck** (1862–1949), whose *Pelléas et Mélisande* inspired Debussy's opera, and who won the Nobel Prize for Literature in 1911; and Michel de Ghelderode (1898–1962), a prolific avant-garde dramatist who penned over 60 plays, many of them peopled with disturbing and cruel characters, like *La Farce de la Mort qui faillit trépasser* (The Farce of Death Who Almost Died; 1925).

Dance

The absence of a strong dance tradition or classical ballet company has enabled Brussels to develop as a world centre for contemporary dance. The pioneer of this movement was Maurice Béjart (1927–2007), a French choreographer in residence at La Monnaie opera house from 1960–87, whose *Ballet du XXe siècle* (Ballet of the Twentieth Century) inspired an enthusiasm for modern dance. Mudra, the dance school that Béjart founded in 1970, launched a generation of new dancers, including Anne Teresa De Keersmaeker, whose formal yet feminine style confirmed Belgian dance as a new cultural force.

Other local choreographers include **Wim Vandekeybus**, whose Ultima Vez company creates intense, physical dance, **Jan Lauwers** and his Needcompany, which straddles theatre and dance with deconstructed productions featuring actors, dancers and musicians, **Meg Stuart**, a US citizen whose Damaged Goods company has been based in Brussels since 1994, and **Thierry Smits**, whose Compagnie Thor explores the limits of the human body.

Venues

Chapelles des Brigittines

Petite Rue des Brigittines 1; tel: 02 213 86 10; www.brigittines.be; Mon–Fri 10am–6pm and evenings durin[g] performances; free; bus: 27, 48; map p.135 C3

Primarily a dance venue for French community companies, this lovely Baroque church has been able to expand its contemporary programme since it acquired a stylish new extension.

Kaaitheater

Square Sainctelette 20; tel: 02 201 59 59; www.kaaitheater.be; metro: Yser, tram: 51, bus: 47, 88; map p.133 D4

Flemish-run centre that is a reference point for ground-breaking contemporary dance, music and theatre from Belgium and abroad. It[s] studio theatre (Rue Notre-Dame du Sommeil) features less established artists.

KVS

Rue de Laeken 146; tel: 02 210 11 00; www.kvs.be; metro: Yser, tram: 51, bus: 47, 88; map p.135 D1

A stunning modern renovation of the Royal Flemish

Left: the world-famous Maurice Béjart ballet.

Last-minute, half-price tickets for plays, concerts and shows can be purchased from the ticket office of Flagey, Place Sainte-Croix, or the Arenberg Cinema, Galerie de la Reine 26. Check what's available at www.arsene50.be. Purchases in person only; no phone or internet bookings.

Theatre has been matched by a forward-looking programme of theatre and dance that reaches across the linguistic barrier.

Le Rideau de Bruxelles
Rue Ravenstein 23; tel: 02 507 82 00; www.bozar.be; metro: Gare Centrale, tram: 92, 94; bus: 38, 71; map p.135 D3
The theatre within Bozar is suited to small-scale productions by contemporary playwrights, both French-language and foreign in translation.

Théâtre de la Place des Martyrs
Place des Martyrs 22; tel: 02 223 32 08; www.theatredesmartyrs.be; metro: De Brouckère, tram: 3, 4, bus: 63, 66, 71; map p.135 D1
This lovely theatre is known for quality theatre by established dramatists, including classics in French translation.

Théâtre de Poche
Chemin du Gymnase 1A; tel: 02 649 17 27; www.poche.be; tram: 23, 24, 94, bus: 38
Tucked in the Bois de la Cambre, this French-language theatre challenges stereotypes and convention with socially engaged drama by international playwrights.

Théâtre de Toone
Impasse Sainte-Pétronille, 66 Rue du Marché-aux-Herbes; tel: 02 511 71 37; www.toone.be; tram: 3, 4, bus: 48, 95; map p.135 D2
A puppet theatre in Brussels dialect, run by the eighth generation of the family who began it. The plays can be understood by French- and Dutch-speakers, but there are performances in English too.

Théâtre les Tanneurs
Rue des Tanneurs 75; tel: 02 512 17 84; www.lestanneurs.be; metro: Lemonnier, bus: 27, 48; map p.135 C3
This Marolles theatre for new dance and theatre (mainly French-language) has a young vibe (and a good bar).

Théâtre National
Boulevard Emile Jacqmain 111–115; tel: 02 203 53 03; www.theatrenational.be; metro: De Brouckère or Rogier, tram: 3, 4, bus: 47, 88; map p.135 D1
The French community flagship arts venue has capacity for large-scale theatrical productions and touring dance companies.

Théâtre Royal du Parc
Rue de la Loi 3; tel: 02 505 30 30; www.theatreduparc.be; metro: Parc, tram: 92, 94; map p.135 E2
The only real traditional theatre in town (also French-language) occupies a delightful 18th-century playhouse facing the Belgian Parliament.

Right: Théâtre de Toone.

Transport

Thanks to its central location in a small, well-connected country, Brussels is blessed with superb international rail, air and road links. Less than two hours by high-speed train to major cities in France, the Netherlands, Germany and the UK, it is a good base for visiting the Low Countries and northern France. Within the city, the public transport network is excellent, reasonably priced and ever-improving. Although many locals hate to leave their cars at home, there is no need for private transport in the city's central districts as most destinations can be reached by metro, tram or bus.

Getting There

BY RAIL

The most comfortable way to arrive in Brussels is by high-speed train. You can travel from London St Pancras, Ebbsfleet or Ashford to central Brussels in under two hours on the **Eurostar** rail service, which passes through the Channel Tunnel to arrive in Brussels Gare du Midi (South Station). There are up to 10 trains from London a day, and tickets include onward travel with the national rail network (SNCB/NMBS) to any station in Belgium, valid for 24 hours after the Eurostar departure. Through-tickets are also available from many UK stations. Children under 3 travel free (although are not guaranteed a seat), and there are reduced price tickets for those aged 4–11. Seat reservations are essential and worth booking in advance to benefit from cheaper tickets, which are limited in number. For timetables and reservations, see www.eurostar.com, tel: 08705 186 186 or from outside UK +44 1223 617 575 (8am–9pm). Note that there is a £5 charge for booking by phone.

BY SEA

Travelling by car and ferry can be economical if several people are travelling together Cross-Channel ferries from the UK to Belgium and northern France are engaged in a permanent price war with each other, and in competi-

Below: there are regular daily flights to and from destinations in the UK, US and Canada.

Left: Eurostar connections are quick and easy from Brussels.

Carbon offsetting – donating money to a project that reduces carbon dioxide emissions by the same amount as emitted by your air or car journey – is an interim solution for concerned individuals and businesses who want to reduce their climate impact. A number of organisations will help you calculate the CO_2 emissions of your journey, collect your donation and invest in renewable energy projects in developing countries. Pure (www.puretrust.org.uk), My Climate (www.myclimate.org) and Atmosfair (www.atmosfair.de) are among the most reputable.

tion with Le Shuttle services through the Channel Tunnel.

Transeuropa Ferries (tel: 01843 595 522; www.transeuropaferries.com) operates up to four crossings daily from Ramsgate to Ostend, with a journey time of four hours. Ostend is 110km (70 miles) from Brussels.

P&O Ferries (tel: 08716 645 645 or from outside the UK +44 1304 863 000; www.poferries.com) run a nightly service (every other night in January) from Hull to Zeebrugge (also 110km/70 miles from Brussels), which takes around 12 hours.

P&O Ferries also serves the busy Dover–Calais route, competing on the narrowest crossing point of the Channel with **Seafrance** (tel: 0871 423 7119 or from outside the UK +44 8705 711 711; www.seafrance.com); each operates over 20 ferries daily; crossings take 90 minutes. Calais is 200km (125 miles) from Brussels and the journey by car takes around 3 hours. Dunkirk, at 157km (97 miles), is served from Dover by **Norfolkline** (book on tel: 0844 847 5042 or from outside UK +44 208 127 8303; www.norfolkline.com), which runs about 11 crossings each way daily, taking 1 hour 45 minutes.

BY ROAD

Car

Brussels is located on the E40 cross-Europe motorway that connects Calais to Kazakhstan. Motorists from Britain can travel through the Channel Tunnel on the Eurotunnel-operated **Le Shuttle** from Folkestone to Calais, a drive-on, drive-off train service that takes 35 minutes, or about 1 hour from motorway to motorway. You can turn up and buy a ticket, but it is worth booking ahead at busy times of the year to avoid a wait and get a cheaper deal. Payment is made at toll booths, which accept cash, cheques or credit cards. The price applies to the car, regardless of the number of passengers or car size. **Eurotunnel**, tel: 08705 353535 (UK), www.eurotunnel.com.

Le Shuttle runs 24 hours a day, all year, and there are between two and five departures an hour, depending on the season and time of day. From Calais, allow 3 hours to drive to Brussels.

Coach

A cheap way to travel to Brussels is by coach. **National Express Eurolines** runs four services daily from London Victoria Coach Station, and the journey takes about 7 hours. There are discounts for young people and senior citizens, and the ticket includes the ferry crossing (via Dover). For more information and to book, tel (from the UK; National Express): 08717 818181 (8am–8pm); www.nationalexpress.com or (from outside the UK) www.eurolines.com. From Belgium, tel: 02 274 13 50.

BY AIR

Most international airlines fly into **Brussels Airport** (Belgium tel: 0900 700 00, elsewhere tel: +32 2 753 77 53; www.brusselsairport.be) at Zaventem, 14km (9 miles) from the city centre.

Taken together, British Airways, bmi, Brussels Airlines and VLM operate virtually an

The 'priority to the right' rule – although simple – baffles even the most experienced foreign driver who spends time in Belgium. As well as the obligation to give way to all public transport vehicles, motorists must give way to any vehicle coming from the right, except on a major road where there is a jagged white line at the junction indicating a stop line. The rule is widely used in Brussels; its defenders say it helps calm traffic, as drivers are obliged to slow at every junction to check for a car arriving from the right. Detractors see it as a recipe for chaos and accidents.

hourly day service between Brussels and London – less frequently to other cities around Britain. Aer Lingus flies between Dublin and Brussels. There are direct daily flights from many cities in North America and Canada, among them New York, Washington, Chicago, Atlanta and Toronto.

Beneath the airport is a railway station, from which the 'Airport Express' service takes (a not particularly 'express') 20 minutes to reach Brussels centre, running from around 4.45am to midnight. Contact www.sncb.be; tel: 02 528 28 28.

The number 12 Airport Line bus operated by public transport company STIB runs every 30 minutes Mon–Fri from 5am–8pm and makes just five stops, terminating at Place du Luxembourg in the EU quarter (alight at Schuman and take a metro to reach the historic centre). Special tickets must be purchased. After 8pm and on weekends and public holidays, the route of bus 21 (more stops) is extended from Nato to the airport.

Ryanair flies from Manchester, Glasgow, Dublin and Shannon to **Charleroi** (or Brussels Charleroi, as the airline calls it), about an hour by coach from Brussels. Contact Voyages l'Elan, tel: 071 35 33 15; www.voyages-lelan.be or buy a ticket on the bus.

Getting Around

PUBLIC TRANSPORT

The city's three main rail stations – Gare du Nord, Gare Centrale, Gare du Midi – are hubs for the local public transport system, and are themselves connected by a train line cutting through the centre. It is possible to catch a train to anywhere in the country from each of the stations. Indeed, there are cross-country services connecting coastal resorts in the west to Aachen in the east, passing through all three main Brussels stations en route. See timetables and book on tel: 02 528 28 28; www.sncb.be.

Within Brussels, municipal transport company STIB (MIVB in Flemish; tel: 070 23 2000; www.stib.be) operates the

Brussels' metro network is a vast open-access art gallery: all stations are decorated with works by contemporary Belgian artists created since the 1970s. They vary from a fantasy cityscape relief by comic-strip artist François Schuiten (Porte de Hal) to abstract tiled murals (Schuman) and a particularly spooky collection of statues of the royal family (Stuyvenbergh).

Below: a Brussels Card offers good value if you plan to travel around the city.

Above: the city's tramway offers a speedy and direct way of getting around the city.

metro, tram and bus network, a well-organised system that has been revised in the past year to reflect improvements. Services run from 6am–midnight. Certain trams run below ground in some areas, where they are referred to as the 'pre-metro'. All stops are request stops: raise your arm to indicate to the driver that you wish to board the bus or tram. A night-bus service, Noctis, runs on Fri–Sat evenings on 17 routes, from midnight to 3am.

Tickets are a fixed price for an hour's journey (including transfers – stamp on each entry), and may be purchased from bus or tram drivers (do not present more than 5 euros), but are cheaper if bought in advance, from metro stations, STIB information offices or many newsagents. Various combinations are possible – 1-, 5- or 10-trip tickets (several passengers can share a multi-trip card), or a 1- or 3-day pass. Accompanied children under 6 travel for free with no ticket. The Brussels Card also includes free public transport for 24, 48 or 72 hours.

SEE ALSO MUSEUMS AND GALLERIES, P.77

Flemish bus service De Lijn (www.delijn.be) runs routes from central Brussels to the Flemish belt around Brussels (to Tervuren, Grimbergen and Leuven, for example), while Walloon bus service TEC (www.infotec.be) does the same for routes to Wallonia (Waterloo and Wavre, for example).

TAXI

The main taxi companies in Brussels – all of which bear the official Brussels sign on their roof – are **Autolux**, tel: 02 411 12 21; **Taxis Bleus**, tel: 02 268 00 00; **Taxis Oranges**, tel: 02 349 43 43; **Taxis Verts**, tel: 02 349 49 49. Tips and service are included in the price of the journey, although a small extra tip is appreciated.

SEE ALSO NIGHTLIFE, P.91

Collecto is a night-time shared taxi service (11pm–6pm) designed to supplement the night-bus network. It operates pick-ups from dozens of public transport stops and drops passengers at any address in the Brussels region. Taxis must be booked at least 20 minutes before pick-up (on the hour or half-hour); indicate your chosen pick-up point and the number of people travelling. Fares are a flat €5 or €8 depending on distance of journey, payable when you board. Departure points are indicated at www.collecto.org.

Walks and Tours

The city of Art Nouveau, Art Deco, comic strip and good food is inclined to reveal its charms only slowly or on repeated inspection. For those who have limited time, a good way to understand Brussels is to take a guided tour, by foot, bus, bike or boat, joining a group led by a specialist heritage or other organisation. The city centre is compact and easily visited on foot, but it is also hilly, and many of the architectural treasures are located slightly out of the centre, in the communes of Etterbeek, Ixelles and Saint-Gilles. This section introduces the main guided tour operations.

Arau
Boulevard Adolphe Max 55; tel: 02 219 33 45; www.arau.org
Insightful bus and walking tours in English that reflect on Brussels city planning are run by urban campaigning group Arau (Atelier de la Recherche et d'Actions Urbaines – Studio for Urban Research and Action). Its architectural experts are knowledgeable and committed, and tell a story that many run-of-the-mill tour organisations might prefer to ignore. English-language bus tours last 3 hours and include Art Nouveau and Art Deco tours, among others; walking tours last 1½ or 2½ hours and cover the Marolles, the buildings and history of the EU institutions, the Grand'Place and Art Nouveau districts. Tickets can be purchased online or via the tourist office, and advance booking is recommended.

Arkadia
Rue Hôtel des Monnaies 120; tel: 02 537 67 77; www.arkadia.be
This art history association runs mainly French walking tours conducted by art historians, but also two in English, one on Horta and Art Nouveau, the other on 'secret Brussels'. They are rather infrequent, however, so check dates in advance.

Above: architecture tours offer a valuable insight into the city.

Brussels City Tours
Rue de la Colline 8; tel: 02 513 77 44; www.brussels-city-tours.com
This company runs hourly guided bus tours of the city (a grand tour as well as the hop-on, hop-off Brussels Line service) plus half-day and day-long excursions to Waterloo, Antwerp, Ghent, Bruges, Amsterdam and Luxembourg. They will also collect from centrally located hotels. Download the brochure for details of the options – or pick up a copy at the tourist office – and book in advance.

Golden Tours
Tel: 0486 05 39 81; www.goldentours.be
This open-topped yellow bus runs a daily hop-on, hop-off tour (with headphones) from 10am–4pm to visit the key sights in Brussels centre, the EU district, the royal quarter in Laeken and the Atomium.

Left: comic mural.

Best Views of Brussels
Top floor of the Musée des Instruments de Musique *(see p.80)*
Parapet alongside the Palais de Justice *(see p.24)*
Top ball of the Atomium *(see p.25)*
Dome of the Basilique du Sacré-Cœur *(see p.39)*
Cinquantenaire Arch, accessed via the Musée Royale de l'Armée et de l'Histoire Militaire *(see p.83)*

Guides Brussels Belgium
Hôtel de Ville, Grand'Place; tel: 02 548 04 48; www.brusselsinternational.be
Official tourist-office tour guides can tailor their large number of ready-made tours to your interest, whether that is Brussels under Habsburgs rule, Jewish Brussels or the current fashion scene.

MP3 Guides
Three audio walking guides have been produced for the tourist office by D*Tours (www.d-tours.org), one for the Grand'Place, one for the Marolles and the third for the Sainte-Catherine district. The sound recordings, which contain evocative sounds of the city and interviews with local people, can be rented with headphones and an MP3 player from the tourist office, or purchased as a direct download from the tourist office website www.brusselsinternational.be – on the link Brussels MP3 walks.

Pro Vélo
Rue de Londres 15; tel: 02 502 73 55; www.provelo.org
Brussels is not as cycle-friendly as the flat towns in Flanders, with its cobbles, tram lines and erratic motorists. Nevertheless, more and more people are taking to two wheels, and on a fine day it can be the best way to visit the city. Cycling organisation Pro Vélo runs mainly French-language tours from March to October on rented bikes (or your own) departing from its Rue de Londres HQ. Themes include beer and breweries, Art Deco and Modernism, 'secret Brussels', women in Brussels, fountains and sculpture, as well as specific tours of the city's different neighbourhoods. Tours in English can be arranged for groups.

Vizit
Tel: 09 234 17 28; www.vizit.be
This Ghent-based organisation offers culinary tours of Brussels, including two each Saturday in English for individuals. The two-hour afternoon tour allows visitors to taste local delicacies (snails, chocolate, cheese) at the same time as learning about history and local life; the evening tour includes a visit to four restaurants in the Marolles for a separate dinner course.

Below: chocolate shops are just one of the delights of the European capital.

HOUSE
HOMARD
LE BOURGEOIS
aux
Armes de
SAINT
LAURENT

Atlas

The following streetplan of Brussels makes it easy to find the attractions listed in our A–Z section. A selective index to streets and sights will help you find other locations throughout the city

Map Legend

	Motorway		Railway
	Dual carriageway		Metro
	Main road		Bus station
	Minor road		Airport
	Footpath		Tourist information
	Pedestrian area		Sight of interest
	Notable building		Cathedral / church
	Transport hub		Mosque
	Park		Synagogue
	Hotel		Statue / monument
	Urban area		Hospital
	Non urban area		

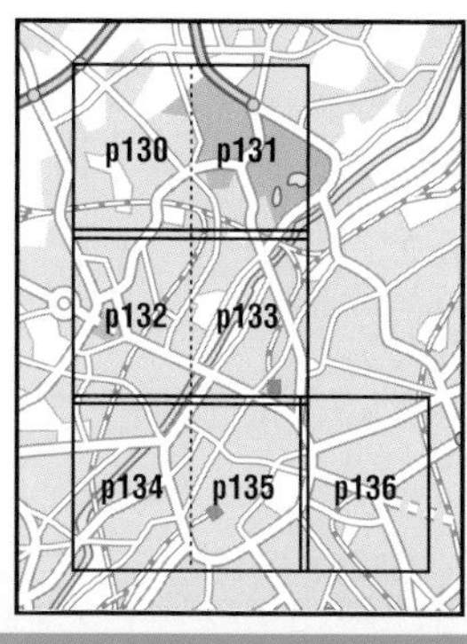

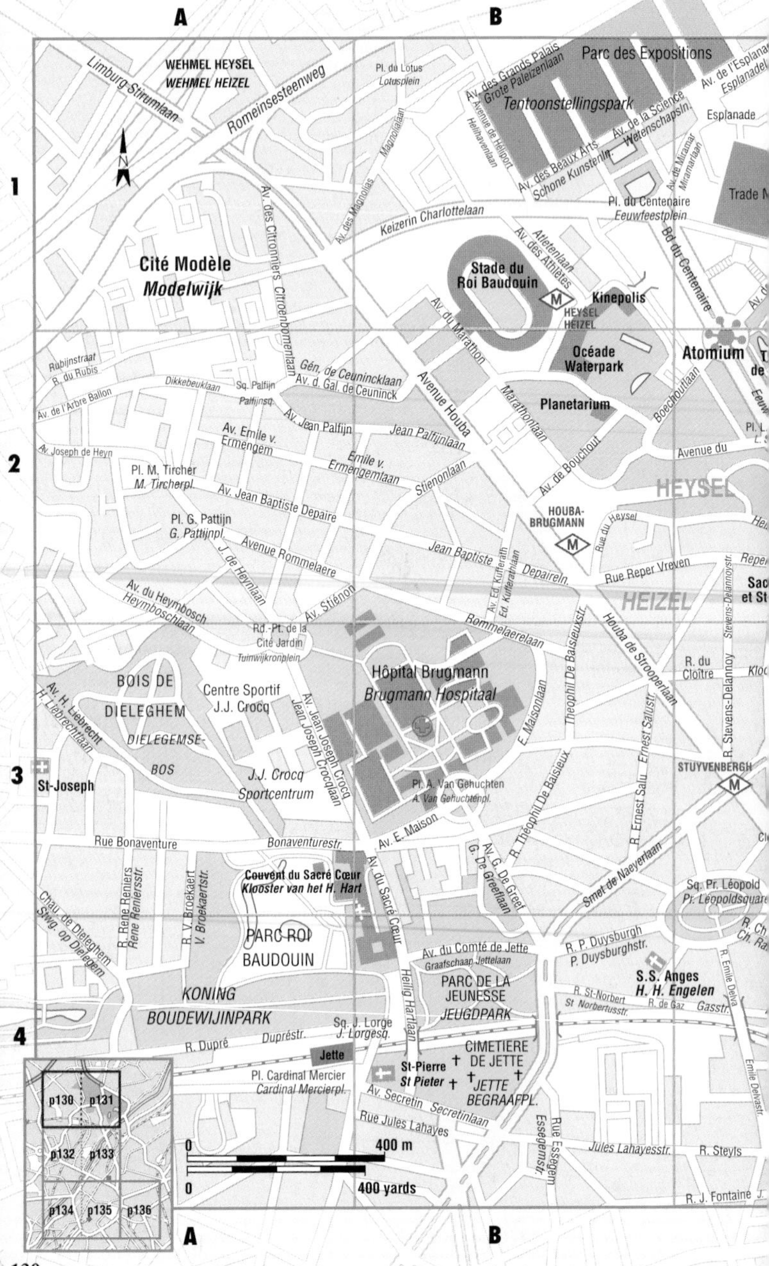
A
B
WEHMEL HEYSEL
WEHMEL HEIZEL
Parc des Expositions
Tentoonstellingspark
Cité Modèle
Modelwijk
Stade du
Roi Baudouin
Kinepolis
HEYSEL
HEIZEL
Océade
Waterpark
Atomium
Planetarium
HOUBA-
BRUGMANN
Hôpital Brugmann
Brugmann Hospitaal
BOIS DE
DIELEGHEM
DIELEGEMSE-
BOS
Centre Sportif
J.J. Crocq
J.J. Crocq
Sportcentrum
St-Joseph
STUYVENBERGH
Couvent du Sacré Cœur
Klooster van het H. Hart
PARC ROI
BAUDOUIN
KONING
BOUDEWIJINPARK
PARC DE LA
JEUNESSE
JEUGDPARK
S.S. Anges
H. H. Engelen
Jette
St-Pierre
St Pieter
CIMETIERE
DE JETTE
JETTE
BEGRAAFPL.
0
400 m
0
400 yards
p130
p131
p132
p133
p134
p135
p136
1
2
3
4

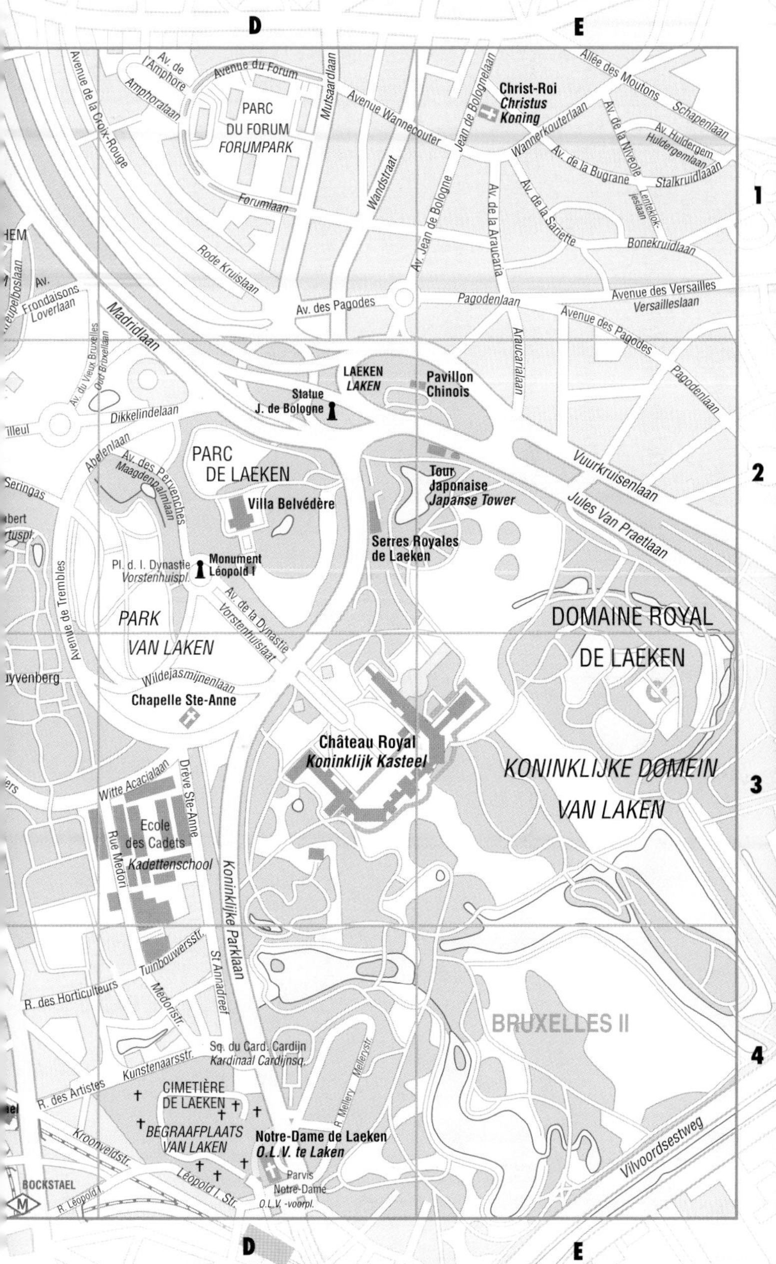
D
E
1
2
3
4
Avenue de la Croix-Rouge
Av. de l'Amphore
Amphoralaan
Avenue du Forum
PARC
DU FORUM
FORUMPARK
Forumlaan
Mutsaardlaan
Wandstraat
Avenue Wannecouter
Wannerkouterlaan
Jean de Bolognelaan
Christ-Roi
Christus
Koning
Allée des Moutons
Schapenlaan
Av. de la Nivéole
Av. Huldergem
Huldergemlaan
Av. de la Bugrane
Stalkruidlaan
Lentekloklaan
Av. Jean de Bologne
Av. de la Araucaria
Av. de la Sariette
Bonekruidlaan
Rode Kruislaan
Av. des Pagodes
Pagodenlaan
Avenue des Versailles
Versailleslaan
Avenue des Pagodes
Araucarialaan
Pagodenlaan
Av. Frondaisons
Loverlaan
Madridlaan
Av. du Vieux Bruxelles
Oud Brussellaan
LAEKEN
LAEKEN
Statue
J. de Bologne
Pavillon
Chinois
Dikkelindelaan
Abelenlaan
Av. des Pervenches
Maagdenpalmlaan
PARC
DE LAEKEN
Villa Belvédère
Tour
Japonaise
Japanse Tower
Vuurkruisenlaan
Jules Van Praetlaan
Serres Royales
de Laeken
Pl. d. l. Dynastie
Vorstenhuispl.
Monument
Léopold I
Avenue de Trembles
Av. de la Dynastie
Vorstenhuislaan
PARK
VAN LAKEN
DOMAINE ROYAL
DE LAEKEN
Wildejasmijnenlaan
Chapelle Ste-Anne
Château Royal
Koninklijk Kasteel
KONINKLIJKE DOMEIN
VAN LAKEN
Witte Acacialaan
Drève Ste-Anne
Ecole
des Cadets
Kadettenschool
Rue Medori
Koninklijke Parklaan
Tuinbouwersstr.
St Annadreef
R. des Horticulteurs
Medoristr.
BRUXELLES II
Sq. du Card. Cardijn
Kardinaal Cardijnsq.
Kunstenaarsstr.
R. des Artistes
Mellerystr.
R. Mellery
CIMETIÈRE
DE LAEKEN
BEGRAAFPLAATS
VAN LAKEN
Notre-Dame de Laeken
O.L.V. te Laken
Kroonveldstr.
Léopold I. Str.
Parvis
Notre-Dame
O.L.V. -voorpl.
Vilvoordsestweg
BOCKSTAEL
R. Léopold I
M

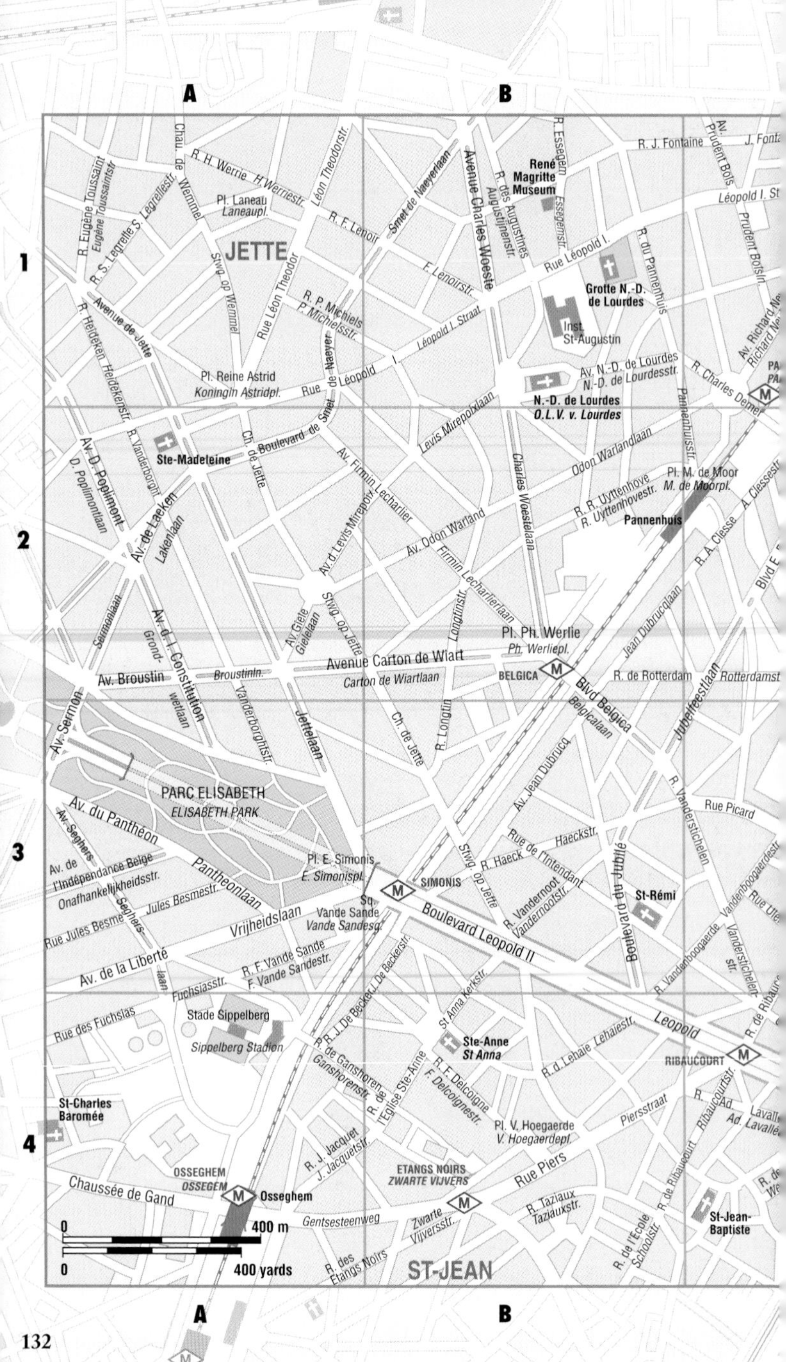

A
B
1
2
3
4
JETTE
René Magritte Museum
Grotte N.-D. de Lourdes
Inst. St-Augustin
N.-D. de Lourdes
O.L.V. v. Lourdes
Ste-Madeleine
Pannenhuis
Pl. Ph. Werlie
Ph. Werliepl.
BELGICA
Avenue Carton de Wiart
Carton de Wiartlaan
Blvd Belgica
Belgicalaan
PARC ELISABETH
ELISABETH PARK
Pl. E. Simonis
E. Simonispl.
SIMONIS
Boulevard Leopold II
St-Rémi
Stade Sippelberg
Sippelberg Stadion
Ste-Anne
St Anna
RIBAUCOURT
St-Charles Baromée
OSSEGHEM
OSSEGEM
Osseghem
Chaussée de Gand
Gentsesteenweg
ETANGS NOIRS
ZWARTE VIJVERS
Rue Piers
St-Jean-Baptiste
ST-JEAN
0
400 m
400 yards

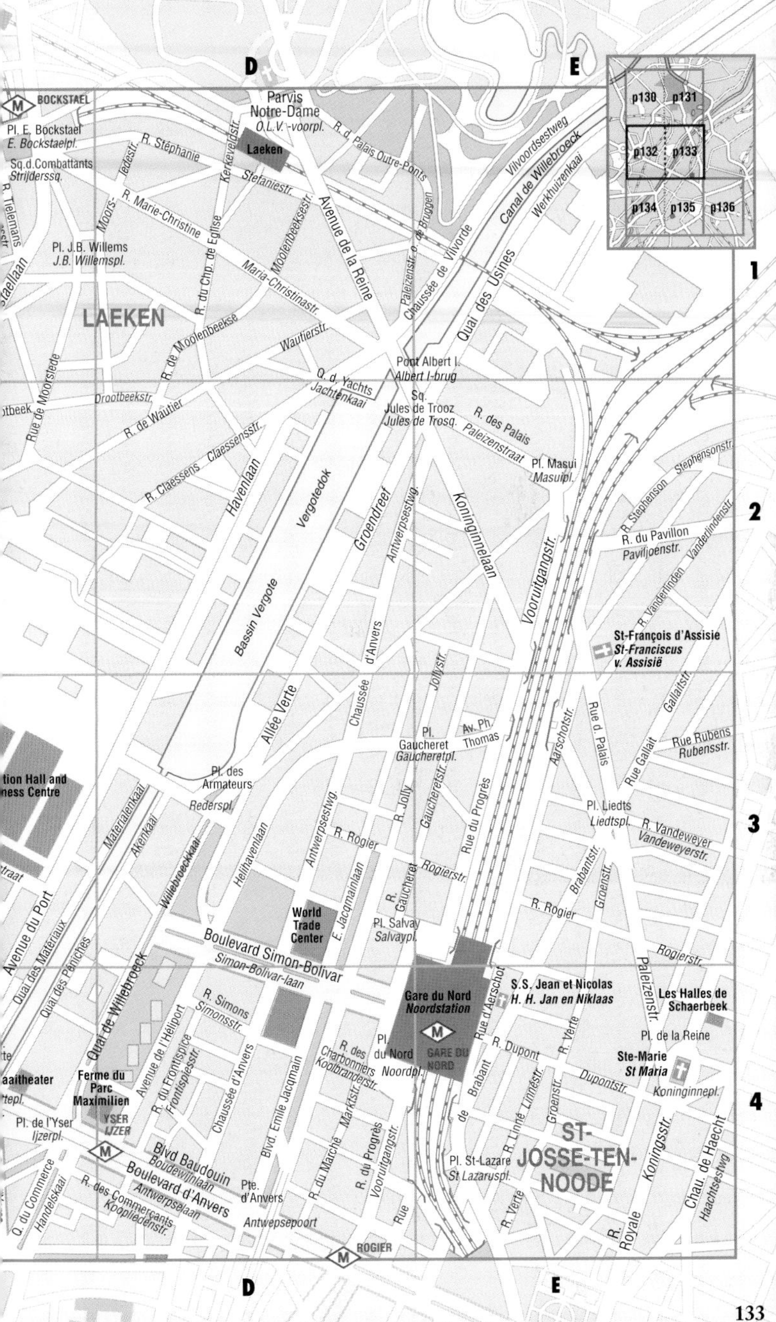
D
E
p130
p131
p132
p133
p134
p135
p136
BOCKSTAEL
Pl. E. Bockstael
E. Bockstaelpl.
Sq.d.Combattants
Strijderssq.
Parvis
Notre-Dame
O.L.V.-voorpl.
Laeken
R. Stéphanie
Stefaniestr.
R. d. Palais Outre-Ponts
R. Marie-Christine
Maria-Christinastr.
Pl. J.B. Willems
J.B. Willemspl.
LAEKEN
Avenue de la Reine
Chaussée de Vilvorde
Quai des Usines
Canal de Willebroeck
Vilvoordsestweg
Werkhuizenkaai
Pont Albert I.
Albert I-brug
Q. d. Yachts
Jachtenkaai
Sq.
Jules de Trooz
Jules de Trosq.
R. des Palais
Paleizenstraat
Pl. Masui
Masuipl.
Wautierstr.
R. de Wautier
Drootbeekstr.
Rue de Moorslede
R. Claessens
Claessensstr.
Havenlaan
Vergotedok
Groendreef
Antwerpsestwg.
Koninginnelaan
Vooruitgangstr.
R. du Pavillon
Paviljoenstr.
R. Stephenson
Stephensonstr.
R. Vanderlinden
Vanderlindenstr.
St-François d'Assisie
St-Franciscus
v. Assisië
Bassin Vergote
Chaussée d'Anvers
Jollystr.
Allée Verte
Pl. Gaucheret
Gaucheretpl.
Av. Ph. Thomas
Aarschotstr.
Rue d. Palais
Gallaitstr.
Rue Gallait
Rue Rubens
Rubensstr.
Pl. des Armateurs
Rederspl.
Pl. Liedts
Liedtspl.
R. Vandeweyer
Vandeweyerstr.
R. Rogier
Rogierstr.
R. Jolly
Gaucheretstr.
Rue du Progrès
Brabantstr.
Groenstr.
Materialenkaai
Akenkaai
Willebroekkaai
Helihavenlaan
World Trade Center
E. Jacqmainlaan
R. Gaucheret
Pl. Salvay
Salvaypl.
Avenue du Port
Quai des Matériaux
Quai des Péniches
Boulevard Simon-Bolivar
Simon-Bolivar-laan
Gare du Nord
Noordstation
GARE DU NORD
Rue d'Aerschot
S.S. Jean et Nicolas
H. H. Jan en Niklaas
Paleizenstr.
Les Halles de Schaerbeek
Pl. de la Reine
Ste-Marie
St Maria
Koninginnepl.
Quai de Willebroeck
R. Simons
Simonsstr.
Avenue de l'Héliport
R. du Frontispice
Frontispiesstr.
Chaussée d'Anvers
Blvd. Emile Jacqmain
R. des Charbonniers
Koolbranderstr.
Pl. du Nord
Noordpl.
R. Dupont
Dupontstr.
R. Verte
Rue de Brabant
R. Linné
Linnéstr.
Ferme du Parc Maximilien
YSER
IJZER
Pl. de l'Yser
Ijzerpl.
Blvd Baudouin
Boudewijnlaan
Boulevard d'Anvers
Antwerpselaan
R. des Commerçants
Koopliedenstr.
Q. du Commerce
Handelskaai
Pte. d'Anvers
Antwerpsepoort
R. du Marché
Marktstr.
R. du Progrès
Vooruitgangstr.
ROGIER
Pl. St-Lazare
St Lazaruspl.
ST-JOSSE-TEN-NOODE
Koningsstr.
R. Royale
Chau. de Haecht
Haachtsestwg
1
2
3
4

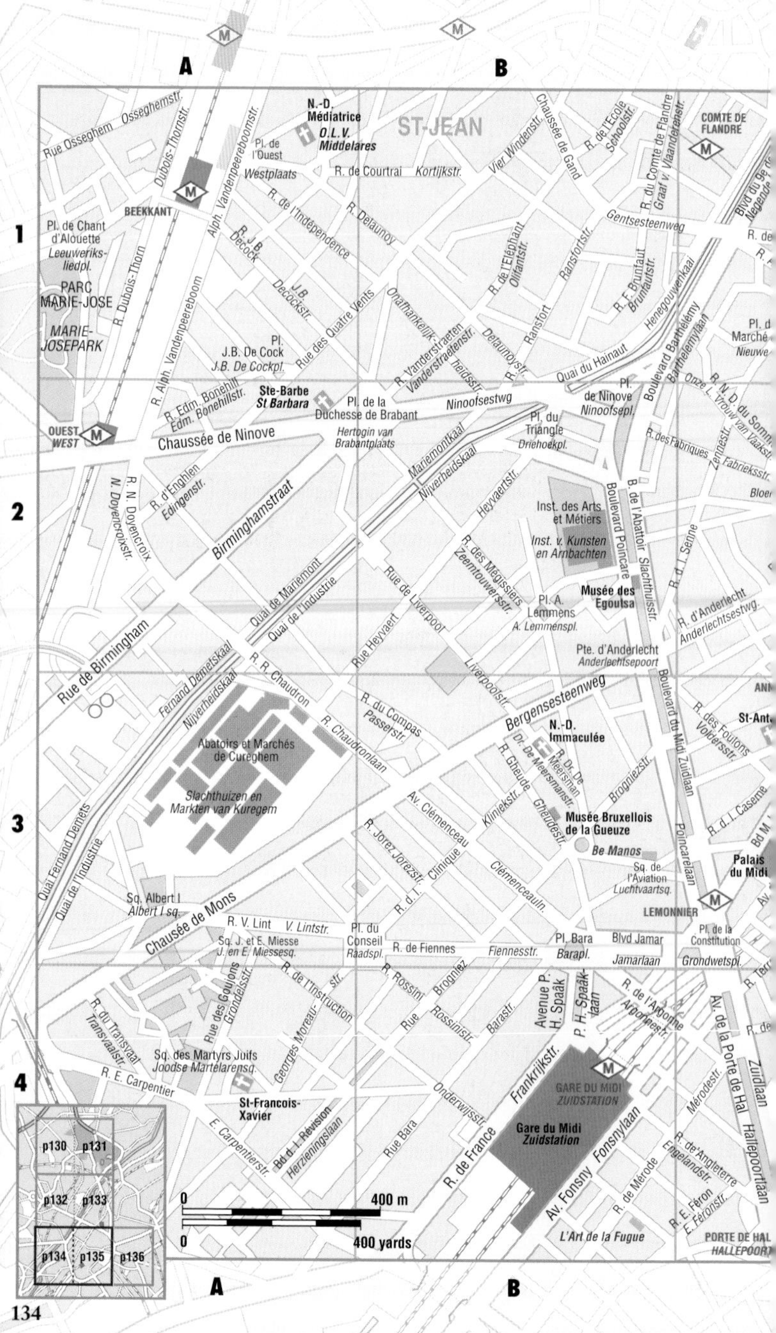
A
B
1
2
3
4
ST-JEAN
N.-D. Médiatrice
O.L.V. Middelares
Pl. de l'Ouest
Westplaats
R. de Courtrai
Kortijkstr.
BEEKKANT
COMTE DE FLANDRE
Pl. de Chant d'Alouette
Leeuweriks-liedpl.
PARC MARIE-JOSE
MARIE-JOSEPARK
Pl. J.B. De Cock
J.B. De Cockpl.
Ste-Barbe
St Barbara
Pl. de la Duchesse de Brabant
Hertogin van Brabantplaats
OUEST WEST
Chaussée de Ninove
Ninoofsestwg
Pl. du Triangle
Driehoekpl.
Pl. de Ninove
Ninoofsepl.
Quai du Hainaut
Inst. des Arts et Métiers
Inst. v. Kunsten en Ambachten
Musée des Egoutsa
Pl. A. Lemmens
A. Lemmenspl.
Pte. d'Anderlecht
Anderlechtsepoort
Birminghamstraat
Rue de Birmingham
Bergensesteenweg
N.-D. Immaculée
Abatoirs et Marchés de Cureghem
Slachthuizen en Markten van Kuregem
Musée Bruxellois de la Gueuze
Be Manos
Sq. de l'Aviation
Luchtvaartsq.
LEMONNIER
Palais du Midi
Sq. Albert I
Albert I sq.
Chausée de Mons
R. V. Lint
V. Lintstr.
Sq. J. et E. Miesse
J. en E. Miessesq.
Pl. du Conseil
Raadspl.
R. de Fiennes
Fiennesstr.
Pl. Bara
Barapl.
Blvd Jamar
Jamarlaan
Pl. de la Constitution
Grondwetspl.
Sq. des Martyrs Juifs
Joodse Martelarensq.
St-Francois-Xavier
GARE DU MIDI
ZUIDSTATION
Gare du Midi
Zuidstation
L'Art de la Fugue
PORTE DE HAL
HALLEPOORT
0
400 m
0
400 yards
p130
p131
p132
p133
p134
p135
p136

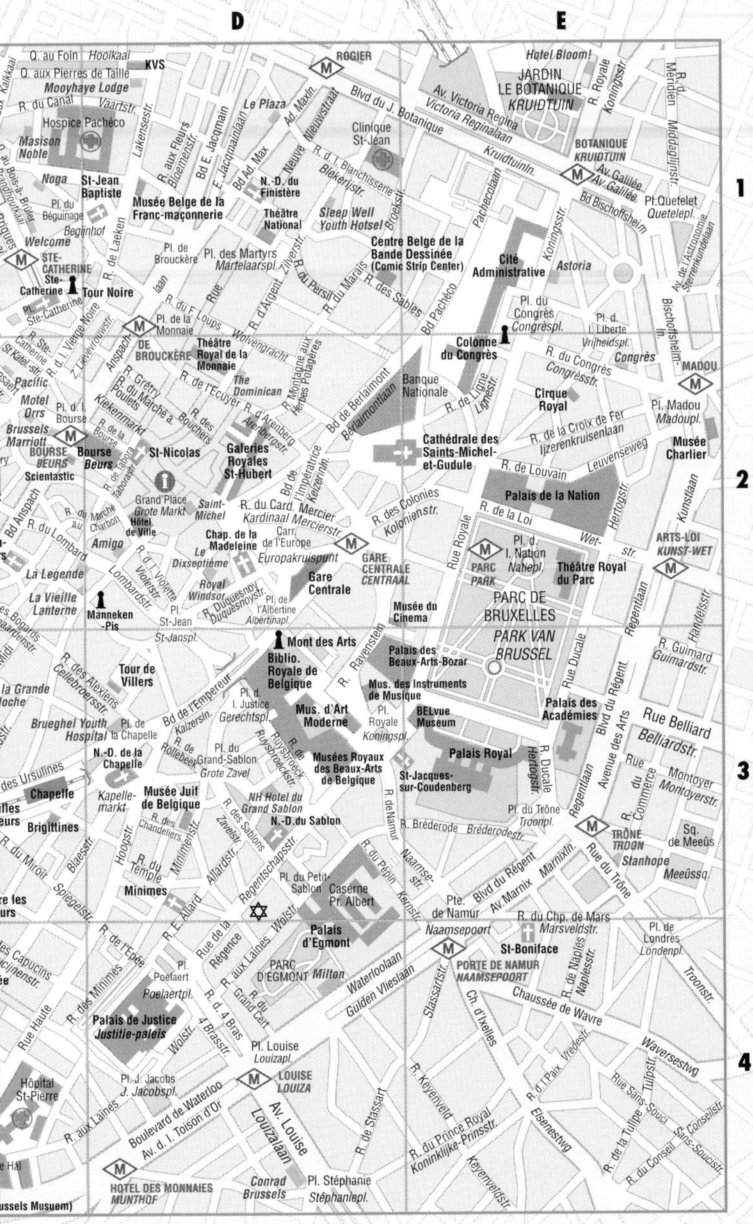

D
E
1
2
3
4
Q. au Foin Hooikaai
Q. aux Pierres de Taille
KVS
Mooyhaye Lodge
R. du Canal Vaartstr.
Hospice Pachéco
Masison Noble
Noga
St-Jean Baptiste
Pl. du Béguinage Begijnhof
Welcome
STE-CATHERINE
Ste-Catherine
Tour Noire
Pl. Ste-Catherine
Musée Belge de la Franc-maçonnerie
Pl. de Brouckère
Pl. des Martyrs Martelaarspl.
Le Plaza
N.-D. du Finistère
Théâtre National
Sleep Well Youth Hotsel
ROGIER
Clinique St-Jean
Blvd du J. Botanique
Av. Victoria Regina
Victoria Reginalaan
Hotel Bloom!
JARDIN LE BOTANIQUE KRUIDTUIN
R. Royale Koningsstr.
R. d. Meridien Middaglijnstr.
BOTANIQUE KRUIDTUIN
Kruidtuinln.
Av. Galilée
Bd Bischoffsheim
Pl. Quetelet Queteletpl.
Centre Belge de la Bande Dessinée (Comic Strip Center)
Cité Administrative
Astoria
Av. de l'Astronomie Sterrenkundelaan
Pl. de la Monnaie
DE BROUCKÈRE
Théâtre Royal de la Monnaie
The Dominican
R. du Marais
R. des Sables
Bd Pachéco
Pl. du Congrès Congrèspl.
Pl. d. l. Liberte Vrijheidspl.
Colonne du Congrès
R. du Congrès Congrèsstr.
Congrès
MADOU
Pacific
Motel Orrs
Pl. d. l. Bourse
Brussels Marriott
BOURSE BEURS
Bourse Beurs
Scientastic
St-Nicolas
Galeries Royales St-Hubert
Banque Nationale
Cathédrale des Saints-Michel-et-Gudule
Cirque Royal
R. de la Croix de Fer Ijzerenkruisenlaan
Pl. Madou Madoupl.
Musée Charlier
R. de Louvain
Leuvenseweg
Palais de la Nation
Grand'Place Grote Markt
Hôtel de Ville
Saint-Michel
R. du Card. Mercier Kardinaal Mercierstr.
Carr. de l'Europe Europakruispunt
R. des Colonies Kolonienstr.
R. de la Loi Wetstr.
ARTS-LOI KUNST-WET
Amigo
Chap. de la Madeleine
Le Dixseptième
La Legende
La Vieille Lanterne
Manneken-Pis
Royal Windsor
Pl. de l'Albertine Albertinapl.
Pl. St-Jean St-Janspl.
GARE CENTRALE CENTRAAL
Gare Centrale
Musée du Cinema
Pl. d. l. Nation Natiepl.
PARC PARK
Théâtre Royal du Parc
PARC DE BRUXELLES PARK VAN BRUSSEL
Mont des Arts
Biblio. Royale de Belgique
Palais des Beaux-Arts-Bozar
Mus. des Instruments de Musique
Tour de Villers
A la Grande Cloche
Brueghel Youth Hospital
Pl. de la Chapelle
Pl. d. l. Justice Gerechtspl.
Mus. d'Art Moderne
Pl. Royale Koningspl.
BELvue Museum
Palais Royal
Palais des Académies
Rue Belliard Belliardstr.
N.-D. de la Chapelle
Chapelle
Brigittines
Pl. du Grand-Sablon Grote Zavel
Musées Royaux des Beaux-Arts de Belgique
St-Jacques-sur-Coudenberg
Montoyer Montoyerstr.
Musée Juif de Belgique
NH Hotel du Grand Sablon
N.-D. du Sablon
R. Bréderode Brédérodestr.
Pl. du Trône Troonpl.
TRÔNE TROON
Sq. de Meeûs
Stanhope
Minimes
Pl. du Petit-Sablon
Caserne Pr. Albert
Pte. de Namur
Bvd du Régent
Av. Marnix
Rue du Trône
Palais d'Egmont
R. du Chp. de Mars Marsveldstr.
Pl. de Londres Londenpl.
Naamsepoort
St-Boniface
PORTE DE NAMUR NAAMSEPOORT
Pl. Poelaert Poelaertpl.
PARC D'EGMONT
Milton
Waterloolaan
Gulden Vlieslaan
Chaussée de Wavre
Palais de Justice Justitie-paleis
Rue Haute
Pl. Louise Louizapl.
LOUISE LOUIZA
Hôpital St-Pierre
Pl. J. Jacobs J. Jacobspl.
Boulevard de Waterloo
Av. d. l. Toison d'Or
Av. Louise Louizalaan
R. de Stassart
R. du Prince Royal Koninklijke-Prinsstr.
Waversestwg
HOTEL DES MONNAIES MUNTHOF
Conrad Brussels
Pl. Stéphanie Stéphaniepl.
Brussels Musuem)

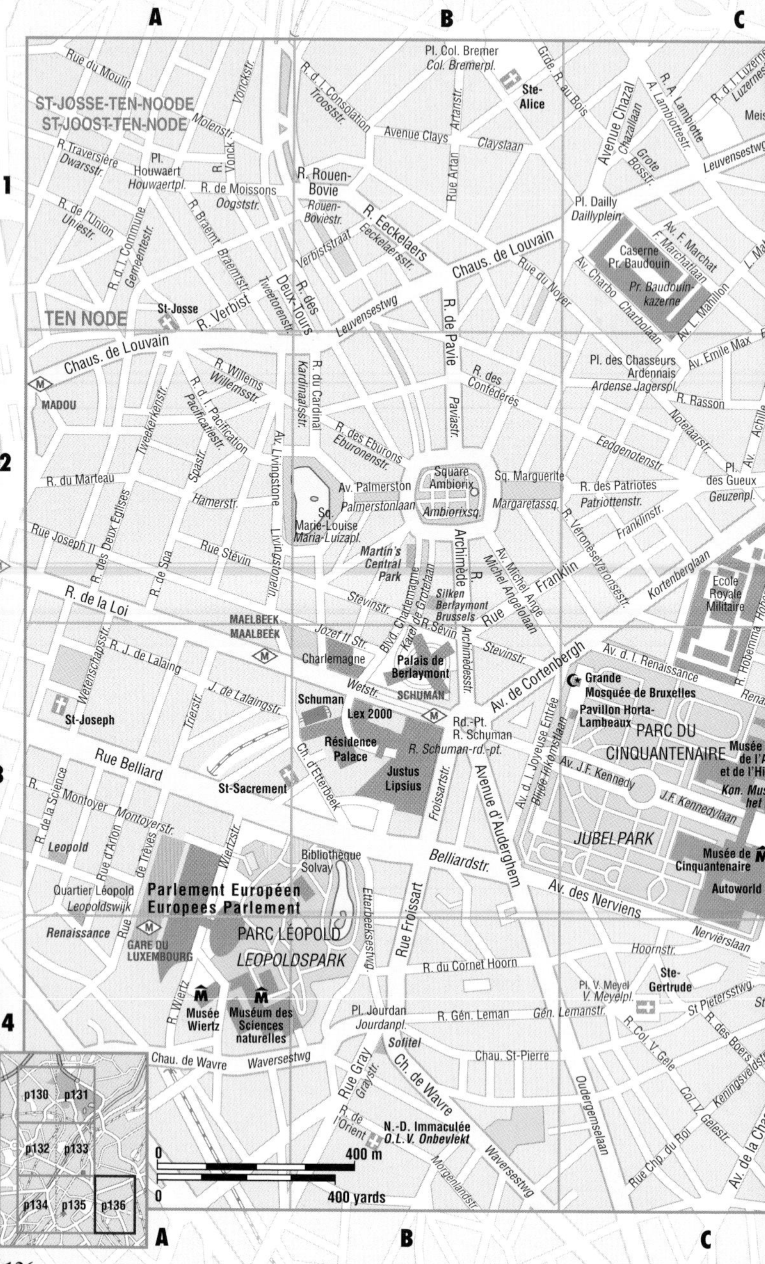

A
B
C
1
2
3
4
ST-JOSSE-TEN-NOODE
ST-JOOST-TEN-NODE
TEN NODE
MADOU
MAELBEEK
MAALBEEK
SCHUMAN
Square Ambiorix
Ambiorixsq.
Sq. Marie-Louise
Maria-Luizapl.
Martin's Central Park
Silken Berlaymont Brussels
Palais de Berlaymont
Charlemagne
Schuman
Lex 2000
Résidence Palace
Justus Lipsius
St-Josse
St-Joseph
St-Sacrement
Ste-Alice
Ste-Gertrude
Caserne Pr. Baudouin
Pr. Baudouin-kazerne
Grande Mosquée de Bruxelles
Pavillon Horta-Lambeaux
PARC DU CINQUANTENAIRE
JUBELPARK
Ecole Royale Militaire
Musée de Cinquantenaire
Autoworld
Bibliothèque Solvay
Parlement Européen
Europees Parlement
PARC LÉOPOLD
LEOPOLDSPARK
Quartier Léopold
Leopoldswijk
Renaissance
GARE DU LUXEMBOURG
Leopold
Musée Wiertz
Muséum des Sciences naturelles
Sofitel
N.-D. Immaculée
O.L.V. Onbevlekt
Chaus. de Louvain
Rue Belliard
Belliardstr.
R. de la Loi
Av. de Cortenbergh
Avenue d'Auderghem
Av. des Nerviens
Nerviërslaan
Chau. de Wavre
Waversestwg
Ch. de Wavre
Pl. Jourdan
Jourdanpl.
R. Gén. Leman
Gén. Lemanstr.
Chau. St-Pierre
Rue Froissart
Oudergemselaan
0
400 m
400 yards
p130
p131
p132
p133
p134
p135
p136

Selective Index for Street Atlas

French

Flemish

Index

J

K

L

M

N

O

P

Q

R

S

T

U

V

W

Z

Insight Smart Guide: Brussels
Written by: **Katharine Mill**
Edited by: **Joanna Potts and Rachel Lawrence**
Proofread and indexed by: **Neil Titman**
Photography by: All pictures © **APA/Julian Love, Mark Read, Glyn Genin, Abe Nowitz, Corrie Wingate** and **Britta Jaschinski** except: **AKG** 58TL 58TR; **Alamy** 42/43, 48/49, 50B, 50/51, 56/57; **Bridgeman** 81; **Corbis** 118/119; **Documentation, Brussels** 59TR; **Frédéric Latinis-Nu** 86/87; **Getty** 122/123; **istock photo** 5CL, 5TL, 34/35, 49B, 83T, 90T, 90BL, 91B, 99, 105, 111, 122B, 125; **Leonardo** 67TR, 69B, 67TL, 66B, 63T, 61BR, 61BL; **Shutterstock** 22/23, 24/25T, 25B, 26/27, 118B; **Stephen DAU** 92T, 92/93; **Mary Evans** 59BL
Picture Manager: **Steven Lawrence**
Maps: **James Macdonald**
Series Editor: **Jason Mitchell**

First Edition 2009

Printed in Singapore by Insight Print Services (Pte) Ltd

Worldwide distribution enquiries:
Apa Publications GmbH & Co. Verlag KG (Singapore Branch) 38 Joo Koon Road, Singapore 628990; tel: (65) 6865 1600; fax: (65) 6861 6438
Distributed in the UK and Ireland by:
GeoCenter International Ltd
Meridian House, Churchill Way West, Basingstoke, Hampshire RG21 6YR; tel: (44 1256) 817 987; fax: (44 1256) 817 988
Distributed in the United States by:
Langenscheidt Publishers, Inc.
36–36 33rd Street 4th Floor, Long Island City, New York 11106; tel: (1 718) 784 0055; fax: (1 718) 784 0640

Contacting the Editors
We would appreciate it if readers would alert us to errors or outdated information by writing to:
Apa Publications, PO Box 7910, London SE1 1WE, UK; fax: (44 20) 7403 0290; e-mail: insight@apaguide.co.uk

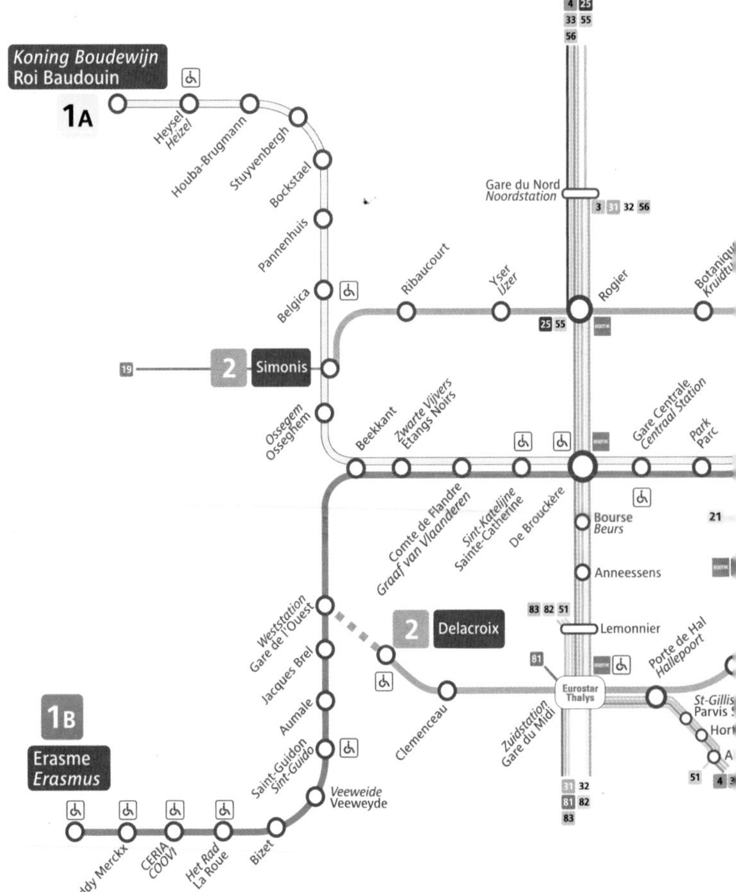

Koning Boudewijn
Roi Baudouin
1A
Heysel
Heizel
Houba-Brugmann
Stuyvenbergh
Bockstael
Pannenhuis
Belgica
2
Simonis
19
Ossegem
Osseghem
Ribaucourt
Yser
IJzer
Rogier
Botaniqu
Kruidtu
4 25
33 55
56
Gare du Nord
Noordstation
3 31 32 56
25 55
Beekkant
Zwarte Vijvers
Etangs Noirs
Comte de Flandre
Graaf van Vlaanderen
Sint-Katelijne
Sainte-Catherine
De Brouckère
Gare Centrale
Centraal Station
Park
Parc
Bourse
Beurs
21
Anneessens
83 82 51
Lemonnier
Weststation
Gare de l'Ouest
2
Delacroix
Jacques Brel
Aumale
Saint-Guidon
Sint-Guido
Veeweide
Veeweyde
Clemenceau
81
Eurostar
Thalys
Zuidstation
Gare du Midi
Porte de Hal
Hallepoort
St-Gillis
Parvis
31 32
81 82
83
51
1B
Erasme
Erasmus
Eddy Merckx
CERIA
COOVI
Het Rad
La Roue
Bizet

MIVB ST